SKILLS FOR SUCCESSFUL SCHOOL LEADERS

Second Edition, Revised 1994

JOHN R. HOYLE
Professor of Educational Administration
Texas A & M University, College Station, Texas

FENWICK ENGLISH
Professor, Educational Administration
University of Kentucky, Lexington, Ky.

BETTY STEFFY
Associate Professor, Educational Administration
University of Kentucky
Lexington, Ky.

AMERICAN ASSOCIATION OF SCHOOL ADMINISTRATORS
1801 NORTH MOORE STREET, ARLINGTON, VIRGINIA 22209-9988 (703) 875-0748

OTHER PUBLICATIONS

On School Leadership:
Challenges for School Leaders
Profiling Excellence in America's Schools
AASA Professional Standards for the Superintendency

School Administrators:
Leaders for Learning (Videotape)
Strategic Planning for America's Schools (book and videotape)

Administrative Team Development Series:
Selecting the Administrative Team
The Board's Role in Selecting the Administrative Team
Compensating the Administrative Team

Superintendent Career Development Series:
Guidelines for the Preparation of School Administrators
Selecting a Superintendent
The Superintendent's Contract
Compensating the Superintendent
The Administrative Leadership Team
Evaluating the Superintendent
The Role of a Consultant in a Superintendency Search

Key Board-Administrator Publications:
Roles and Relationships . . . School Boards and Superintendents (1994 updated version)
Goal Setting and Self Evaluation of School Boards
Principles of Effective School District Governance and Administration
Holding Effective Board Meetings
Building Better Board-Administrator Relations

These publications and more are available from the American Association of School Administrators (AASA), 1801 North Moore Street, Arlington, Virginia 22209-9988. Price lists available. Discounts on multiple copy orders. AASA members receive the monthly magazine of the profession, *The School Administrator,* and many other member services.

AASA Stock Number: 021-00132

Library of Congress Card Catalogue Number: 84-73431

ISBN Number: 0-87652-083-2

Graphics and design by Congressional Arts Enterprises, Inc.

TABLE OF CONTENTS

PREFACE

Beginning in the early part of the 1980s, a series of thunderclap reports rolled across the nation castigating public education and educators for poor performance. Another echo was heard in 1989 when the U.S. Department of Education released its "wall chart" report, a "good news, bad news" type of assessment. Schools were not any worse, stated the U.S. Secretary of Education, but they were not getting any better.

Many in the spate of reports during the decade cited lack of administrative leadership as one of the root causes for the problems. Not only were administrators ill prepared for their roles, some charged; they were not exercising their leadership functions effectively to achieve maximum results.

The American Association of School Administrators, as the nation's largest association of education administrators, was concerned. Though they felt that schools and performance were not as bad as portrayed, most agreed there was room for improvement.

Just what were the essential skills school administrators needed to ensure not only their own success, but the success of schools and students under their direction? When AASA initially researched this question, we found that there was a void. No single entity existed that delineated clearly what areas were, indeed, critical to success.

AASA filled the vacuum, commissioning John Hoyle, Fenwick English, and Betty Steffy to write *Skills for Successful School Leaders*. It was a first. It proved to be a winner. This is the revised, second edition updated after four years of use in the field by colleges and universities, professors and practitioners, students, and educational institute leaders. It addresses the concern raised by professors Kent D. Peterson and Chester E. Finn, Jr., who said it was "ironic" that no such work existed previously that gave those responsible for administrator preparation "clear notions about what essential knowledge constitutes higher achievement among their own students." The one commendable effort to rectify this, they wrote, was "offered by AASA" in its work "spanning eight major areas of knowledge and skills."

AASA believes that most successful leaders are not born that way — they emerge. After years of education, training, and on the-job seasoning, they move to the forefront as a result of their experiences, or they become lost in the ever-changing environment that characterizes education today. AASA hopes this textbook will enable more to move forward as skilled and accomplished leaders.

In *Skills for Successful School Leaders,* AASA offers the following eight skills it believes are essential: positive school climate; building local, state, and national support; developing curriculum; instructional management; staff evaluation; staff development; resource allocation; and research, evaluation, and planning. In essence, these constitute a theory–curriculum for administrator preparation and staff development courses based on the *Guidelines for the Preparation of School Administrators* established in 1983 by the AASA Advisory Committee on Higher Education Relationships. This book contains research, ideas for successful practices, and suggested activities to provide actual experiences in each area of study.

It also represents only part of the process for the preparation of successful leaders. It is imperative that school administrators continue to pay attention to the rise and fall of issues, the rapid development of technology, and the changing values of our society. Membership in AASA, careful monitoring of professional journals, and active participation in professional seminars and institutes are critical to survival in today's chaotic school world.

AASA believes that school administration is one of the most important professions in the world. Through the unfailing endeavors of skilled leaders, America will continue to have an educated and productive people. As a result, our free and democratic society will continue to flourish.

American Association of School Administrators

INTRODUCTION

Skills for Successful School Leaders attempts what might seem the impossible, although its repeated use throughout the nation since 1985 indicates otherwise: the clear recitation and description of eight critical skill areas necessary for school leaders to master and apply.

It is believed that these are the areas in which today's administrator must be conversant, must have insights into, and must practice with sophistication if he or she is to lead successfully.

In addition to being a valuable resource for practicing administrators, this textbook also presents a comprehensive set of skills and program components to serve as a guide to improve campus-based administrator preparation programs. The reader should know, however, that these guidelines are not presented as the "ultimate" gauge for all quality administrator preparation and development programs. But it is true that, in the absence of other guides, they already have had a profound influence across the nation.

For example, these guidelines and this book influenced the Leadership in Educational Administration Development (LEAD) national network of 50 projects, which was funded by the U.S. Department of Education. The competencies, skills, and program preparation components have been the spark for papers presented at numerous education conventions; and doctoral students have completed dissertations to validate the importance of the skills in helping superintendents, principals, and college professors and administrators become successful leaders.

It appears that the eight knowledge and skill areas, plus the recommendations for program components, have become an accepted guide for "best practice" by many professors of educational administration and directors of institutes, workshops, and academies. *Skills for Successful School Leaders* also has helped provide the stimulus needed to reform inservice programs across the country, many of which have come under attack in the series of national reports during the last decade. More importantly for the practitioner, busy administrators at all levels have relied on this book for their own personal skill development plans.

One of the greatest impacts of the book is its use as the research base for the creation in 1987 of the AASA National Executive Development Center (NEDC). It is estimated that some 16,000 central office administrators nationwide could feel the impact of the NEDC programs, which could, literally, redefine the professional development process for administrators.

AASA believes that the skills and program suggestions contained in *Skills for Successful School Leaders* can continue to be the structure to guide others in determining what an administrator preparation or development program should include; to suggest who should do the teaching; and to help maintain a proper balance between the knowledge gained in the classroom or institute and actual on-the-job performance.

Each administrator needs a well-defined educational philosophy or ideology to make the deeply personal decisions that may not be handled by the AASA knowledge base and skills alone. This second edition reaffirms and builds on the philosophical, ethical, and performance dimension of school leadership to assist those charged with preparation and development programs.

The term *vision* has become important in the literature on leadership. Two popular analyses of successful businesses and their leaders, *Corporate Cultures*[1] and *In Search of Excellence*,[2] have recognized that few things are as useful as vision. So we have treated vision in Chapter 9 of this edition because it does permit a school leader to see beyond the immediate situation and to take a proactive, rather than merely a reactive, stance.

Chapter 10 now provides examples of outstanding university preparation programs and academic institutes that have incorporated various elements of the AASA skills and delivery components in their programs. Next, the reader will find information on the goals and progress of the new National Policy Board for Educational Administration. The actions of this board will have far-reaching influence on administrator preparation and development programs in the closing years of this century. The reader will find a step-by-step plan to build a state-of-the-art graduate preparation and development program based on collaborations among professional administrator associations, LEAD projects, public schools, and universities.

Finally, new references and resources have been added to each chapter to guide the reader to recent research and best practice development in each of the eight skill areas.

How To Use this Book

We view this book as a contribution to preparation and development programs already in existence, and hope that professors and staff development directors will use it to review their current programs and determine if the recommended competencies and skills are being tested and addressed. As stated in the 1983 AASA *Guidelines for the Preparation of School Administrators:*

> AASA recognizes the danger inherent in developing guidelines that may vary substantially from the programs provided by some institutions. Professionalism depends on creativity and the capacity of individuals and institutions to capitalize on these unique strengths. Since uniform standards rigidly applied may impair the flexibility that program needs to meet local or regional needs, AASA desires that these guidelines not be used to limit program development or the expertise of a given faculty.

The message is clear: National and state accrediting bodies should consider

AASA's document a guide to program improvement and not a uniform rigid standard for all to meet.

Although we have not tried to cover each of the eight areas definitively, we have attempted to develop the major concepts and present key research supporting each skill area. No single textbook could include all of the research base and practical applied solutions found in the literature of educational administration and the related fields. Just as no single theory of leadership accounts adequately for all of the leadership dimensions of successful performance, no single set of administrative or supervisory skills will solve each and every problem facing school leaders today.

However, we have attempted to describe what professors and practitioners believe are vital and common ingredients for successful school management and leadership. While our attempt to simplify and generalize may strike some as too simplistic, we believe that school leaders who possess these eight major skills will have the necessary cognitive structure to confront any uncertainty in facing the future.

Because this book represents a distillation of the perceived "essentials" of modern school leadership by consensus of both professors and practitioners, it can be used by both as follows:

To establish for practitioners:
• A baseline of job standards for various administrative positions within a school district.
• A basis for assessing job performance.
• A base for designed staff development, and a needs assessment instrument.
• A base to focus attention on the recruitment, training, and performance of school administrators at the national level.

To establish for professors:
• Criteria to examine the content of preparation courses.
• Criteria to recruit faculty members to prepare school leaders.
• A base for required research in areas that lack sufficiently grounded theory, or in which skills have become obsolete.

In specifying the skills described in the book, many subskills overlapped from one to the other. For example, collective bargaining, cited in Chapter 3 as a "political skill," also is mentioned in Chapter 8 because it involves specific legal concepts and practices. This crisscrossing of subskills means that the skills used to categorize the dimensions of school leadership are of a higher order of magnitude in grouping areas of training and practice, but are not absolutely discreet. Certain analytical skills are almost generic to all problem-solving situations in school administration. The lack of discreteness underscores the cumulative nature of the higher order skill areas as well as their integrative nature.

Finally, the designation of the skills and knowledge areas described in this book has, and will continue to serve, as a "content bridge" for communication between practitioners and professors about the value and meaning of modern school leadership. Too many times in the past, both parties "talked past each other." This resulted quite often in research with little or no practical value, and practitioners repeating past mistakes because of lack of adequate preparation or self-renewal. We hope professors and students in university graduate training programs, practicing administrators, participants in school districts and state training institutes, and other professional organizations and agencies involved in administrator training will find this a vital resource in ensuring that these competencies and skills are addressed.

Resources

1. T.E. Deal and A.A. Kennedy, *Corporate Cultures*, (Reading, Mass.: Addison-Wesley, 1982).

2. T.J. Peters and R.H. Waterman, *In Search of Excellence: Lessons from America's Best-Run Companies*, (New York: Harper & Row, 1982).

CHAPTER ONE

THE PREPARATION DILEMMA

School leaders of the future must lead others to plan and execute programs that will improve the chances for every American youth's success. To lead in times of dramatic change in family structure; to face pressures created by educational reforms and increased societal demands, requires a new kind of educator. The leader of tomorrow must form a vision of the schools we need and motivate others to join in the pursuit of that vision.

The major attribute required of leaders was best characterized by Father Theodore Hesburg, former president of the University of Notre Dame, when he observed that "the very essence of leadership is [that] you have to have a vision. It's got to be a vision you articulate clearly and forcefully on every occasion. You can't blow an uncertain trumpet."[1]

In this book we are concerned first with university-based preparation programs, and second with ongoing staff development for school administrators. Above all, we are concerned with administrative preparation as a continuum that is everlasting.

The university preservice component is charged with teaching the structure of the discipline of educational administration and serving as the research arm of the profession. Graduate students are introduced to the historical, philosophical, theoretical, political, economic, legal, technological, and organizational components of the field of study. This scholarly inquiry separates the educator from a trained "technocrat." The intellectual activities of writing, researching, and wrestling with value-laden issues of leadership and decision-making are best conducted in a university environment where qualities of the mind are revered. This quest for scholarship should, however, never be in isolation from inservice, continuous professional growth activities for practicing administrators. New skills are needed as others are mastered or are no longer critical to successful performance. New skills and knowledge are always needed to prepare school leaders for next week and next year.

New skills derived from a solid knowledge base like the one provided by this text will better prepare school leaders to conceptualize and act on the educational problems such as inadequate human and financial resources, growing numbers of "at-risk" children, and the increasing demands from staff, school boards and state education departments to improve student performance. The quest for excellence in administrator preparation should know no bounds. University leaders, then, must combine the best executive development ideas from business and from professional associations with current preparation programs to help place the preparation of school leaders high on state and national political and social agendas.

Universities, professional associations, and public schools must make greater efforts to encourage talented, eager young teachers to look toward administrative leadership roles. Quality preparation programs will attract quality students such as these, but more must be done to recruit from the teaching pool, with increased emphasis on women and minorities. These leaders will be needed to replace the 40-50 percent turnover of principals and superintendents that will occur over the next 15 years.

Reform Efforts

Since the first edition of *Skills for Successful School Leaders* appeared in 1985, the concern regarding the inadequacy of administrator preparation programs has lead to several state and national reform efforts. The most far-reaching was the report of the National Commission on Excellence in Educational Administration, *Leaders for America's Schools*.[2] The 27-member Commission, composed of leaders both within and outside the education profession, was asked by the University Council for Educational Administration to examine the quality of educational leadership in America. The commission found preparation programs with outstanding professors and students. It also found others woefully inadequate to prepare tomorrow's school leaders. Among the troubling aspects found throughout the field were the lack of:

- A definition of good educational leadership.
- Leader recruitment programs in the schools.
- Collaboration between school districts and universities.
- Minorities and women in the field.
- Systematic professional development programs for school administrators.
- Quality candidates for preparation programs.
- Preparation programs relevant to the job demands.
- Sequence, modern content, and clinical experience.
- A system of licensing that promotes excellence.
- A national sense of cooperation.

The Need for Public School/University Collaboration

It is clear that closer collaboration between public schools and universities to improve administrator preparation is crucial. Leading scholars and practitioners are calling for a careful blend of rich and intense theoretical and applied research environments that are found both on university campuses and in school districts. Many leaders in higher education and public schools maintain that the trend by education faculty to conduct "prestige" research unrelated to the real world of schools must be changed. Cecil Miskel, dean of the School of Education at the University of Michigan, states that, "Once we accept the idea that schools of education must become professional schools granting professional degrees, we can get squared away on the job of preparing school administrators."[3] Dan Griffiths, chairman of the National Commission on Excellence in Educational Administration, agrees, stating, ". . . departments of educational administration must turn back to the schools and establish relationships."[4]

The Theory/Practice Balance

Part of the problem in isolating these training factors is discussed by Jack Culbertson, former executive director of the University Council for Education Administration (UCEA), in the article, "Theory in Educational Administration: Echoes from Critical Thinkers."[5] He suggested that the theory movement in the study of educational administration launched in Chicago in 1957 has failed to live up to its advance billing. He notes that even though the theory movement has not reached a final answer about precise applications of theory to practice, researchers did "launch an exciting search directed at a very significant question: What knowledge is of most value for the field of educational administration?" In a subsequent paper, Culbertson said that, "Tomorrow's most significant research and training challenges reside primarily in the leadership practices and settings of school systems and secondarily in the research and training practices of professors of educational administration"[6]

Thus, the stage was set for new approaches to the issues of administrative theory development and effective practice. Conventional wisdom from interpreting research findings and successful practice has been the basis upon which training programs are designed. Two of the best sources on the problems in administrator preparation and the latest findings on research and successful practice to identify leadership skills and functions of successful practice are *Approaches to Administrative Training*[7] and *Leaders for America's Schools.*[8]

Common Versus Specialized Skills

Since the 1950s, when educational administration became a serious field of study in its own right, educational writers have isolated common elements found in education, business, public, and hospital administration.[9] Among these are organizational theory, theories and methods of organizational change, management information sytems, organizational behavior, and human resource management. In 1961, a UCEA Task Force on Common and Specialized Learnings included educators from various kinds of administrative positions and training programs. After a two-year study, it agreed that "about two-thirds of the learning to be acquired would be needed in common by all students and that specialized content for specific positions or functions would amount to approximately one-third."[10] Some writers have devloped skills specific to the school principal, school supervisor, assistant superintendent, and superintendent.

The National Association of Secondary School Principals (NASSP) Assessment Center bases its administrator development programs on 12 critical skills, simulation techniques and exercises, and a comprehensive program to train assessorship such as those which exist between professional schools in the university and their practitioners.[11]

NASSP's Assessment Center works with the University of Nebraska, the University of Utah, and Texas A&M University to demonstrate its concept in a campus setting. The assessment centers emphasize a series of simulated activities that include measuring abilities in decision making, human relations, instructional management, time management, and staff evaluation. A group of expert assessors observe prospective or practicing principals for several days to determine administrative potential and skill levels.

The Association for Supervision and Curriculum Development (ASCD) has identified skills for successful instructional leaders. The National Association of Elementary School Principals (NAESP) also has been active in identifying critical skills needed for successful elementary school leadership. NAESP produced an outstanding document that states its position about essential ingredients in a quality elementary or middle school. It combines the findings of current research in effective schools with the practical on-site experience of working principals.[12]

The AASA Guidelines for Preparation

In reviewing books, monographs, and papers to develop the AASA preparation guidelines, it was evident that there was a total lack of structure or system to determine what an administrator training program should include, who should do the training, and what the relationship is between the training and on-the-job performance. While discrete skills enable administrators to succeed in different specialties, almost all administrative roles require a common set of competencies and skills. It is hoped that, by establishing these common skills, order will be brought to the professional discipline of educational administration and practicing and aspiring administrators will be encouraged to establish a comprehensive practical knowledge base. The *Guidelines* have gained wide acceptance by practitioners and professors alike. Their acceptance has been documented in seven nationals studies.[13]

Leadership Outcome Goals

AASA's *Guidelines* publication presents a list of "Leadership Outcome Goals" for successful school leaders. School leaders should both understand the *theoretical foundations* and *demonstrate the application* of these specific performance goals:

1. Establish and maintain a positive and open learning environment to bring about the motivation and social integration of students and staff.

2. Build strong local, state, and national support for education.

3. Develop and deliver an effective curriculum that expands the definitions of literacy, competency, and cultural integration to include advanced technologies, problem solving, critical thinking, and communication skills, and cultural enrichment for students.

4. Develop and implement effective models/modes of instructional delivery that make the best use of time, staff, advanced technologies, community resources, and financial means to maximize student outcomes.

5. Create programs of continuous improvement, including evaluation of both staff and program effectiveness as keys to student learning and development.

6. Skillfully manage school system operations and facilities to enhance student learning.

7. Conduct and make use of significant research as a basis for problem solving and program planning of all kinds.

For each leadership outcome goal, the guidelines include related competencies and skills. A chapter is devoted to each goal with the exception of goal number five, which includes two areas of concern and will be treated in separate chapters. Thus, the seven goals become eight and are referred to as the *eight skill area*s. Of course, the degree of importance of each skill area varies from one administrative position to another. However, all administrators should attempt mastery in each.

The AASA National Executive Development Center

Based on these skill areas, AASA developed the National Executive Development Center (NEDC) for experienced school administrators who wished to build on their strengths and increase their awareness of personal and professional knowledge, attributes, and skills. The first pilot executive development center was established at the University of Texas, Austin, in 1986. The center's emphasis was on professional growth through diagnosis of strengths and weaknesses, and the development of a professional growth plan. The program was self-directed and self-paced with time-sequenced activities to enhance professional growth. The essential knowledge base was derived primarily from the competencies and skills as outlined in this book. Through several validation studies, it was determined that the essential knowledge base for administrators should be combined into five leadership task areas or domains: 1) instructional leadership; 2) general administrative leadership; 3) human relations leadership; 4) liberal education; and, 5) personal capabilities. Each leadership area was broken down into task areas, tasks, and subtasks (competencies).

Once individuals accomplished the goals as validated by mentors, peers, and themselves, they exited the system or recycled through the model for continued growth. This program is no longer offered by AASA.

Other AASA Programs

Other AASA programs that affect administrator preparation and effectiveness are the popular National Academy for School Executives (NASE) seminars and institutes, National Curriculum Audit Center, National Strategic Planning Center for Education, Superintendents' Academy, and the College of Senior Educational Executives.

The National Academy for School Executives. The AASA National Academy for School Executives (NASE) was created in 1968 to provide professional development for practicing school administrators. The academy, the concept which was proposed by the AASA Committee for the Advancement of School

Administrators (CASA), was designed to be a self-supporting arm of AASA. Since its inception, NASE has conducted hundreds of programs for more than 30,000 school administrators. Program topics are identified through a needs and interests survey of AASA members and other educational administrators. NASE professors are selected for their expertise and presentation style, and are evaluated and retained on the basis of their performance. The professors represent higher education, public education, and other agencies. NASE offers three basic types of professional development programs for members: seminars, institutes, and contract programs.[14]

The National Curriculum Audit Center. The National Curriculum Audit Center provides curriculum audit certification programs and external audits for school leaders. A curriculum audit is an objective examination of the curriculum design and delivery system of a school or school district. The process leads to the development of specific recommendations for improving curriculum affairs and advancing education effectiveness.

The AASA/NASE certification program is an intensive training course designed to prepare school leaders for the auditing experience. Instruction is led by curriculum audit expert Fenwick English, and involves a variety of teaching strategies, individual application exercises, and group activities.

As well, NASE, in cooperation with the University of Cincinnati, offers school districts a comprehensive audit of their curriculum. Fenwick English heads up the audit team, which provides school leaders with information and data as the first step toward planning for school improvement.[15] An audit examines management practice and system results and provides specific recommendations to enhance quality assurance in the school program. It it not a financial audit, although it is governed by the same principles and standards. The audit team uses documents, interviews, and site visits as major sources of data to determine the extent to which there is congruence among the written, taught, and tested curricula.

The National Strategic Planning Center. The National Strategic Planning Center for Education, under the direction of noted professor, author, and lecturer, William Cook, helps school leaders to concentrate a district's efforts and resources on agreed-upon goals. This planning process is successful in assisting school districts to develop and internalize a process that will enable them to control their future tie to self-improvement.

Superintendents' Academy. The National Superintendents' Academy, sponsored by AASA/NASE, is an intensive two-week training program that prepares new superintendents to meet the day-to-day challenges of the job, and provides insight and a competitive edge to those who aspire to the superintendency. Top-notch training is available in implementing strategies to ensure a dynamic start in the superintendency; organizing a district and motivating staff for productivity; "reading" the school board, community, and staff; determining the organizational climate of a district; and managing and improving curriculum and instructional programs, to name a few of the major topics covered.

Nationally known and recognized experts and practitioners in the field of education serve as instructors, such as Fenwick English, Terry Deal, and Bob Tschirki, among others.

College of Senior Educational Executives. A unique retreat for veteran superintendents, the College of Senior Educational Executives is an advanced leadership program designed for superintendents with 10 or more years of experience. The thrust of the college is on personal and professional assessment, renewal, and challenge; fine tuning leadership knowledge; setting new directions in leadership performance; and leading through mentoring.

Participants meet and learn from other educational leaders in America, and are challenged to grow by a variety of experts in such specialties as communication, organizational climate and culture, and wellness and personal planning.

A number of points can be made about the various AASA services. First, they are the best example of a professional group in education exercising widespread influence over the professional development of its members. Second, AASA delivery services are more responsive to the needs and interests of its members than are traditional university-based programs. Third, these programs are based on the premise that practicing school administrators can learn much from each other. The heavy reliance on the use of practicing school administrators as NASE professors most clearly reflects this assumption. Fourth, skill building and program implementation receive considerable emphasis in these programs. Finally, NASE programs underscore the importance of professionalization through shared experience during meetings and informal gatherings of participants.

New Viewpoints in Preparation

AASA also plays a vital role in administrator preparation in a much broader sense. Several scholars and professional associations are collaborating by advancing positive proposals and programs for improvement and reform. Charles Achilles, in *Leaders for America's Schools,* says that he is convinced that now is the time for new viewpoints, new models, and new structures in educational administration. "All involved in this very large enterprise need to build from a sturdy tripod: Why, what, and how!"[16]

Achilles and other leaders in educational administration support the position taken in this book that professional preparation at the universities is only part of the education of a school administrator. The well-prepared school leader is able to meet changes and new challenges by staying up to date. The university programs emphasize intellectual development and the research base, but the applied skills must be learned largely in a field setting.

Resources

1. American Association of School Administrators, *Challenges for School Leaders* (Arlington, Va.: American Association of School Administrators, 1988), p. 21.

2. National Commission on Excellence in Educational Administration, *Leaders For America's Schools* (Tempe, Ariz.: The University Council for Educational Administration, 1987), pp. xvi-xvii.

3. C. Miskel, "Research and the Preparation of Educational Administrators," paper presented at the annual meeting of the University Council for Educational Administration in Cincinnati, Ohio, October 1988, p. 22.

4. D.E. Griffiths, "Educational Administration: Reform PDQ or RIP," paper presented at the annual meeting of the American Educational Research Association in New Orleans, La., April, 1988, p. 16.

5. J. Culbertson, "Theory in Educational Administration: Echoes from Critical Thinkers," *Educational Researcher* 12, 10 (1983), pp. 15-22.

6. J. Culbertson, "Tomorrow's Challenges to Today's Professors of Educational Administration," paper presented at the annual meeting of the National Council of Professors of Educational Administration in Kalamazoo, Mich., August 1988, p. 1.

7. J. Murphy and P. Hallinger, eds., *Approaches to Administrative Training* (Albany,: SUNY Press, 1987).

8. D.E. Griffiths, R.T. Stout, and P.B. Forsyth, eds., *Leaders for America's Schools* (Berkeley, Calif.: McCutchan Publishing Corp., 1988).

9. Four works on this subject are written by E. Miklos, Training-in-Common for Educational, Public, and Business Administrators (Danville, Ill.: Interstate Printers, and Publishers, Inc.), ERIC/CEM-UCEA Series on O'Donnell. Principles of Management (New York: McGraw-Hill Book Co., 1959); J. March, "Analytical Skills and the University Training of Educational Administrators," The Journal of Educational Administration 1, 8 (1974), pp. 30-54; and J. Wilson, "Administrative Functions and Tasks Common to the Positions of President, Vice-President of Academic Affairs, Academic Deans, and Department Chairpersons in Public Institutions of Higher Education" (doctoral dissertation, Texas A&M University, 1980), pp. 139-143.

10. V. Miller, Common and Specialized Learnings for Educational Administrators (Columbus, Ohio: University Council for Educational Administration, 1962), pp. 6-7.

11. P. Hersey, "The NASSP Assessment Center Develops Leadership Talent," Educational Leadership 39 (1982), pp. 370-371; also see J. Wiles and J. Bondi, *Principles of School Administration* (Columbus, Ohio: Merrill Publishing Co., 1983), Ch. 14, "Training Modern School Leaders."

12. National Association of Elementary School Principals, *Standards for Quality Elementary Schools: Kindergarten Through Eighth Grade* (Reston, Va.: National Association of Elementary School Principals, 1984).

13. W. Edgell, "Educational Administration Professors' Perceptions of the Importance of the Competencies and Related Skills in the Guidelines for the Preparation of School Administrators" (doctoral dissertation, Texas A&M University,

1983); M.J. McClellan, "A National Study of Public School Superintendents' Perceptions of the Relevance of the Competencies and Related Skills in the Guidelines for the Preparation of School Administrators (doctoral dissertation, Texas A&M University, 1983); D.L. Piper, "Programs in Educational Administration: State-of-the-Art Perspective," presented to the National Council of Professors of Educational Administration, Missoula, Mont., August 1983; J. Fluth, "Public Senior High School Principals' Perceptions of the Importance of the Competencies and Related Skills in the Guidelines for the Preparation of School Administrators" (doctoral dissertation, Texas A&M University, 1985); S. Sclafani, "AASA Guidelines for the Preparation of School Administrators: Do They Represent the Important Job Behaviors of Superintendents?" (doctoral dissertation, The University of Texas, 1987); M. Hall, "Effective High School Principals: Perceptions of the Importance of the Competencies and Related Skills in the Guidelines for the Preparation of School Administrators" (doctoral dissertation, Texas A&M University, 1988); A.D. Pollock, "Perceptions of Selected Community, Technical, and Junior College Trustees and Administrators concerning the Relevancy of the Competencies and Skills of the American Association of School Administrators' Guidelines for the Preparation of School Administrators (doctoral dissertation, Texas A&M University, 1989).

14. J. Hoyle, "The AASA Model for Preparing School Leaders," in J. Murphy and P. Hallinger, eds., *Approaches to Administrative Training* (Albany: SUNY Press, 1987).

15. F.W. English, *Curriculum Auditing* (Lancaster, Pa., Technomic Publishing Co., Inc., 1988). Also see M.L. Paddock, "Full Accounting for Curriculum," *The School Administrator* 1, 45, (1988), pp. 12-13.

16. C.M. Achilles, "Unlocking Some Mysteries of Administration and Administrator Preparation: A Reflective Prospect," in D.E. Griffiths, R.T. Stout, and P.B. Forsyth, eds., *Leaders for America's Schools* (Berkeley, Calif.: McCutchan Publishing Corp., 1988) p. 62.

SKILLS IN DESIGNING, IMPLEMENTING, AND EVALUATING SCHOOL CLIMATE

School climate may be one of the most important ingredients of a successful instructional program. A broad term, climate refers to the environment of the school as perceived by its students, staff, and patrons. It is the school's "personality." Without a climate that creates a harmonious and well-functioning school, a high degree of academic achievement is difficult, if not downright impossible, to obtain.

Some of the skills necessary to accomplish this include:

- Human relations, organizational development, and leadership skills.

- Collaborative goal setting and action planning.

- Organizational and personal planning and time management skills.

- Skills in participatory management and the use of variations in staffing.

- Climate assessment methods and skills.

- Skills in improving the quality of relationships among staff and students to enhance learning.

- Multicultural and ethnic understanding.

- Group process, interpersonal communication, and motivation skills.

A positive climate or "feeling" in a school district and in each school in the district is vitally important. However, designing a positive, successful climate within a school, much less an entire school district, is easier said than done. School leaders alone cannot create an open school climate. At best they can set the tone for their staffs to create an open climate. That tone may be described best as morale and work motivation for school personnel and students. Positive morale and work motivation promotes an ethos that promotes higher achievement by teachers and students. Leading effective schools researchers write that a key to effective schools is:

> A school climate conducive to learning -- one that is free from disciplinary problems and that embodies high expectations for student achievement.[1]

Climate Theory Base

The writings of prominent motivational theorists, Abraham Maslow, Douglas McGregor, and Frederick Herzberg, have strongly influenced educational practice and research.[2] Notable experts in organizational dynamics led by Kurt Lewin laid the foundation for additional educational research and practice.[3] Motivational theorists have developed compelling explanations of human behavior driven by individual needs. Maslow describes the force that drives people to goals in terms of a "hierarchy of needs." The theory, simply stated, is that people have a series of sequential needs, which, when the most basic ones are fulfilled, actuate them to strive to fulfill the next higher need in the sequence (see Figure 1).[4]

Figure 1.
Maslow's Hierarchy of Needs.

Maslow's theory has been extended to examine the hygienic and psychological factors that motivate workers, and research by Frederick Herzberg of Case Western University suggests that the factors involved in producing job satisfaction and motivation are separate and distinct from the factors that lead to job dissatisfaction.[5] He has found that work achievement and responsibility are among the leading factors that motivate a worker (see Figure 2).

Figure 2.
Maslow's Needs And Herzberg's Motivators.

Self-Fulfillment Needs	Work itself, achievement	
Self-Esteem Needs	Advancement, status recognition	Motivators
Social Needs	Supervision, company policies	Non-Motivators
Safety Needs	Job security, working conditions	
Physiological Needs	Salary and benefits	
Maslow's Hierarchy of Human Needs	Herzberg's Motivators and Non-Motivators	

Theories X, Y, and Z

Douglas McGregor's "Theory X" and "Theory Y" explain two sides of human nature. "Theory X" takes the position that people dislike work and are lazy and must be pushed and directed. "Theory Y" embraces the notion that people enjoy work as much as play and are creative, autonomous, and goal seekers.[6]

"Theory Z," a relatively recent development in management literature by William Ouchi, incorporates concepts of Maslow's needs theory and McGregor's Theory Y. Theory Z emphasizes the development of "quality circles" to create small groups composed of management and workers, working as problem-solving teams (see Figure 3).[7]

Figure 3.
McGregor's Theories X and Y and Ouchi's Theory Z.

Theory X	Theory Y	Theory Z
1. People dislike work and will avoid it	1. Work is as natural as play	1. Workers and management work together in teams
2. People must be forced to work	2. People are self-directed and will strive to accomplish objectives	2. Managers clarify, and gain workers' support of company objectives
3. People want to be directed and will avoid responsibility	3. People will learn to accept and seek responsibility	3. Management and workers take a long run company view

The major difference between theories Y and Z is that Theory Y is an example of the leadership style of one individual. Theory Z focuses on the culture of an entire organization and the way it functions to reach maximum efficiency and productivity.

Others have written that people will choose to behave in response to the motivational forces that are strongest.[8] Writers in industrial settings note that workers frequently are forced by management to behave in immature ways that fit the premises of "Theory X." Managers are urged to apply ideas similar to "Theory Y" that will produce mature and more highly motivated self-directed behavior in the workers.[9] Each of these theorists has sought answers to the reasons people are motivated to join organizations, stay in them, and become productive contributors. That is, they have tried to capture the elusive variables that explain worker morale and work climate.

Motivation Theory

During the past 20 years progress has been made in understanding morale and work motivation, which in combination create the work climate. However, knowledge gained in other settings has not been transferred adequately to educational settings and to school leaders. A few researchers have attempted to transfer those research efforts to educational settings.[10] Though much work remains to be done in testing work motivation theories in education, Cecil Miskel of the University of Michigan asserts, "Encouraging signs are evident that work motivation theory is a viable and growing area . . . ."[10]

AASA has produced a Critical Issues Report titled *Building Morale–Motivating Staff* that presents excellent ideas for building staff morale.[11] The 12 chapters include educator and business management views on morale builders and morale killers, case studies on successful staff motivation programs, suggestions on managing conflict, examples of the "right" kinds of inservice to build morale, and many other topics. While most of the practical ideas in the report are steeped in theory, researchers are seeking ways to validate and adapt these types of successful practices to school districts. The opportunities are ripe for scholars to make significant contributions to the theory base on what school administrators can do to become leaders in building morale and motivating staff to produce positive school climates.

Job Enrichment and Career Ladders

Current motivation research findings indicate clearly that work factors which motivate workers are:

- The work itself.
- Recognition for good work.
- Achievement/responsibility.
- Promotion.

This theory base offers school leaders valuable insights into enriching the jobs of all staff members within a school. The development of "career ladders" for teachers and administrators is a viable system to encourage staff growth and opportunity for more responsibility, achievement, and promotion.

Climate and Student Achievement

Psychologists have also studied the impact of environment or climate on human personality. Kurt Lewin, a noted authority on organizational dynamics, believed that human behavior is a function of the interaction of person and environment. His research spawned a generous body of literature on the subject.[12] Researchers have gathered data through self-report questionnaires, observations, interviews, and experimental manipulations of organizational variables in educational settings. Other writers indicate that institutional and individual characteristics interact in schools and determine student learning.[13] In spite of the tremendous amount of energy expended by researchers of school climate, the exact effect of school climate on student achievement has yet to be determined.[14]

Climate Improvement Skills

However, there is enough evidence to convince professors and school leaders that administrators can promote and sustain a more positive school climate to improve student achievement by:

● Conducting surveys to measure school climate.

● Developing long range goals for climate improvement.

● Working patiently to help other administrators and teachers implement sound classroom management.

● Setting a consistent example of leadership and a sense of caring.

● Believing in the strengths and talents and good intentions of staff members.

● Creating an open communication network through frequent personal contact to keep informed about professional and personal concerns and needs.

These examples of leadership will pay off in higher levels of student achievement and higher staff morale.

Few doubt that positive school climate has a positive effect on student performance. A major four-year study in which private and public schools were compared reinforced this belief by declaring that:

> Recent studies indicate that the most effective schools are distinguished, not by elaborate facilities, extensively trained teachers, small classes, or high levels of financial support, but by *outstanding social climate*.[15]

Thus the abundance of research in many organizational settings has established the thesis that motivation affects human performance. People will respond to what satisfies their personal needs. School leaders must continue to investigate how staff and students feel about themselves, their tasks, and their school environments. Top performers need an open supportive climate. This belief is vital in designing, implementing, and evaluating school climate improvement programs.

Designing and Implementing School Climate Improvement Programs

School administrators from the superintendent to the department chairpersons hold equal responsibility in a district when it comes to designing a school climate improvement program. However, if superintendents and board members are reluctant to create an open atmosphere, it could inhibit creating successful climates. A school leader's ability to influence policymakers, professional staff, and the various publics is the key to designing and sustaining a school climate improvement program.

The importance of designing a positive school climate can hardly be overstated, for a school's climate has a powerful impact upon the teachers' and students' feelings of self-worth and mutual respect, which promote effective teaching and learning. When effective teaching and learning are occurring, the accomplishment of school goals is inevitable. The most common findings emerging from school effectiveness research is that effective schools have clear goals and a positive "can do" attitude on the part of staff and students that the goals will be attained.

Human Relations, Organizational Development, and Leadership Skills

What are other key steps that school leaders must take to create a positive climate? Although no substantial research exists on the best steps to take, the general consensus in the literature and among social scientists is that the *team approach* is "in." School leaders agree that use of good human relations and leadership skills are important to improve school climate.

The first step in promoting good school climate is to create an awareness of climate and to assess the climate of your school or school district. To do this, there are many model instruments, some of which we discuss in this chapter. After positive and negative climate features have been identified, the school team – administrators, teachers, and sometimes parents and students – should decide what areas they wish to improve and how they will do it.

Among the major methods to improve human relations and school climate are models and skills presented in the CFK Ltd. Model, the Denver Plan, Group Problem-Attack Training, and Organizational Development.

School Climate Improvement Models and Skills

CFK Ltd.'s Model. This excellent model, which combines research with action, focuses on the role of the superintendent and other central office personnel in building a positive school climate throughout a school district. It provides a step-by-step guide for school teachers who wish to develop a healthy school climate.[16] The CFK model is based on work by the climate improvement teams who use the CFK Ltd. School District Profile in the field. The model's major components:

• The climate improvement teams are initially composed of central office staff and then branch to include site administrators and teachers.

• The teams meet in members' homes or at school in an informal, relaxed atmosphere and discuss data collected from the profile.

• Each participant completes a self-evaluation profile and the group leadership is rotated to teach human relations and communications skills to each group member to enhance commitment and increase personal involvement.

The idea, which came before the concept of "quality circles" and "Theory Z," is to involve every administrator and teacher in the district who wishes to participate. The underlying purpose of climate improvement team activities is to create open classroom climates conducive to student growth and development.

The Denver Plan. Another successful districtwide climate improvement program has been designed and implemented under court direction in the Denver school district.[17] According to Evie Dennis, the Denver plan was established to "improve understanding of racial and ethnic groups by students and staff." They used the following steps:

• Each campus or School Inservice Committee (SISC) in the district created a human relations council composed of administrators, teachers, parents, and students from the racial, ethnic, and age categories living in the school attendance area.

• Training sessions were held for representatives from each council to teach group leadership skills and planning techniques (for example, Nominal Group Technique [NGT], attitude survey techniques, and climate assessment strategies).

• Motivation skills were stressed to help the representatives present a positive "winning attitude" when training council members.

• After the training sessions, videotapes, reading materials, and climate self-report questionnaires were made available to the representatives to train other council members.

• The councils meet monthly with the major goal of bringing people together in each attendance area to improve the school climate and to provide all students with opportunities for success.

Group Problem-Attack Training (GPAT). Another design for school climate improvement is Group Problem-Attack Training (GPAT).[17] GPAT incorporates research findings from educational administration, social psychology, organizational development, organizational behavior, and leadership. The following procedures are employed:

- Each problem identifies points of conflict and communication problems that impair positive school climate.

- The groups "attack the problems" within the restraints of board policy, school law, and budget.

- The sessions are held monthly or more frequently if needed.

- Conflict resolution is used to diffuse the problems among the entire staff, giving each person a "piece of the rock" in resolving conflicts.

GPAT is based on the premise that if the leadership can hold people together long enough to bring the best collaborative thinking to the problem, the solution will be more effective and create higher morale and a more open school climate.

Prior to the formation of the GPAT sessions, an assessment of administrators', teachers', and students' perceptions is made. The resulting data provide a districtwide and school "view" of climate and administrative leadership. It also creates some structure for the sessions and focuses on solutions to problems and not on individuals. The data also point out differing "views" of the same climate among administrators, teachers, and students. Thus, diagnosis of school climate helps answer the question: Where are we? This assessment can be done by administering self-report inventories such as the Organizational Climate Description Questionnaire (OCDQ), the Learning Climate Inventory (LCI), and other similar instruments, (see pp. 28-33).

Another rather simple, but effective, data – gathering technique is the open-ended questionnaire. Using these three questions encourages creative and varied responses:

1. If you could rent the Goodyear Blimp and fly it over your school district, what three messages would you flash on its side to tell the public about the accomplishments made in your school climate in the past two years?

2. What two or three changes would you like to see made to improve your school climate by the year 1995?

3. What barriers do you see that may stop you from improving your school climate by the year 1995?

The responses to the self-report questionnaires and the three questions can reveal formal and informal "climate" information important to the GPAT process.

Organizational Development (OD). Organizational development, one approach for designing effective school climate programs, is a series of planned strategies for the diagnosis, intervention, change, growth, and self-renewal of organizations.[19] To open a school (or school district) to OD invites an inspection of value structures, authority relationships, processes communication, staff idiosyncrasies, and so on. Because it opens up everything for inspection, growth and trust can be established. Successful OD programs require several important ingredients:

- People must see strong reasons to improve.

- The decision to enact an OD activity must be made jointly by the consultant, the manager, and the subordinates.

- Ideally, OD activities should start at the top and work down in an organization.

- The real thrust of OD activities is to tap the resources of the people in the organization.

- OD is a collaborative process of managing the culture of the organization—not something that is done to somebody, but a process of people working together to improve their mutual effectiveness.[20]

Thus, OD programs designed to improve individual and group effectiveness can be effective in improving school climate.

Other suggestions for designing a positive school climate have been compiled from activities that have worked for people in the field. These are some of the suggestions culled from their ideas:

- *Rebirth of the organization*. Let the staff know that organizational change is afoot by stating new goals and presenting a plan of action.

- *Building a history*. Shared experiences among staff members—such as pre-school retreats—can establish a warm glow of camaraderie that will help boost morale.

- *Building trust*. Use established management training exercises to help build trust.

- *Communications*. Quality, not quantity, is important.

- *Reinforcement*. Maintain group cohesion through staff meetings with informal, participant-generated agendas.

- *Pride*. The administrator can involve each participant in owning a piece of the action by explicitly commending staff-development innovations and improvements.[21]

The design and implementation of these and similar human relations, organizational development, and leadership skills will promote school climate improvement programs if school staff members feel "ownership" and believe in themselves and their leaders.

Collaborative Goal Setting and Action Planning

Goals are not good unless they are agreed upon and reachable. It is also important that all staff members and other individuals affected by the goals are involved in setting the goals. Therefore, school leaders must have skills in collaborative goal setting and action planning to ensure broad involvement and support.

Many states have legislated that local school districts develop goals. For example, the school accreditation process in Texas requires each district to establish goals for student development. Each district arranges for constructive involvement of school and community representatives to select and adopt official goals for a five-year time period. The goals are sent to the Texas Education Agency along with an action plan describing the implementation and monitoring of the five-year plan for goal accomplishment. Most school leaders have gone beyond the basic requirement of "constructive involvement of representatives" and have total community participation.

Several school districts have involved virtually hundreds of thousands of people in their goal-setting processes. In addition to community leaders, separate groups of citizens, teachers, and students were selected through a random sampling process to ensure a good balance from the three categories. The citizen sample represented all geographic areas, ethnic groups, educational levels, occupations, and other characteristics of the population residing in the school district. School leaders employed the skills of collaborative goal setting and action planning to work with these groups. The adage, "United we stand, divided we fall," has never been so important for school leaders as it is today. As more people turn away from public schools and search for alternatives, school leaders must build stronger coalitions to ensure that the common school remains a source of community pride and truly represents the educational needs of its community.

A more useful goal attainment model available in R. L. Hammond's chapter "Evaluation at the Local Level" in *Education Evaluation: Theory and Practice* includes these first steps:

- Determine what needs to be evaluated.
- Define the important variables.
- Write objectives in behavioral terms.
- Measure the behavior described in the objective.
- Determine the extent of goal attainment.

A second model is presented in chapter nine in Figure 5.[22] Other suggested readings and activities on goal setting and action planning are presented under skill B on the Skill Accomplishment Checklist at the end of this chapter.

Organizational and Personal Planning and Time Management

Good organizers who use time efficiently and wisely help create good school climates. Staff and students need order and must use class time to accomplish learning tasks. Time on task and academic learning time must become primary concerns. Unless we become more adept at planning the school year and day, teachers and students may be facing seven or eight hours for 220 days. We are not using school time as efficiently as we know how. If school climate is to be improved, use of school time must be carefully planned. Some successful time management tips are as follows:

● Inform each staff member about state and local time on subject requirements and the importance of effective use of learning time.

● Request each staff member to develop a time management schedule for one month.

● Conduct an inservice program on efficient planning and time use.

● Initiate an observation system using audio and video recordings of classroom activities.

● Request each staff member to complete an annual time efficiency report.

Helpful hints for successful time management are described in *School Leadership: Handbook for Survival* published by the Clearinghouse on Educational Management at the University of Oregon. Drawing from numerous studies, the handbook recommends these steps:

1. Set goals and put them in priority lists.

2. Develop a daily time log.

3. Manage time wasters (for example, visitors and phone calls, meetings, paperwork, inability to say "no," inability to schedule, inability to delegate, and procrastination).

AASA's publication *Time on Task* also provides useful hints for successful time management.

Participative Management, Variations in Staffing

School leaders must know the goals of their schools and which decisions they wish to share. They also have a responsibility for helping staff at all levels in the district to understand the parameters of shared leadership. Some staff members may not wish to participate in some decisions. C. I. Barnard, in *The Functions of the Executive* refers to this as the "Zone of Indifference." Barnard refers to areas of decision making in which staff members take great interest and have expertise to contribute as the "Zone of Sensitivity." [23, 24]

No matter the reason, it is most important to know the talents and interests of all staff members (central administrators, principals, teachers, and others) and use that information to involve them on specific problem-solving teams or task forces. It is equally important for school leaders to know when to share the responsibilities that come with leadership. A warm, sensitive, "good person" who lacks participatory skills can literally "give the school away" in the name of shared decision making. Decisions about personnel, legal areas, board policy, teacher associations or unions, and decisions that require highly specialized personnel are examples of areas where shared decisions are not appropriate. Thus, to design an effective school climate improvement program, a school leader must identify and involve staff who have both the interest and expertise. The following techniques are helpful in assisting school leaders determine which staff members to include in various decisions:

● Conduct a survey to assess staff interest in being involved on committees to investigate specific school operations (for example, curriculum development, staff evaluation, planning, scheduling, community activities).

● Determine the areas of expertise of each staff member and place the names under specific categories.

● Develop a computerized interest and talent bank based on the above steps.

● Construct committees based on both interest and expertise in specific problem areas.

These suggestions for improved participative management and the use of personnel can also be used to develop a community leader resource talent bank to assist in problem-solving and action plans that will also create good will and strong coalitions for the district.

Variations in Staffing

For more than 20 years researchers and administrators have investigated ways to differentiate the roles and responsibility of staff to allow for individual differences and interests. With renewed interest by state legislatures, school boards, and motivational researchers to find some form of merit pay for superior performers, school leaders are turning to "career ladders" or differentiated staffing systems. For example, opportunities are created for teachers to seek promotion through a step-by-step climb to the position of master teacher. Master teachers would gain more status, higher salary, and more responsibility. They would serve as instructional supervisor models and evaluators of other classroom teachers. They would also be required to obtain advanced degrees and remain current through self-study and inservice programs. A team composed of other master teachers, administrators, and university professors would select master teachers and evaluate their progress.

Climate Assessment Methods and Skills

Within any school district, no two learning climates are exactly alike. Schools have organizational personalities, which include unique organizational styles and human dynamics. One of the most definitive works to investigate the relationship between environment and student achievement is *Educational Environment and Effects: Evaluation Policy and Productivity*.[25] The book is a series of investigations that deal with environments outside the school as well as with various aspects of environment within the classroom.

Most efforts to evaluate school climate have included either observational or self-report methods and instruments. Observational instruments are "low inference" because they are used to record directly observable specific behaviors or incidents. Self-report methods and instruments are labeled "high inference" because they ask the respondents to judge how they feel or perceive the climate to be.

Observational Instruments and Techniques. The use of observation instruments to evaluate school climate is based on the assumption that it is possible to infer feelings or "affect" by watching the overt behaviors of students, teachers, and administrators in school settings. While it is true that people behave differently in different school settings, it is often difficult to make inferences about teachers' or students' motives with respect to specific behaviors. However, by noting a pattern of behavior across a variety of classroom settings, observers can draw inferences about feelings of staff and students. A book titled *Assessing Affective Characteristics in the Schools* is an excellent source on the topic of affective assessment that is inextricably linked to evaluating school climates.[26]

Classroom Interactions. The anthology *Mirrors of Behavior* contains 92 observational systems. Of these, 76 have been used for observation of instruction in learning climates. The most detailed and frequently used observational instrument is Flander's Interaction Analysis System (IA).[28] The IA system became a base for many similar systems used to record the sequences of behavioral events in the classroom.

● Trained observers record classroom interaction or videotape classroom activity for analysis.

● The system focuses on how the teacher influences student actions and distinguishes "direct" and "indirect" influence.

● The classifications of categories include seven types for teacher talk and three types for student talk.

Even though researchers find mixed evidence of the significance between teachers' interaction patterns and students' performances, many still believe that too much teacher talk can stifle student spontaneity and initiative. Teachers can benefit from having an occasional analysis of their teaching behaviors, but these benefits come only if well-trained observers conduct multiple observations and plan carefully as to what will be observed, who will do the observing, and how often the observations will occur. For some administrators the time and expense involved in completing observational procedures may seem impractical; however, observations are an invaluable method for uncovering some of the mystery between classroom climate and student achievement.

Useful Questionnaires. There are many types of observational instruments for checking the climate of a school or district. Some are geared toward specific variables; others are more global. Exhibit 1,(page 28)"The School Climate Observation Checklist," is an example of a relatively simple observational instrument for observing more global climate variables. With some alterations for grade levels, it can be used to gather various general indicators about a school's or district's climate. *Building Morale...Motivating Staff;* an AASA Critical Issues Report, contains an instrument to measure organizational health. The data gathered on these types of observational checklists combined with data gathered from other sources can provide detailed information about the climate of a specific school or school district.

Nonstandardized and Standardized Self-Report Instruments. Self-report instruments usually take the form of a series of statements, adjectives, or questions. They gather a person's perception of what is, what was, or what ought to be. However, there are almost as many self-report instruments to measure learning climates as there are climates to measure. This is a result of researchers and practicing administrators believing that they can develop an instrument that asks the "right" questions for their situations. Several widely used instruments to measure school climate are based on theory but have no checks for validity and reliability. The CFK Ltd. School Climate Profile is an example of an instrument developed by professors and practitioners.

Nonstandardized Secondary School Climate Instruments. Exhibit 2, The Secondary School Attitude Inventory (SSAI), is an example of a nonstandardized student self-report instrument (page 31). The SSAI asks students in grades 7-12 to agree or disagree with statements on a Likert scale describing general kinds of activities that characterize their class. The activities are used to assess two dimensions of school climate: stress on effective classroom conditions and on futures oriented higher order thinking skills. Teachers can also respond to the items to compare their perceptions on the two dimensions with their students' perceptions. The instrument contains 30 items and can be handscored in a short time.

Designing Your Own Questionnaire. A strong case can be made for nonstandardized "homemade" or "situational" questionnaires, particularly those constructed to assess attitudes or opinions on a set of specific issues of local concern. Several self-report questionnaires or instruments of this nature are available in the comprehensive *Handbook of Organizational Development in Schools.*[29] Opinionnaires to measure attitude change before and after new programs can be "tailormade" to answer specific, valid questions. The items can be written by a group composed of teachers, students, parents, principals, and superintendent. These items can relate directly to the philosophical, instructional, and human variables that affect school climate.

Standardized Self-Report Instruments. Two classes of standardized climate instruments stand out. They are *student self-report* and *teacher self-report* instruments.

• STUDENT SELF-REPORT INSTRUMENTS FOR MIDDLE, JUNIOR, AND SENIOR HIGH SCHOOLS. One of the more promising and frequently used instruments to measure the classroom climate through the eyes of students is the *Learning Environment Inventory (LEI)*.[30] The LEI, which measures student attitude (grades 7-12) through a number of classroom dimensions, is convenient and easy to administer. If possible, though, it should be machine scored. There are seven items in each of the 15 dimensions. The names of some of the dimensions and their internal consistency are: intimacy (.78); friction (.78); satisfaction (.80); difficulty (.66); and apathy (.83). In several studies LEI scores were found to be better predictors of student achievement than were IQ scores. Researchers and school leaders will find the LEI to be a helpful tool in evaluating a learning climate.

Other valid and reliable student self-report instruments deserve mention. They are the *High School Characteristics Index (HSCI), Classroom Environment Scale (CES)* and the *Class Activities Questionnaire (CAQ)*.[31, 32, 33] The instruments can be used, with some caution, in grades 6-12. The HSCI contains 300 items and requires a sophisticated scoring process.

The CES consists of 90 true-false items grouped into nine subscales. All nine subscales discriminate significantly among classrooms in three parallel forms:

—The Real Form (Form R) asks teachers and students how they perceive the climate.

—The Ideal Form (Form I) asks them what they perceive to be an ideal classroom climate.

—The Expectations Form (Form E) asks prospective members of a class what they think the classroom climate they are about to enter is like.

The Class Activities Questionnaire (CAQ) assesses both the cognitive and affective dimensions of the learning climate using "lower-inference" items. The CAQ asks students for a statement of agreement or disagreement on a four-point Likert scale describing general kinds of activities that characterize their class. The items measure student and teacher perceptions of the levels of cognitive development being stressed. The seven cognitive dimensions, adapted from Bloom's taxonomy, range from low to high. Other items on the CAQ measure the classroom climate dimension. The reliability coefficients range from .76 to .88 for each of the four major dimensions of lower thought processes, higher thought processes, classroom focus, and classroom climate. The value of the CAQ is that teachers are able to compare their views of cognitive levels and classroom climate with the students'. views.

• STUDENT SELF-REPORT IINSTRUMENTS FOR ELEMENTARY SCHOOLS. The LEI has been adapted for use with elementary students. This new instrument, called the My Class Inventory (MCI), has 45 items and 5 subscales. The scales are valid and reliable measures of elementary student perceptions of the class climate.

Another student self-report instrument is the *Elementary School Environment Survey (ESES)*.[34] The ESES contains 100 items that indicate five dimensions of environmental press: Practicality, Community, Awareness, Propriety, and Scholarship. These instruments are reliable and could prove helpful to researchers and practitioners. However, the ESES is lengthy and requires a sophisticated scoring process.

● SELF-REPORT SYSTEM FOR GENERAL USE. Rensis Likert Associates (RLA, Inc.) has a *School Profile Inventory* that includes questionnaires for students, principals, superintendents, central staff, teachers, and parents.[35]A Likert School Profile data printout is made available through Rensis Likert Associates, Inc. The instruments are well-designed, lengthy, and must be scored through RLA, Inc. The RLA approach gives a total system view of climate, which can be valuable in policy development. The authors recommend the LEI, MCI, and CAQ as the most useful standardized student self-report instruments for both researchers and school leaders.

● TEACHER SELF-REPORT INSTRUMENTS. These instruments hold the greatest promise in evaluating school climates. Teachers are the principal agents of climate because the way they perceive their situation affects their behavior and effectiveness. Research findings in social psychology and administrative theory disclose a close relationship between self-perception and behavior or performance. Some humanistic psychologists and educators believe that performance is entirely dependent on self-perception. It is sound theory to assume that a self-actualized, enthusiastic, productive teacher will have a greater positive impact on learners than a teacher who possesses none of these characteristics. No matter how we define or characterize good and bad teaching, it is difficult to see how an unfulfilled, dissatisfied teacher could have a positive effect on students. Thus, valid, reliable teacher self-report instruments are important in evaluating learning climate.

The most popular and widely used instrument for evaluating school climate has been the *Organizational Climate Description Questionnaire (OCDQ)* developed by Halpin and Croft.[13] The OCDQ contains 69, four-point Likert items assigned to eight subscales developed by factor analytic methods. The rationale underlying the OCDQ assumes that school climate is closely related to the perceived behaviors of teachers and principals. Six school climate profiles have emerged through using the instrument in various studies. They are Open Climate, Autonomous Climate, Controlled Climate, Familiar Climate, Closed Climate, and Paternal Climate.

The OCDQ is more applicable to elementary or smaller middle or junior high schools. The results tend to be inconsistent when the OCDQ or any teacher self-report instruments are used in large schools, especially high schools because teachers have less opportunity to interact professionally and socially. Consequently, the chances are greater that "disengagement" scores will be high and "esprit" scores low. These measures produce a profile of a Closed Climate school. For this reason, researchers and building principals (in large high schools) are reluctant to profile a large high school climate as open or closed based solely on the OCDQ, LCI, or other teacher self-report scores. However, in spite of this weakness, the instrument remains strong in identifying importing factors impacting school climate as perceived by teachers.

Administrators view climate differently. Researchers using the OCDQ found discrepancies between the way the teachers view the school climate and the way principals perceive it, according to Wiggins.[13] The feedback from both is useful in planning inservice programs for teachers. The OCDQ, like other teacher self-report instruments, must be used in the context of the total school environment. A "Familiar" or "Paternal" climate may be the best climate in certain kinds of schools and the worst in others. Influences external to an individual school must also be considered when drawing conclusions about school climate.

Administering the OCDQ is easy and requires approximately 30 minutes, but the scoring requires computer procedures and skilled interpretation.

Another teacher self-report instrument is the *Organizational Climate Index (OCI)* developed by Stern and Steinhoff.[36] The OCI presents teachers with 300 true-false items about their school. The items describe first and second order factors to assess the climate. Because the instrument requires more than an hour to complete, it has not been widely used. A well-designed study of innovative schools using the OCI was conducted by Ron Roland of Albany State University.[37] He had difficulty gathering the data because of the amount of teacher time required. The theory base and strength of the OCI offer the researcher an excellent instrument to find more specific measures of school climate. However, its length prevents practical application in many schools.

One helpful teacher self-report instrument is the *Learning Climate Inventory (LCI)*[38] (See sample in Exhibit 3). The LCI was developed to assess the learning climate in elementary and secondary schools. It was initially used as an organizational development tool in several Ohio school districts to gather staff perceptions of learning climate in each building and in the district. Profiles for each school based on the data gathered were constructed and given to the staff in interpretive conferences. The instrument contains 20 items with a seven-point Likert–type scale. The original instrument contained 45 items, and pilot tests and factor analytic procedures reduced them to 20 with five factors. The reliability coefficients for each factor range from .50 to .75. Test-retest reliabilities range from .75 to .92. The five factors are:

1. Leadership: The extent to which the teachers perceive the leadership behaviors of the administrators.

2. Freedom: The extent to which teachers feel free to experiment and determine their own instructional activities in their classrooms.

3. Evaluation: The extent to which teachers and students are involved in teacher and administrator evaluation.

4. Compliance: The extent to which teachers feel the pressure to conform to the rules of the system.

5. Cooperation: The extent to which teachers are supported in their efforts to team-teach and use resource people.

The LCI is designed to gather teachers' perceptions about their administrators, peers, and teaching situation. An advantage of the LCI is its brevity. When compared to the 69–item OCDQ and the 300–item OCI, the 20–item LCI takes only 10 to 15 minutes to complete. With many longer instruments respondents tend to hurry and are less considerate in their responses, especially if the instruments are administered at the end of the day during "a faculty meeting."

Another frequently used and excellent teacher self-report instrument is the *Pupil-Control Ideology (PCI)*[40] The PCI is a 20-item instrument that measures pupil-control orientation along a continuum from custodial to humanistic. It differs from the OCDQ and LCI in that it focuses solely on teacher-student relations. The concept of pupil-control ideology has proven to be a powerful predictor of a school's tone or feeling. A strong relationship has been formed between humanism in the pupil-control orientation schools and the openness of a schools' organizational climate.[41]

Measures of Administrative Leadership. Decision making is an important component of a learning environment. The *Problem-Attack Behavior Inventory (PABI)* is a useful instrument for gathering teacher perceptions of how the principal makes decisions.[42] The instrument consists of 15 items that make up five factors are:

- Problem-recognition behavior.
- Problem-analysis behavior.
- Group participation behavior.
- Active behavior.
- Evaluative behavior.

The PABI has been successfully used to differentiate the behavior of five high school principals whose behaviors were hypothesized to be similar because of the similarities in their personal characteristics and the homogeneity of their schools. In a study that created interest in the feminist movement to encourage the hiring of more women administrators, PABI results found that women elementary principals recognize problems more frequently than do men and re-evaluate their decisions more often.[43] Also, factors in PABI and LBDQ have been found to be statistically correlated.[44] The PABI can be adapted to measure perceptions of a superintendent's or other central office administrators' problem-attack skills.

Although the PABI is a simple and proven inventory to gather teacher perceptions of a building principal's behavior, administrators should take care in interpreting the data. A principal who "always" recognizes or acts on a problem may not be the most effective leader. Data must be interpreted in context with other variables such as teacher satisfaction, school goal accomplishment, or student behavior.

Another instrument developed to measure administrative leadership and its effect on climate is the *Leader Behavior Description Questionnaire (LBDQ)*. Fred Fiedler, a leader in leadership research, after dozens of investigations in controlled situations, concluded that the effective leadership style depends on three conditions:

- Relationship between the leader and group members.

- Nature of the task to be accomplished—whether it is structured or unstructured.

- Position power of the leader. [45]

Because the leader and the group are so inextricably linked the LBDQ is effective in gathering the teachers' views of a principal's leader behavior.

From the LBDQ, which consists of a series of short descriptive statements concerning the behavior of leaders, two dimensions or factors — "Initiating Structure" and "Consideration" — have emerged. [46] Initiating Structure refers to a leader's behavior in delineating the relationship between himself or herself and members of the workgroup. This dimension also includes how a leader defines patterns of organization, channels of communication, and methods of procedure. Consideration refers to behavior indicative of friendship, mutual trust, respect, and warmth in the relationship between a leader and staff members.

From data gathered in numerous studies, it is obvious that Initiating Structure and Consideration are essential to the behavior of leaders. The two dimensions are not arranged on a continuum, but are separate. The two types of behavior may be plotted on a horizontal and vertical axis to mark a leader's score in either of four quadrants. Most effective leaders will score high on both Initiating Structure and Consideration. [47]

The LBDQ, like other teacher self-report instruments, remains no more than a tool to gather an observer's perceptions. All studies, no matter how carefully administered, have limitations, and any findings should be carefully interpreted. The LBDQ, however, should be in the arsenal of every researcher and administrator who attempts to analyze a school climate. It is easy to administer and the scoring is not complicated. These climate and leadership assessment questionnaires can provide valuable information about ways to improve interpersonal relationships which is presented in the following section.

Improving the Quality of Relationships Among Staff and Students to Enhance Learning

School leaders must be willing to model behavior for those who are expected to follow them. They must "walk the walk" not merely "talk the talk". The attributes of good leadership begin early in the lives of people and the secrets of training great leaders eludes the best university and academy training programs. Some researchers focus on the "situational" nature of leadership while others study the personal and physical traits of leaders. More than 40 years ago writers argued that leaders should be good listeners, that they need to understand the social structure of industry, and above all else they must achieve understanding of the sentiments of workers. This thesis remains important today. It is the central theme in the book titled *In Search of Excellence: Lessons from America's Best Run Companies*. [48]

Therefore, there is little doubt that school leaders must possess the following skills:

- They must be good listeners.
- They must understand the social structure of the school and community.
- They must be attuned to the sentiments of the staff, students, and patrons.

Since each person is unique with different needs and ambitions, school administrators need to model their skills in listening, caring, and team building to enhance improved staff performance and student learning.

Multicultural and Ethnic Understanding

We must ensure that the schools provide multicultural and multiethnic information in curriculum and staff development programs. Especially critical are skills in shared decision making and in creating a supportive school climate to accommodate the racial and ethnic differences of young people and their communities are critical.[49] Administrators must possess the skills to be effective in providing education for the ethnic groups in our nation:

- Finding data sources in the community to monitor the number of different cultural ethnic groups.
- Understanding the cultural backgrounds of the school population.
- Developing networks with church leaders and social service agencies.
- Seeking curriculum materials and textbooks relevant to minority cultures.
- Avoiding biased materials that place women or minorities in inferior positions.

Working With Others

The search is endless for the secret to communicate with and motivate people to work toward the accomplishment of school goals. We claim that we value and believe in our staffs but turn around and psychologically "drop kick" to get anything done. We talk about applying the humanizing elements of Theory Y and Theory Z but apply the dictator tactics of Theory X. We assert that we trust people and believe that they will enjoy their work as much as play but then suspiciously watch them to make sure that they do it our way. How often do we hear a school administrator mournfully say, "I knew they couldn't be trusted. I should have done it myself." Assumptions made about the abilities and motives of staff are important in determining how we act toward others. If we are cynical about the motives of other administrators, teachers, and board members, then we will fail to lead them in accomplishing school goals. If, on the other hand, we like ourselves, flaws and all, and believe in our abilities, then we will like other people, flaws and all, and believe in their abilities to get the job done. School leaders need to know that their interpersonal communication sends out clear signals about how much they trust and believe in others. A high level of faith in others is a must if schools are to be good places to work and learn.

Group Process, Interpersonal Communication, and Motivation Skills

Administrators work each year with hundreds of groups whose purposes range from planning a party to discussing a law suit against the district. Skills in group process are vital to ensure that each member of a group feels free to contribute and is valued as a person of worth. If a meeting is called and the administrator determines the agenda, dominates the discussion, and decides the outcome, then why not send a memo announcing the decision in the first place? If school leaders believe that they have all of the talent and knowledge in the school, then they will not see the need to delegate and share the load. Geese may be smarter than many school leaders. A flock of geese flying in formation knows the meaning of believing in each other. The lead goose creates a draft or vacuum for the geese following on the left and right. When the lead goose tires, another takes the lead role and the journey continues. By this wonder of nature a flock of geese can fly 78 percent farther than a single goose can fly alone. Thus, the research on group process and maturation concludes that:

• School leaders who trust and believe in others and model these traits will accomplish far more and develop devoted followers.

• A true leader shows the way and encourages others during the journey.

Therefore, skills in group process, interpersonal communication, and motivation must be tested and sharpened if we want to see ourselves as school leaders. We must know ourselves if we are to know others.

Conclusion

In this chapter, we introduced three main issues in school climate: (1) rationale and examples of school climate design and implementation; (2) behaviors required of administrators to improve school climate; and (3) observations and self-report processes and instruments to evaluate school climates.

The first issue makes the sound assumption that an open climate in a school district and in each school is a major factor in promoting improved teacher and student performance. Hundreds of research efforts have failed to show precise causal relationships between specific characteristics of school climates and student achievement. That is, few answers exist to the questions about the exact processes and strategies to open communications among central office administrators, principals, assistant principals, and teachers to improve school climate and student performance.

However, there is enough climate research evidence to convince professors and school administrators that the ways in which administrators behave establish a positive or negative school climate. How they manage time and resources and relate to other administrators, teachers, and students correlate with successful schools with open supportive climates. Repeated studies on effective schools support the conviction that administrators set the tone for creating a school climate conducive to learning, with clear goals, free from disciplinary problems, and embodying high expectations for teachers and students.

Finally, most efforts to evaluate school climates have included either observational or self-report methods and instruments. Observational strategies are important to make inferences about the behaviors of students, teachers, and administrators in school settings. Even though it is often difficult to make these inferences because the observers must be well trained, observation strategies can prove valuable in gaining information about school climates. Careful thought must be given to what will be observed, who will do the observing, and how often the observations will occur.

If a choice has to be made between the two methods, self-report instruments are more appropriate for evaluating school climate. Non-validated "homemade" student and teacher self-report instruments can be valuable in investigating specific school climate problems. Several valid and reliable instruments are presented in this chapter to help researchers and school administrators isolate specific climate factors that need to be altered or eliminated to build open climates. Since the relationship between a learning climate and learner outcomes is global and complex, a combination of observation, self-report instruments, and common sense is the recommended strategy for evaluating the climate of the district and each school. Skills in measuring and maintaining a positive school climate are second to none in importance to good school management.

Exhibit 1.
School Climate Observation Checklist.

(Note: Information can be gathered by observations and interviews.)
Directions: Check each item appropriately as it applies to your school. Scoring directions are at end.

1. Amount of Open Space for Instruction in the Building

_____	100%
_____	50%
_____	10%
_____	0%

2. Instructional Group Size (Note: Indicate by percentage of time in each.)

_____	Large group, more than 30 students
_____	Medium group, 16-29 students
_____	Small groups, 2-15 students
_____	Individual

3. Staff Organization

_____ Extensive use of team teaching
_____ Moderate use of team teaching
_____ Limited use of team teaching
_____ No team teaching

4. Grouping

_____ Determined by continuous assessment of student achievement
_____ Determined by occasional assessment of student achievement
_____ Determined by limited assessment of student achievement
_____ Determined by normed tests at beginning of school year

5. Noise in Classrooms

_____ Noise level is comfortable
_____ Noise level is disorderly
_____ Noise level is distracting
_____ Noise level is silent

6. Seating in Classrooms

Students are:
_____ Seated on floor
_____ Seated on "homey" furniture
_____ Seated in movable desks or tables
_____ Seated at fixed stations

7. Instructional Materials

_____ Wide variety of teaching material
_____ Multiple texts
_____ Extensive use of A-V equipment including computers
_____ Instruction is confined to single text

8. Teaching Strategies

_____ Wide variety of teaching strategies in all classrooms
_____ Moderate variety of teaching strategies in all classrooms
_____ Limited variety of teaching strategies in all classrooms
_____ No variety of teaching strategies in all classrooms

9. Student Movement

_____ Students are free to move about as they wish
_____ Students may move freely with teacher's permission
_____ Students have limited movement with teacher's permission
_____ Students have little opportunity to move about

10. Teacher Work Areas

_____ Used by more than 20 teachers
_____ Used by 11-19 teachers
_____ Used by 5-10 teachers
_____ Used by less than 5 teachers

11. Instructional Time to Promote Mastery by Students

_____ Extensive use of flexible instructional time
_____ Moderate use of flexible instructional time
_____ Limited use of flexible instructional time
_____ No flexible instructional time

12. Use of Media or Resource Center

_____ Heavily used by students all day long
_____ Heavily used by students during portions of school day
_____ Limited use by students
_____ Rarely used

13. Teaching and Learning Time

_____ No classroom time is taken from instruction by outside influences
_____ Little classroom time is taken from instruction by outside influences
_____ Considerable time is taken from instruction by outside influences
_____ Too much time is taken from instruction by outside influences.

14. Instructional Goals

_____ Instructional goals are clear and understood by all students
_____ Instructional goals are clear and understood by most students
_____ Instructional goals are not clear and understood by a few students
_____ Instructional goals are not clear and students are confused

15. Community Resources

_____ Resource people are used extensively
_____ Resource people are used occasionally
_____ Resource people are used rarely
_____ Resource people are never used

16. Inservice Education for Staff

_____ Extensive use of inservice for morale building and cooperative problem solving
_____ Moderate use of inservice for morale building and cooperative problem solving

_____ Occasional use of inservice for morale building and cooperative problem solving

_____ Morale building and cooperative problem solving are never stressed

Scoring:

1. Items 4, 5, 8, 11, 13, 14, 15 and 16 are scored by giving four (4) points if the first choice is checked and one (1) point if the last choice is checked. The higher total score indicates a more open and business-like climate.

2. Items 1, 2, 3, 6, 7, 9, 10, 12 are checked but given no weight. The evaluator uses the information as background or context for the scored item.

___

Exhibit 2.
Secondary School Attitude Inventory

For Grades 7-12 (Student Self-Report)

For each sentence below, circle the letters which show the extent to which you **Agree** or **Disagree**

Circle SA — If you **strongly agree** with the sentence

Circle A — If you **agree** moderately with the sentence

Circle D — If you **disagree** moderately with the sentence

Circle SD — If you **strongly disagree** with the sentence

1. The students usually enjoy their class assignments. (CI) SA A D SD
2. Most students feel free to take part in discussions. (CI) SA A D SD
3. The teacher talks all of the class time. (CL) SA A D SD
4. The teacher stresses memorization too much. (CL) SA A D SD
5. Every member of the class is treated fairly by the teacher. (CI) SA A D SD
6. Students are expected to explore new ideas. (CL) SA A D SD
7. The teacher encourages us to solve problems and to think creatively. (CL) SA A D SD
8. The teacher disciplines troublemakers. (CI) SA A D SD
9. Only the smart student get special treatment. (CI) SA A D SD
10. Students are allowed to make some class decisions. (CI) SA A D SD
11. The teacher expects all students to learn. (CL) SA A D SD
12. Students cooperate with each other. (CI) SA A D SD
13. The teacher believes that all students can learn the classwork well. (CL) SA A D SD
14. The students believe that they can learn the classwork well. (CL) SA A D SD
15. The teacher motivates all students to learn. (CL) SA A D SD

16. Students are encouraged to consider
    more than one solution to problems. (CL)   SA A D SD
17. Students are encouraged to use step-by-step
    logic to solve problems. (CL)   SA A D SD
18. The teacher discourages student discussion
    about classwork. (CL)   SA A D SD
19. Students are under too much pressure to
    make good grades. (CI)   SA A D SD
20. Students feel they can have fun and laugh in class. (CI) SA A D SD
21. Classmates are friendly to each other. (CI)   SA A D SD
22. Students feel threatened in the class. (CI)   SA A D SD
23. The teacher is patient in helping all students. (CI) SA A D SD
24. Certain students try to push others around. (CI) SA A D SD
25. The class makes students feel good about their future. SA A D SD
    (CI)
26. Students are often confused about what
    the teacher is trying to teach. (CL)   SA A D SD
27. The teacher enjoys teaching the class. (CI)   SA A D SD
28. Students look forward to this class. (CI)   SA A D SD
29. The classwork usually relates to the real world. (CL) SA A D SD
30. The teacher cares about all students. (CI)   SA A D SD

29. The classwork relates to the real world. (CL) SA A D SD
30. The teacher cares about all students. (CI)   SA A D SD

Scoring: For each item assign a score of 4 to SA, 3 to A, 2 to D, and 1 to SD. Determine the mean scores for each item.

- Climate items (CI) 1, 2, 5, 8, 10, 12, 20, 21, 23, 25, 27, 28, and 30 should have mean scores of 3 or better.

- Climate items (CI) 9, 19, 22, and 24 should have mean scores of 2 or 1.

- Cognitive level items (CL) 6, 7, 11, 13, 14, 15, 16, 17, and 29 should have mean scores of 3 or better.

- Cognitive level items (CL) 3, 4, 18, and 26 should have mean scores of 2 or 1.

Source: John R. Hoyle, Texas A&M University.

Exhibit 3.
Sample from the Learning Climate Inventory.

On the following page are statements that may be used to describe the learning climate in your school. Your task is to respond as accurately as you can. Your responses should be based on the general impression that you have formed about the learning climate during the current school year.

Scale

Never	Seldom	Occasionally	Often	Always
1	2	3	4	5

Sample Items:

Circle the appropriate number

1. You are free to experiment with teaching methods and techniques in your classroom.   1 2 3 4 5

3. You are encouraged to "teach to the test" to improve student achievement.   1 2 3 4 5

4. You feel free to discuss students' learning difficulties with your principal.   1 2 3 4 5

5. You participate in the administrative decisions affecting your classroom teaching.   1 2 3 4 5

10. You are discouraged from teaching higher level critical thinking skills to your students.   1 2 3 4 5

11. Your teaching is evaluated by a mutually agreed upon set of objectives.   1 2 3 4 5

13. Your principal keeps the teaching staff working together as a team to improve the learning climate.   1 2 3 4 5

15. Building inservice programs are planned to help you improve the teaching-learning process in your classroom.   1 2 3 4 5

16. Your creative teaching techniques are highlighted (praised) by your principal.   1 2 3 4 5

17. You are invited to evaluate the performance of your principal.   1 2 3 4 5

20. Are you satisfied with your teaching situation?   1 2 3 4 5

© 1973 John R. Hoyle

Skill Accomplishment Checklist for Chapter Two

Competency and Skills	Reading and Activities for Mastery
Competency: Designing, implementing, and evaluating a school climate improvement program that includes mutual efforts by staff and students to formulate and attain school goals.	Readings: See resources 9, 11, 13, 16, 18, 29. Activities: 1. Learner could design a workable climate improvement plan based on readings and local conditions. 2. Visit local corporations to discuss their climate improvement plan.

Skill A: Human relations, organizational development and leadership skills.

Readings: See resources: 2, Owens, 1987, Chapters 5, 6, 7, 8, and 9; Silver, 1983, Chapters 6-9; also see 7, 19, 30, 45.

1. Learner could establish task groups for planning a curriculum or instructional change. The learner would be observed to determine skill development.

2. Learner could develop simulation games to role play various leadership styles (i.e. Theories X, Y, and Z).

Skill B: Collaborative goal setting and action planning.

Readings: See resources 6, 9, 11, 16, 23, 24, 47.

Activities:

1. Learner could design a community education needs assessment project that inludes a plan for implementing the recommendations.

2. Learner could simulate a presentation about an action plan to the school board. (Use video camera to provide feedback to learner.)

Skill C: Organizational and personal planning and time management

Readings: See *New Perspectives on Planning in Educational Organizations,* Far West Lab., 1885 Folsom Street, San Francisco, Calif., 84103, 1980; see Cunningham and Payzant, 1983, also, Krajewski, et al., 1983, on the topic of managing time, pps. 44-51; see Chapter 2 for these two references; Also see AASA's *Time on Task*, 1982, for ideas on using instructional time more effectively and "Time management," in *School Leadership* and *Handbook for Survival*, published by the Clearinghouse on Educational Management, University of Oregon. This source offers current hints for effective time management for school administrators.

Activities:

1. Learner could demonstrate practical uses of GANTT charts, PPBS, or PERT in a curriculum or program evaluation project.

2. Learners could organize their time management schedules for one month.

3. Learners could attend a NASE time management workshop.

Skill D: Participative management, variations in staffing

Readings: See K. Davis, "Management by Participation," in *Organization Theories*. (Columbus, Ohio: Merrill, 1970) pps. 122-140; and see Owens, Chapter 9, 1987 and Silver, Chapter 7, 1983; also resources 19, 23, 24, 47.

Activities :

1. Ask learner to make presentation on

	participative management — its strengths and weaknesses. 2. Learner could develop a GPAT or OD plan for problem solving in a district.
Skill E: Climate assessment methods and skills.	Readings: See resources 13, 25, 27, 30, 32, 33, 38, 39, 44, 47. Activities: 1. Learner could administer, score, and interpret the OCDQ, LCI, and LDBQ. 2. Learner could design a student and teacher self-report instrument, 3. Learner could use Climate Observation Checklist and compare results with the LCI in one school.
Skill F: Improving the quality of relationships among staff and students to enhance learning.	Readings: See resources 1, 10, 12, and 15; also see J. Goodlad, *A Place Called School*, 1984 and W. Bickell, ed., "Effective Schools," *Educational Researcher*, 12, 4, (1983).
Skill G: Multicultural and ethnic understanding.	Readings: See resource 49; and Hoyle and McMurrin, 1983; Bell, 1980; and Naisbitt, 1982 (references found in Appendix A); Also see R. Simms and G. Contreas, *Racism and Sexism,* (Washington, D.C., National Council for the Social Studies, *Bulletin No. 61,* 1980); and Campbell, et al., *Introduction to Educational Administration,* 1983, Chapter 19. Activities: 1. Learner could present a report on the cultural diversity of America. 2. Class could discuss the meaning of cultural plurality and ethnicity. 3. Learner could design a K – 12 curriculum that includes multicultural elements.
Skill H: Group process, interpersonal communication and motivation skills.	Readings: See resources 4, 5, 6, 7, 8, 9 10, and 11. Activities: 1. The learner could report on the comparisons among the theories of Maslow, McGregor, Herzberg, and Ouchi (i.e. Theory Z). 2. The learner could design a staff recognition and motivation plan for a school or district. 3. The learner could attend a NASE seminar on group process, team building, or staff motivation.

Resources

1. B. Rowan, S. T. Bossart, and D.C. Dwyer, "Research on Effective Schools: A Cautionary Note," *Educational Researcher* 12, 4 (1983), p. 24.

2. See R. G. Owens, *Organizational Behavior in Education*, (3rd Edition), (Englewood Cliffs, N.J., 1987), pp. 91-122; P. Silver, *Educational Administration*, (1983), pp. 295-350; and W. K. Hoy and C. G. Miskel, *Educational Administration: Theory and Practice (3rd Edition)*, (New York: Random House, 1987), pp. 175-215.

3. K. Lewin, *A Dynamic Theory of Personality* (New York: McGraw-Hill, 1935); also see H. Murray, *Explorations in Personality* (New York: Oxford University Press, 1938); G. G. Stern, "The Measurement of Psychological Characteristics of Students and Learning Environments," *Measurement in Personality and Cognition*, S. J. Messick and J. Ross (eds.) (New York: Wiley, 1962), pp. 27-68; J. W. Getzels and H. A. Thelen, "The Classroom as a Unique Social System," *The 59th Yearbook of the National Society for the Study of Education*, Part II (1960) p. 53; also see, J. W. Getzels, "Administration as a Social Process," *Administrative Theory in Education*, A. Halpin (ed.) (Chicago: Rand McNally, 1973).

4. A. H. Maslow, *Motivation and Personality* (New York: Harper and Row, 1954).

5. F. Herzberg, "One More Time: How Do You Motivate Employees?", *Harvard Business Review* 46, 1 (1968) pp 53-62.

6. D. McGregor, *The Human Side of Enterprise* (New York: McGraw-Hill, 1960).

7. W. Ouchi, *Theory Z: How American Business Can Meet the Japanese Challenge* (New York: Avon Publishing, 1982).

8. V. Vroom, *Work and Motivation* (New York: John Wiley & Sons, Inc., 1964).

9. C. Argyris, *Integrating the Individual and the Organization* (New York: John Wiley & Sons, Inc., 1964).

10. T. Sergiovanni, "Factors Which Affect Satisfaction and Dissatisfaction of Teachers," *Journal of Educational Administration* 5, (1967) pp. 66-82; G. L. Schmidt, "Job Satisfaction Among Secondary School Administrators," *Educational Administration Quarterly* 12 (1976) pp. 66-85; C. G. Miskel, "Motivation in Educational Organizations," *Educational Administration Quarterly* 18, 3 (1982 pp. 65-88.

11. B. Brodinsky, *Building Morale—Motivating Staff,* Critical Issues Report (Arlington, Va: American Association of School Administrators, 1983).

12. Murray, 1938; Stern, 1962; and Getzels and Thelen, 1960 and Getzels, 1973. See resource 3.

13. A. W. Halpin, "The Organizational Climate of Schools," *Theory and Research in Administration* (New York: McMillan, 1966) pp. 131-249; and A. W. Halpin and D. B. Croft, *The Organizational Climate of Schools* (Chicago: University of Chicago, Midwest Administration Center, 1963); L. W. Hughes, "Organizational Climate—Another Dimension in the Process of Innovation?", *Educational Administration Quarterly* 4 (1968) pp. 17-28; T. W. Wiggins, "A Com-

parative Investigation of Principal Behavior and School Climate," *The Journal of Educational Research* 66, 3 (1972) pp. 103-105; G. J. Anderson and H. J. Walberg, "Learning Environments," *Evaluating Educational Performance*, edited by H. J. Walberg, (Berkeley, Calif.: McCutchan, 1974) p. 81; H. D. Nielsen and D. H. Kirk, "Classroom Climates," *Evaluating Educational Performance*, edited by H. J. Walberg (Berkeley, Calif.: McCutchan, 1974), p. 57; J. Hoyle, "Organizational and Spatial Characteristics of Urban Learning Environments," *The Journal of Educational Administration* 15 (1977) p. 124; and R. H. Moos, "Educational Climates," *Educational Environments and Effects*, edited by H. J. Walberg (Berkeley, Calif.: McCutchan, 1979), p. 49; and W. K. Hoy and C.G. Miskel, *Educational Administration, Theory, Research, and Practice*, (3rd Edition) (New York, Random House, 1987) Chapter 8.

14. This problem is discussed by Silver in *Educational Administration: Theoretical Perspective on Practice and Research*, pp. 227-272; and J. R. Hoyle, "Organizational and Spatial Characteristics in Urban Learning Environments," pp. 124-125.

15. D. A. Erickson, "A New Strategy for School Improvement," *Momentum* (December 1981) p. 46.

16. Two works discuss the model: T. A. Shaheen and P. W. Roberts, *School District Climate Improvement: A Challenge to the School Superintendent* (Denver, CFK Ltd,. 1974); and Phi Delta Kappa, *School Climate Improvement: A Challenge to the School Administrator* (Bloomington, Ind., 1974); Both works include the CFK School District Climate Profile as well as many excellent readings and assessment instruments.

17. Directed by Dr. Evie G. Dennis, executive director, Department of Human Relations and Student Advisory Services, Denver Public Schools.

18. The GPAT process is described in three sources: J. R. Hoyle, "Your Interpersonal Behavior is Showing," *American Secondary Education* 2, 3 (1972), pp. 13-15; C. R. Atkinson, "A Study of the Learning Climate and the Problem Attack Behavior of Principals as Perceived by Teachers in Selected Schools Before and After Small Group Work," (doctoral dissertation, Miami University, 1974); and J. Hoyle, "Human Relations Training: Educational Leaders or Followers?" *The School Administrator, (Oct. 1975) p. 19.

19. F. W. English, *School Organization and Management* (Worthington, Ohio: Jones Pub. Co., 1975) pp. 54-107.

20. W. L. French, "Organizational Development: What It Is and Is Not," *Business Review*, published by the University of Washington (Summer 1970), p. 46.

21. R. J. Lindstrom, "Between Cliff-Hanger and Climax," *Thrust for Educational Leadership* 7, 2 (1977) pp. 6-7, 14.

22. For the first model see R. L. Hammond, "Evaluation at the Local Level," in Worthen and Sanders, *Educational Evaluation: Theory and Practice* (Worthington, Ohio: Jones Pub., 1973); the second model see N. S. Metfessel and N. B. Michael, "A Paradigm Involving Multiple Criterion Measures for the Evaluation of the Effectiveness of School Programs," *Educational and Psychological Measurement* 27 (1967) pp. 931-943.

23. C. I. Barnard, *The Functions of the Executive* (Cambridge, Mass,: Harvard

University Press, 1938).

24. R. G. Owens and E. Lewis, "Managing Participation in Organizational Decisions," *Group and Organizational Studies* 1, (1976) pp. 56-66.

25. H. J. Walberg (ed.), *Educational Environments and Effects* (Berkeley, Calif.: McCutchan, 1979).

26. L. W. Anderson, *Assessing Affective Characteristics in the Schools* (Boston: Allyn and Bacon Inc., 1981).

27. A. Simon and E. G. Boyer (eds.), *Mirrors of Behavior: An Anthology of Classroom Observation Instruments* (Philadelphia: Research for Better Schools, Vols. 1-6, 1967; Vols. 7-14, 1970; and Supplementary Vols., 1970).

28. N. Flanders, *Analyzing Teaching Behavior* (Reading, Mass.: Addison-Wesley, 1970).

29. R. Schmuck, et al., *Handbook of Organizational Development in Schools* (Eugene, Ore.: National Press Books, 1972).

30. G. A. Anderson, *The Assessment of Learning Environments: A Manual for the Learning Environment Inventory and the My Class Inventory* (Halifax, Nova Scotia: Atlantic Institute of Education, 5244 South Street, Halifax, Nova Scotia, Canada. The price was five dollars in 1973. See H. J. Walberg (ed.), *Educational Environments and Effects*, 1979, for several studies using the LEI. Also see Walberg, 1979, for studies using the My Class Inventory with elementary students.

31. G. G. Stern, M. I. Stein, and B. S. Bloom, *Methods in Personality Assessment* (Glencove, Ill.: Free Press, 1956).

32. R. H. Moos, "Educational Climate," *Educational Environments and Effects*, pp. 79-100.

33. J. M. Steele, CAQ for general information, uses, and limitations, DeKalb, Ill.: Northern Illinois University, 1969; and Steele, House, and Kerins, "Instrument for Assessing Instructional Climate through Low-Inference Student Judgments."

34. R. L. Sinclair, "Measurement of Educational Press in Elementary School Environments," paper presented at the annual meeting of the American Educational Research Association, Los Angeles, 1969.

35. R. Likert and J. Likert, "Profile of a School" (Ann Arbor, Mich.: Rensis Likert Assoc., 1971).

36. G. G. Stern and C. Steinhoff, "Organizational Climate in a Public School System," (USOE Cooperative Research Program Contract No. OE-4-255, Project No. S-083, Syracuse University, 1965); see also R. G. Owens and C. R. Steinhoff, "Strategies for Improving Inner City Schools," *Phi Delta Kappan* 50, 5 (1969) pp. 259-63.

37. R. Roland, "A Study of Organizational Climate and Attitude of Selected Schools in an Innovative District," (doctoral dissertation, Miami University, Oxford, Ohio, 1972).

38. J. Hoyle, "The Learning Climate Inventory," Miami University School Climate Research Project, 1972; the instrument and scoring procedures can be obtained from Climate Research Associates, 1308 Todd Trail, College Station, Texas 77840.

39. Selected studies using the LCI are J. Hoyle, "Are Open Space High Schools

More Open?," *The Journal of Educational Research* 62, 4 (1973) pp. 153-156; "Learning Climate and Problem-Attack Behavior of Principals in Open Space and Traditional Elementary Schools," presented to the National Conference of Professors of Educational Administration, Burlington, Vermont, 1972; C. R. Atkinson, "A Study of the Learning Climate and the Problem-Attack Behavior of Principals as Perceived by Teachers in Selected Schools Before and After Small Group Work," (doctoral dissertation, Miami University, Oxford, Ohio, 1974); T. King, "Learning Climate and Problem-Attack Behavior of Secondary School Principals," (Ed.D. dissertation, Fordham University, New York, 1979); and J. Hoyle, 1977. W. Dudney, "The Principal's Influence Upon the Educational Climate of a School as Perceived by Teachers in San Antonio North Side School District," (Ed. D. dissertation, Texas A&M University, 1986).

40. D. J. Willower, T. I. Eidell, and W. K. Hoy, "The School and Pupil Control Ideology," (University Park, Penn.: The Pennsylvania State University Studies Monograph, No. 24, 1967). Contact Don Willower at the university for more information about the PCI.

41. W. K. Hoy and J. B. Appleberry, "Teacher-Principal Relationships in Humanistic and Custodial Elementary Schools" *Journal of Experimental Education* 39 (1970) pp. 27-31.

42. R. S. Randall, "The Development and Testing of an Instrument to Describe Problem-Attack Behavior of High School Principals," (doctoral dissertation, The University of Texas, Austin, Texas, 1964).

43. J. Hoyle, "Who Shall be Principal: A Man or Woman?", *The National Elementary Principal* 158, 3 (1969) pp. 23-24.

44. C. B. Watts, "Problem-Attack Behavior and Its Relationship to Leader Behavior and Effectiveness Among High School Principals," (doctoral dissertation, The University of Texas, 1964).

45. F. Fiedler, *A Theory of Leadership Effectiveness* (New York: McGraw-Hill, 1967).

46. J. Hemphill and A. E. Coons, "Development of the Leader Behavior Description Questionnaire," in R. M. Stogdill and A. E. Coons (eds.), *Leader Behavior: Its Description and Measurement* (Columbus, Ohio: The Ohio State University Press, 1957).

47. A. W. Halpin, "How Leaders Behave," *Theory and Research in Administration* (New York: MacMillan, 1966).

48. T. Peters and R. Waterman, *In Search of Excellence* (New York: Harper and Row, 1982).

49. For an explanation of the unique characteristics of African-American culture, see G. Gay and W. Baber, (eds.), *Expressively Black: The Cultural Basis of Ethnic Identity,* (New York, Praeger Pub., 1987); also see C. I. Bennett, Comprehensive Multicultural Education, (Boston, MA: Allyn and Bacon, 1986).

50. J. Sweeney, *Tips For Improving School Climate*, (Arlington, Va: American Association of School Administrators, 1987).

CHAPTER THREE

SKILLS IN BUILDING SUPPORT FOR SCHOOLS

Building public support for schools is not something an effective school administrator does "on the side." It should, in fact, be the first act of survival.

Education is one of many institutions in our society that function as part of the political establishment, requiring support from the public at large. More than a generation ago, the economy and the birth rate were both booming, the mystique of the professional educator was enough to coax money from taxpayers to do whatever educators felt was necessary. Those days are gone forever.

Today's reality is that the public schools must stand in line with the other public institutions and plead for their share of tax revenue. Taxpayers have become more skeptical of the educational establishment and, whether directly or through elected officials, demand clear answers to such questions as (1) what are you going to do with the money? and (2) what did you do with the money we gave you last year?

The answers to those questions and the way the answers are communicated could spell the difference between an adequate and inadequate school budget. Many veteran school administrators who remember the days of plenty may resent having to justify the existence of programs offered by their schools or even their own existence. But this type of communications has become a fact of life. The art of building public support, therefore, has become the art of survival.

Today's school administrator no longer has the luxury of withdrawing from the political atmosphere that pervades every community with the classic apology, "My job is education." School administration today involves politics and requires effective communications, both internally and externally, and most successful school administrators have learned to master the necessary political skills.

The skills required by any person or institution to gain public support must include an understanding of political theory and the exercise of political skills, whether on a local, state, or national level. The methods used by successful politicians, who build a support base in the community, are not that different from those used by successful school administrators. They become informed, listen carefully, and respond appropriately to the needs of the community, the state, and the nation.

The competency of "building support for schools," essential for successful

49

school administrators, involves primarily mastery of the art of communication and includes the following skills:

a. Developing and implementing school/community and school/staff public relations, coalition building, and related public service activities.

b. Understanding and using politics of school governance and operations.

c. Understanding and using political strategies to pass bond, tax, and other referenda.

d. Developing lobbying, negotiating, collective bargaining, power, policy development, and policy maintenance skills to ensure successful educational programs.

e. Communicating and projecting an articulate position for education.

f. Understanding the role and function of mass media in shaping and forming opinions.

g. Understanding conflict mediation and developing the skills to accept and cope with inherent controversies.

"Public relations" was not listed first by chance. It is, in its broader sense, the one function that encompasses all the others. Whether they realize it or not, those skilled in "politics" must be skilled in "public relations" also.

What Is "Public Relations"?

Public relations is practiced to some degree in virtually every school district in the country, although it may be called something else: school-community relations, public information, or communications. The reluctance of some administrators to accept it for what it is dates back to its earliest days, when public relations was identified with hucksterism and publicity-seeking. In some cases the reluctance results from a fear of communication or bias against being open.

Public relations, in fact, is not at all what P. T. Barnum was all about. Public relations is nothing more than what it says: relating with the public or publics, openly and honestly. Several decades ago, the American Association of School Administrators defined school public relations as a "cooperative development and maintenance of efficient two-way channels of information and understanding between the school, its personnel, and the community."[1]

About 20 years later, the National School Public Relations Association (NSPRA) substituted the word "educational" for "school" and embellished the definition a little further:

> Educational public relations is a planned and systematic two-way process of communication between an educational organization and its internal and external publics. Its program serves to stimulate a better understanding of the role, objectives, and accomplishments of the organi-

zation. Educational public relations is a management function that interprets public attitudes, identifies the policies and procedures of an individual organization with the public interest and executes a program of action to encourage public involvement and to earn public understanding and acceptance.[2]

Nearly a decade later, the first full-fledged textbook in the field of school-community relations expanded even further on the definition of "public relations" in the educational arena and saw it as a "dynamic process" combining these ideas and practices:

1. A way of life expressed daily by staff members in their personal relations with colleagues, pupils, parents, and people in the community.

2. A planned and continuing series of activities for communicating with both internal and external publics concerning the purposes, needs, programs, and accomplishments of a school.

3. A planned and continuing series of activities for determining what citizens think of the schools and the aspirations they hold for the education of their children.

4. The active involvement of citizens in the decision-making process of a school so that essential improvements may be made in the educational program and adjustments brought to meet the climate of social change.[3]

Public relations involves more than what we say or do; it also involves how we say or do it. That point is made abundantly clear in *Public Relations for School Administrators* from the American Association of School Administrators.[4] That book delves into the framework and philosophy of school public relations, discusses the crucial role played by a public relations administrator, and points out the importance of effective public relations in building and maintaining public confidence. Personal communications skills involve nonverbal, listening, interpersonal, and group dynamics skills; dress; consensus building; and making effective presentations.

If communication isn't planned, it becomes haphazard or simply doesn't get done. Getting feedback from both staff and community through surveys, advisory groups, key communicators, and other means keeps a school system close to those it serves. Effective internal communication is a must, since public relations is effective only when it works from the inside out, and every employee must understand his or her important communications responsibilities. Also, if staff members don't know what the goals are and what their responsibilities are in meeting those goals, the school system will never reach them.

Involving and working with many segments of the community is essential. Those segments or publics include: nonparents, parents, members of the business community, older citizens, volunteers, pressure groups, community leaders, members of coalitions, government officials, the news media, and a host of others. Issues management and strategy development are also important parts of the communications process. If issues aren't identified early and appropriate strategies developed, then they end up managing the school system instead of vice versa. Techniques such as producing effective publications and audiovisual materials, making use of the communications potential of computers, and marketing communication are also becoming basic parts of a reasonable public relations effort.

Creating a Public Relations Program

The key words in the NSPRA definition of educational public relations are "planned" and "continuing," meaning that public relations does not just happen. It is the result of a conscious effort by the school district, starting where all other school districts efforts begin — in a policy adopted by the board of education.

Just as there are school district policies establishing codes of conduct or standards for the selection of staff, there should be one avowing the board's commitment to a partnership with the community in the education of its children. The policy need not be detailed or complex. In fact, its strength should lie in the way it can be applied to virtually every aspect of the educational process.

In a book describing award-winning school public relations programs, the National School Public Relations Association suggested that an effective policy need be no more complex than this:

Resolved:

• That the Board of Education recognizes the responsibility of all members of the school staff, both professional and supporting, to keep lines of communication open with the public.

• That every effort shall be made to inform members of the community about the achievements and needs of the school district.

• That members of the community are welcome at all times to visit school buildings and to contribute whatever expertise they possess to the educational process, through volunteer work or service on advisory committees.

• That the school district will make every effort to determine the desires, needs, and attitudes of the community, through both formal and informal means, and will be responsive to the community's needs consistent with financial resources and constitutional responsibilities.

• That the school district is committed to cooperating at all times with the news media to help share the school story in the community.

• That all members of the staff shall be considered valued members of the school family, and shall be kept informed on a continuing basis of all news regarding school board and administrative decisions affecting the district.[5]

Steps in Developing a Public Relations Plan

In developing a public relations plan, school administrators may wish to involve staff and community in these steps:

● Identify those internal and external publics that need to understand or be involved if the schools are to be successful. Internal publics might include: teachers, school board members, custodians, and students. External publics might include parents, nonparent taxpayers, state legislators, the news media, and so on.

● Identify what each of these publics needs to understand for the schools to be successful. This step helps to sort out the content of your message for each.

● Identify communications channels or activities that can be used to communicate. Consider newsletters, the news media, advisory groups, coalitions, staff and community/surveys, open houses, and so on.

● Once communications activities are selected, determine the objectives to be accomplished. Then spell out who will do what by when. Obtain needed resources and get the program underway. Make frequent checks to be sure the approach is on the right track.

The School Public Relations Officer

A growing number of school systems have added a communications person to their top administrative team. This key person, sometimes designated as an assistant or associate superintendent or director, reports to the superintendent and is a member of the cabinet. To advise the school district on its communications, public relations officers must have access to all information and, like superintendents, are concerned with the entire school system. Among their responsibilities are: planning communications programs, providing counsel, developing publications and audiovisual programs, identifying and tracking issues, conducting surveys, developing strategy, working with the news media, providing communications training for staff, and so on.

The Art—and the Science—of Public Relations

Perhaps the most common mistake in public relations is to begin the process by communicating. Understanding the four-step process of public relations is what separates the skilled from the unskilled. Just as a successful politician does not give the same campaign speech to steelworkers and senior citizens, successful school administrators do not make a move without assessing the situation, the audience, and the issues.

The classic definition of public relations divides the process into four basic components:

1. Analyzing
2. Planning
3. Communicating
4. Evaluating

Analyzing

Commercial public relations and marketing firms never take a step without conducting some sort of research to determine how the public views their clients and how they would react to a new product or service. Similarly, a school district will have greater impact on the attitude of its community if it knows what people are thinking and feeling up front.

While it would be simpler to base a public relations effort on truth as the school system sees it, in reality that truth means nothing if the community sees something else. Therefore, the first effort must be to determine the public's perceptions of the issues.

The most scientific way to do that is to conduct a survey of the community and staff to assess attitudes toward the schools and to determine the issues of greatest concern. In virtually all the Gallup polls of the last few years on attitudes toward public schools, the issue most concerning people has been "discipline." Therefore any public relations effort should, to the extent necessary, address that issue. In the same way, if taxpayers feel that high school graduates are entering the job market without basic skills, the schools must respond or risk losing the support of the community.

The analysis phase, however, can reveal more than public perceptions. It can give clues on how to address them. It is no accident that public confidence in education has declined in proportion to the number of adults who do not have children in schools. At the same time, Gallup polls show that adults who have had some direct contact with the schools — through students, community education programs, or open houses — tend to be more supportive. Therefore, it does not take much imagination to envision that public support could be increased by creating ways to bring citizens into direct contact with the schools.

While a formal survey may be the most authoritative way to come up with the information needed to undergird a public relations campaign, it is not the only way. Informal telephone polls can turn up interesting information, as can questionnaires in school newsletters, or meetings with representative members of the community. Depending on the available budget, time constraints, the information-gathering effort will be more or less scientifically reliable. A successful communications effort analyzes the situation and, based upon the analysis, moves into the planning stage.

Planning

In this stage, a school district considers its goals in context of its current situation and the public's perceptions and then charts the course of its communication program.

Exactly what is the desired outcome of the public relations effort? It can be ongoing and comprehensive, such as seeking to renew public confidence in the schools. Or it can be highly specific, such as trying to gain community approval of new school boundaries or a yes vote in a school bond referendum.

To whom is the campaign directed? There are many "publics" in a school's community: parents, staff, students, property owners, renters, nonparents, senior citizens, businesspeople, and so on. The same message doesn't necessarily have the same effect on each audience, so it must be tailored to fit each group's viewpoint—and perceptions.

What is the time frame? If the aim is to win an election in September, the campaign cannot begin in August. A timeline is a must, establishing what phase of the effort should take place when.

Finally, who is responsible for the various activities? Ideally, a districtwide public relations campaign involves more people than just the public information officer or the superintendent. Board members, principals, other administrators, and teachers can be given roles in the effort, as can secretaries, bus drivers, maintenance people, and even students. A diligent planning effort can assign roles to each of these members of the school team and come up with the information and materials they will need to do their jobs.

Once a school district has analyzed the situation and planned its program carefully, the actual communication may begin.

Communicating

The art of communication has many dimensions. It can be said that any message coming from the school is, for better or worse, a communication that can ultimately influence somebody's attitude. Unkempt grounds at a neighborhood elementary school can have as devastating an impact on public confidence as news reports of a drug bust at the high school. No communication has zero impact. It's up to a school district to plan communications that provide an accurate reflection of the schools.

The most rudimentary of public relations efforts rely exclusively on press releases and occasional school district publications. These are, of course, necessary components of any communication effort, but they are far too limited in their impact to carry the entire burden. Even with the most supportive of local media, the public rarely receives the message as the school designed it. In many cases, it is modified to fit the journalistic requirements of the media. Even if reported verbatim, in few cases does the message actually reach all of the desired audience.

Likewise, school newsletters, brochures, or annual reports can have only limited impact on citizens' attitudes. For one thing, it is difficult to produce a written document with universal appeal to all segments of the community. Moreover, sociological research shows that the written word is rarely persuasive at all except to a tiny elite segment of a community. Written documents do, however, reinforce seeds planted by other means.

Face-to-face communications are still the most effective of all "other means." While it may not be possible for school administrators to attempt, like some political candidates, to knock on every door and shake every hand, there are other ways to reach the public on a person-to-person level with the school message. Any personal contact between a member of the public and the school is a communication, and contacts that are orchestrated as part of the planned public relations effort should have a significant impact on the target audience.

Involving community members in school activities as volunteers is an example of a face-to-face communications effort. The same can be said of open houses at school or education fairs at the shopping mall, coffee klatches in the homes of influential citizens, neighborhood advisory councils, or Grandparents' Day at the local elementary school. Bringing adults into the schools at night to learn rug hooking or aerobics or new work skills enables them to see examples of student work on the walls and gives them a feeling of belonging to the school family too.

The communication methods available at an given time are limited only by an administrator's imagination and stamina. There are service clubs that need luncheon speakers and PTAs that need evening programs. There are community influentials who need cultivating, and senior citizens who long to be part of the mainstream again. Each of these contacts can be as valuable in building public support as a dozen annual reports.

They can be, of course, but how do we know if they are? That is where the evaluation phase comes in.

Evaluating

Just as teachers do not assume students have learned the lessons without testing, schools cannot assume that their message has gotten through or had the desired impact on the target audience without checking. And while determining that impact is more difficult than springing a classroom quiz, it is no less important.

Evaluation might come in the form of a decisive defeat at the polls, but there are less traumatic ways of finding out whether a campaign is working. Evaluations could be conducted periodically throughout the school year. Politicians, of course, are famous for polling voters almost constantly during a campaign. There is a very good reason for that. If the campaign is not going exactly according to plan, they want to find out while there is still time to do something about it.

While weekly public opinion polls may be more than an average school system can afford, there are less costly ways to make periodic evaluations. The effectiveness of a presentation, for example, can be determined by handing out an evaluation form to the audience. A brief questionnaire included in a newsletter can provide feedback on a program's effectiveness. Spot telephone surveys and questionnaires sent to selected mailing lists can reveal what kind of impact an effort is having, as can strategy meetings with "key communicators," attuned to the prevailing mood in their neighborhoods.

Even if the results are not as scientifically reliable as a full-blown community survey, they will tell *something* about the way a program campaign is progressing.

It is evident that the evaluation phase of one campaign can be the analysis phase of the next. This, however, is merely indicative of the pervasive nature of public relations. Everything a school district does can be considered part of its public relations program, and everything it does can have an impact on its level of community support. Whether that public relations campaign has the desired result depends on whether it is just allowed to happen, or whether its planning is based on careful analysis and carried out skillfully with frequent evaluations.

A Few Words About Publics

Skilled communicators understand that there is not one "public." In fact, there are many internal and external publics, some with common factors, some very different. In many cases, a message sent to the "community" can have an equal impact on parents and nonparents alike, but others can fall on deaf ears or even provoke a negative reaction if they are directed to the wrong audience.

An obvious example of this might be an information campaign directed to senior citizens. While one might assume that older people listen to the radio a great deal, public service announcements do no good if the only radio stations carrying the announcements are those specializing in rock music.

Part of the planning effort, therefore, is identifying the specific public to be targeted using a specific method and determining how to get that message to hit home. The more focused a message is, the more effective it can be. Conversely, the more universal a message is, the less impact it will have on any one recipient. Time and money determine how narrow a targeting process is possible, but unless the concept is understood, a message could easily have no impact at all.

It's easy to see how certain messages can appeal to one group while angering another. For example, as noted above, external publics include parents—who have a lot at stake in the school system; and nonparents—those whose direct stakes have grown up; and other nonparents—whose direct stakes are either unborn or too young. There are taxpayers, who can be either parents or nonparents, and older citizens, who can be two out of the three but must be considered unique because of other considerations. There are businesspeople who are targeted because of their professional rather than personal status, just as public officials comprise one audience at home and another at work.

Internal Communication

While any discussion of communication generally turns to external publics, internal communication often creates the greatest problems and suffers the greatest neglect.

A school system should organize an effective *internal* communications program because:

• The schools will never reach their goals unless staff members understand what the goals are and their roles in helping reach them.

• Staff members feel a greater sense of ownership when they are involved.

• School staff members have knowledge and skills that can be tapped to make the school system more effective. Working as a team can lead to a sense of synergy, and the staff becomes greater than just the sum of its individual parts.

• The right hand must know what the left hand is doing.

Concerns about morale, increasing levels of stress, and worry about staff burnout have brought greater attention to the key issue of internal communications. To quote one administrator, "You can tell the community how great the math program is, but if staff members don't know about it or feel any ownership for it, they'll kill you. When asked about that math program, they can be expected to say they don't know anything about it, unless they are well informed."

Staff surveys that receive the attention of management, staff advisory committees, and newsletters are just a few of the methods school systems use to communicate with staff members.

Internal communication must include building a team relationship with fellow administrators and working effectively with the board of education. Woven together by effective communication, all will feel more a part of the educational team.

Considering that face-to-face communication is most influential, the broad range of personal contacts made by the many staff members can have a market impact on a school's image. To the general public, every school employee is considered authoritative. Whether the neighbor is a principal or a groundskeeper, what he or she says about the educational system carries a lot of weight.

It makes sense, therefore, for school administrators to consider every member of the staff as important members of the public relations team. They should be kept informed of all the major issues facing the schools—not just those in their specific area of responsibility—and should be made to feel they are a valued part of the school family.

The importance of cultivating that family feeling cannot be overstated, and its impact can be greater than as just a public relations tool. A survey of school principals in 1983 concluded, "Open, honest two-way communication is the bulwark of high morale and is a key to a motivated staff ... A sense of community results from the sharing of common information, common feelings, and common goals. That sense of community can exist within a staff when all feel informed ... when they feel involved ... and when they feel their ideas are heard."[6]

The Role of the Mass Media

It used to be the "press." Today it's the "media." Despite a growing emphasis on electronics, it's the same institution.

The relationship between the schools and the media is important. Schools need the media to help get their messages out to the community. The media, however, are fiercely independent and will reject any implication that they can be "used" by a governmental body. The media operate under a code that emphasizes their freedom from governmental control, a code that puzzles many educators and provokes a question heard ad infinitum at board tables for over a century: "Why can't we ever get any *good* news in the paper?"

There is the temptation, to which many school administrators have succumbed, to approach the local media as adversaries, responding to questions reluctantly and suspiciously. That cynicism, however, merely exacerbates the situation. It is best to avoid a breakdown in communications between the school and the media. One old adage states: Never argue with anyone who buys ink by the barrel and paper by the ton.

It is critical for school administrators to understand the role of the media in this country. Many great Americans have risen to the defense of the free press since our nation was formed, but chances are that whenever a journalist is challenged, this famous statement by Thomas Jefferson will be offered in response:

> The way to prevent these irregular interpositions of the people is to give them full information of their affairs through the channels of the public papers, and to contrive that these papers penetrate the whole mass of the people. The basis of our government being the opinion of the people, the very first object should be to keep that right; and were it left to me to decide whether we should have a government without newspapers or newspapers without a government, I should not hesitate a moment to prefer the latter.[7]

The story goes on, of course, that later in his public life Jefferson became disenchanted with the press, as did many subsequent presidents. But nobody has been able to tamper successfully with the freedoms granted by the First Amendment. It stands to reason that the pique of a local school superintendent is not going to make much of a dent either.

Arguing about whether the media "deserve" First Amendment protection or blaming the media for school problems simply because they reported on them can be a ticket to disaster. Problems should be explored and solved, not blamed on others. Also, the community has a right to know. If schools are doing something that can't be fully reported, perhaps they shouldn't be doing it in the first place.

The Meaning of News

There has never been a definitive answer to the question, "What is news?" Charles A. Dana, when editor of the New York Sun, declared that news was something that made someone exclaim. He later improved on that notion by defining news as "anything which interests a large part of the community and has never been brought to their attention." Gerald W. Johnson, after his years with the Baltimore Evening Sun, gave his definition a shading that emphasized a journalist's pride as well as independence: "News is such an account of such events as a first-rate newspaperman, acting as such, finds satisfaction in writing and publishing."

It is not facetious, therefore, to respond to the question by saying, "News is what's in the newspaper" or "News is what you see on TV." In other words, as one of the basic texts of college journalism puts it, "News is not an event, however stupendous, but the report of that event; not the actual happening but the story or account of that happening which reaches us.[8]

The first thing to understand, therefore, is that news is the creation of the newsperson, not the news source. If a reporter does not see an event as "newsworthy," it becomes a nonevent. If a reporter sees something else as "newsworthy"—something that nobody else might even have noticed—it suddenly becomes "news." School administrators who deal successfully with the media have learned how to spot or create events that are newsworthy and to anticipate the reaction of a reporter to any happening or situation.

Therefore, educators skilled in dealing with the media will not rail at local reporters for being too "negative" or for "looking only for the sensational." And they won't accuse them of "only wanting to sell papers," which is about as foolish as accusing a local auto dealer of "only wanting to sell cars." Instead, they will understand that the nature of news requires reporters to look for the unusual, the new, the different. Much of what schools wish to communicate is interesting and newsworthy, but it is often not unusual enough to warrant a news item. Therefore, schools need to remember their other channels of communication: newsletters, advisory groups, and so on.

It's unfortunate but true that people doing what they are supposed to do is simply not news. When teachers are teaching and kids are sitting quietly in their seats learning, it is not news. But when a student pulls a knife and holds that teacher hostage, that's big news. The media can be expected to converge on the school in droves, and there's a chance that an administrator unschooled in the ways of the press will demand to know, "Where were you yesterday when everything was so peaceful and quiet around here?"

Events entirely out of the ordinary are newsworthy, and no amount of protestation will deter the media. The best thing to do in the event of some kind of disaster, then, is to help the reporter obtain accurate information and avoid reporting rumors. The facts are never as damaging as misinformation or misunderstanding.

A public relations policy adopted by the board of education should require the school system to cooperate with the press. There are few if any occasions in which an administrator is justified in "stonewalling" or keeping information from the media. The point to be remembered is that reporters will get a story with or without the school spokeperson's help. It is to a school system's advantage to see that information reporters get is correct. The law covers questions of student privacy, and the news media would seldom insist that school administrators break the law.

If it sounds as if it's up to the school administrator to accommodate the media and make a special effort to work with them, that is correct. The public school system is part of the government and as such is fair game to the press. The news media are generally privately owned and protected by the Constitution. They do not have to answer to anybody but the people they serve. As television anchorman Walter Cronkite once observed:

> Our job is only to hold up the mirror — to tell and show the public what has happened, and then it is the job of the people to decide whether they have faith in their leaders or government. We are faithful to our profession in telling the truth. That's the only faith to which journalists need adhere.[9]

Dealing with the Media

Understanding the media's role in a free society, school administrators should be able to enjoy mutually satisfactory relationships with local reporters and editors. Here are some guidelines to keep that relationship flourishing:

● *Be honest and open.* An educator who appears to be hiding something is only asking for further investigation. Board policy should include a procedure for dealing with press inquiries, including who speaks for the schools when the superintendent is not available. The policy should also reflect the school system's intent to be open and honest. Never say "no comment" or refuse to answer a legitimate question. A good reporter will keep digging and find the answer elsewhere — and it may not be in the form the school district would like to see it.

● *Be timely.* Understand the media's deadlines. If a television reporter wants to do a story for the 6 p.m. news, you can't put off the interview until after 5 p.m. Nothing angers a reporter more than a news source who returns a call after deadline. A shrewd administrator knows the deadlines of reporters and instructs other staff members and secretaries what to do about messages. Respecting deadlines is one of the easier ways to build good will between school and the media.

● *Be flexible.* By its very nature news is relative. A big story one day may not find space in the paper the next. That means a reporter will not always wait until you're ready to "release" a story. In some cases you have to be ready to answer the questions when they're asked.

● *Avoid jargon.* "Criterion-referenced testing" means as much to a reporter as "dingbat" or "segway" means to an educator. Speak plain English so that there will be no misunderstanding about what you are saying. Jargon often comes across as an indication of the speaker's exalted ego, which does not help promote a good relationship. If you have to use educational terms, be sure to explain them.

● *Don't be defensive.* Help the reporter with the story but don't suggest how it should be written. Never ask to see a story before it's run. Respect the reporter's job, but don't stand in awe of him or her.

● *Avoid speaking off the record.* There are, no doubt, occasions when speaking "off the record" will be advantageous to both parties. A complex issue like the annual budget could be discussed in an off the record briefing before it is released so that the reporter will understand it better. For this to work, however, there must be an atmosphere of mutual trust as well as an understanding of what "off the record" means. It is not a phase to be tossed off lightly. It should not be used as a weapon to prevent a reporter from using something he or she has already learned, because the reporter is under no legal or ethical obligation to honor it. Nothing is ever really "off the record" because reporters can usually obtain the information from other sources.

● *Be available.* The media really appreciates a news source who is available when needed, and an appreciated news source usually gets "good press" instead of carping and criticism. But this means being available during non-working hours or even when the story is one the administrator would rather not see in print. Conceding that there are problems and facing them squarely helps an administrator's credibility not only with the media but with the public. Ignoring problems develops a "Superintendent in Wonderland" atmosphere that could seriously damage the school system in the long run. Also, when schools are presented as perfect, convincing the community that funds are needed becomes more difficult.

• *Don't overreact.* Even the most cooperative public officials are burned once in a while by the media, but if they are smart they control their tempers. Angry phone calls or nasty letters to the editor only fuel the flames. A reasoned response to an inaccurate story or unfair criticism usually gets some space or air time, but it's unreasonable to demand equal space or equal time. In the final analysis, is it really worth destroying a good working relationship? Although at the time it might seem devastating, what will its long-term impact be after all? How many people really saw it? How many really care? And how many people will really let it change their attitudes about the schools? No less a media expert than William L. Rivers noted that public opinion is slow to change, regardless of the nature of new information: "Fragments of new facts and new ideas merge with long-held opinion and long-retained information. The changes that emerge are usually glacial." To share alternative information or points of view, use other means of communication.[10] Chances are good the incident will be forgotten quickly.

In summary, although the media and the public schools are often perceived as natural adversaries, this does not mean they must be antagonists. Each institution has its role in society, and each can help the other perform better. Wise educators know that cooperating with the local media can a give school system reliable conduits of information to its publics. Astute journalists know that education is a good source of news because people in the community want to know what is going on in their schools. It is self-destructive for members of either profession to provoke a feud that deprives schools of their channel of communication and the media of their sources of information.

However, in a head-to-head battle between the educational establishment and the mass media, the media have the advantage. Rooted in the Bill of Rights to the Constitution, it is the same advantage that educators would enthusiastically applaud if the media were on the trail of dishonest councilmembers or crooked judges.

Therefore, school administrators, as agents of the public, have a duty to respect the rights and privileges of the media and to cooperate to the fullest extent possible so that the school story will be told.

But it is also the duty of a school administrator to understand that the media are not the *only* conduits of public information and attitudes and that a school district relying solely on the press can expect limited support in the community. The media must be considered as one of many means of sending a school's message into the community, and the school administrator that keeps this in perspective will have greater success and fewer ulcers.

Education and the Art of Politics

Historically, school administrators have been successful in insulating school operations from local partisan politics. In most locales, even where school leadership and educational issues must be decided at the polls, the law forbids involvement of political parties per se. There is, however, a great deal more to politics than Democrats battling Republicans. While educators, because of their conscience as much as the law, usually avoid the political trenches, they are beginning to realize that political decisions affect their futures and the quality of education.

The politicizing of education began in earnest in the 1970s, when communities throughout the country reacted to shrinking tax dollars by re-evaluating the priorities of the services they support. It shocked many school administrators that education did not automatically get a lion's share. Enrollment was declining while the percentage of people without school-age children was rising. Taxpayers, feeling the pinch of inflation, began to question whether schools were doing the job they were supposed to do. Pressure groups were on the rise. Public confidence in schools declined. Federal and state bureaucrats heaped mandates on the schools without providing money to fund them.

While many individual districts felt the pinch as their local bond or millage elections failed year after year, the issue did not gain national attention until Proposition 13, a tax limitation measure, passed in California. Other states, most notably Massachusetts, followed with similar initiatives soon after. There should no longer have been any doubt in the educational establishment that survival from now on was going to require involvement in the political process.

Again, this is not to say that school people had to run for office or actively work for or against political candidates. But school people needed to realize that issues surrounding financing of public education had to be part of every political campaign. Potentially devastating decisions were being made by political bodies at both local and state levels, while voters who had the opportunity to approve or reject proposed school budgets were becoming more and more negative. The future of public education as we know it was at risk.

While in many parts of the country the focus turned to state capitals for the fiscal transfusion necessary to revive public education, it became evident that the educational establishment often had little or no clout there, either. A study of educational governance in the mid 1970s concluded:

> The various educational organizations are so divided in some states that areas of common interest are not even sought, much less found. Educators and politicians often talk past each other, a condition that has contributed to widespread mistrust of motive and performance on both sides. And state administrators in the different agencies, this probably being nowhere more true than in education, operate in a semiautonomous fashion as if the social problems of a state had little or no relation to one another.[11]

School administrators who insisted on keeping their heads in the political sand were courting disaster. Public education needed somebody to carry its banner in virtually every political arena. Sometimes it was a legislator personally dedicated to education. Sometimes it was a school board member whose familiarity with the political processes opened a few doors. And sometimes it had to be the superintendent or another administrator.

The 1980s, therefore, saw the end of the ivory tower. It had been blown to bits by taxpayer revolts and demands for "accountability." Its former occupants either retired with some bitterness or stepped out into the sunshine and joined the fray. They had become "politicans"—not to seek personal gain or glory, but to place education atop the public's agenda once again. And as the fiscal crisis eased, they began to succeed. Their success was generally tied to their ability to communicate effectively in a personal manner or in a more complex manner such as through coalitions.

Coalition Building

Success in politics often comes from the ability to bring diverse groups together under a common banner. The same can now be said of education, where the art of building coalitions is vital to building a base of support in the community. This was recognized by educational researchers as early as the middle 1960s:

> The problem appears to be one of searching out the responsible publics, the people and the groups in society, broadly conceived, who are most capable of charting the course for the public schools, and then creating the means for converting their expressions into public decisions.[12]

Local educators realize that their relationships with local groups are essential to survival. In many areas, local school system authority is being eroded by state and federal initiatives, state and national teacher unions, and the growth of government through centralization.[13] This means that educators must reach out for help at the local level to gather the clout to have an impact in Washington or in the state capital.

Coalition building reaches into a community to construct networks of influence and support at the local level for school programs. It may also mean creating networks among other educational groups. It would be naive, however, to say that this support comes without a price. While it may not dilute the decision-making power of the school administration, at the very least it opens school affairs to increased citizen participation and possible meddling and the potential of power conflicts between school authorities and the community. As a forum of educational leaders was warned in the late 1970s:

> Why then should school people want to be responsive to what they consider virtually insatiable, potentially less-informed, and legally non-accountable communities? The big carrot in eliciting responsiveness from school people is the support of their clientele. That support is no longer freely given. It is exchanged for something.[14]

It is here where a school administrator's political skills—the arts of compromise and communication, if you will—must come to the fore. Community groups cannot be expected to go out on a limb for public schools without being assured of getting something in return. That "something," of course, does not have to be a distasteful concession, but it might represent a new direction in governance, curriculum, or training that would not have been considered back in the days of the ivory tower.

The year 1983 became known in educational circles as "The Year of the Reports," as nearly 30 studies of national significance dissected public education and put the public schools on the nation's front pages. One of the most common threads running through these reports was the need for the schools to reach out into the community to use available resources beyond those funds granted to them by taxpayers. This statement, although devoted primarily to perceived failings in mathematics and science education, was typical:

> ...the Commission strongly recommends that local school boards foster partnerships between the school board, school administrators, local officials, business and industry, labor leaders, and parents in order to facilitate constructive change. They should encourage business and other institutions not primarily involved in education to become active participants and lend fiscal, political, and other support to the local education system. They should help to further plans for improving educational offerings that stress mathematics, science and technology, rigorous curricula, and high standards of student and teacher commitment and performance. They should encourage parental involvement in all these efforts.[15]

The consummate politician who might be able to elicit support without promising a *quid pro quo* is rare. If the public perceives a life-or-death situation, perhaps they would be drawn to a cause as the only solution. But public education has lost the mystique that once guaranteed support without question. The studies of 1983, right or wrong, seemed to confirm what many people had suggested all along — that public schools needed help and support. The result is that public schools must now enter into dialogues with the various community power structures and bargain for their support.

One of the most effective partners for the public schools is becoming the business community, but even here it does not occur out of altruism. The private sector is supporting public schools in communities all over the country with money, expertise, and outright staff assignments, because it sees how important a strong educational system is to the future viability of the local business community. Thus the appeal for business-school partnerships typically includes this *quid pro quo:*

> The partnership your business establishes with the schools is an investment. And it's an investment that will provide you with great returns—a better work force, an improved tax base for your community, a healthier national economy, a strong national defense, and an increased competitive edge in international competition. Consider this: Not only are future employees for your business in school today; so are future markets for your products and services.[16]

It makes good sense for school districts to offer specialized vocational training coinciding with the skills needed by a local industry. It is, in fact, a common-sense compromise to gain that industry's support for education in general. The art of coalition building, therefore, is the art of being responsive to the needs of those interests that adopt your cause. If that sounds like pure politics, so be it, because it is pure survival.

Guidelines for Successful Coalitions

Here are a few guidelines for a successful coalition:

● Select members who will work in the common good, not just in their own self-interest.

● Be sure members have the information they need to make wise decisons.

● Encourage members to develop strategies for dealing with issues.

● Be positive and look to the future. Don't let the meetings become gripe sessions or excuses to defend the past.

● Keep coalition members, your staff, board, and community informed through a communications network.

● Avoid voting. Work on the basis of consensus. If there is a disagreement, modify the pronouncement, if possible.

● Don't insist that all groups deal with the objectives in the same manner. They may have divergent constituencies. Most can agree, however, on communitywide themes, public service announcements, research projects, and community celebrations.

● Be willing to compromise for the common good. Seek or develop common denominators. Be a good negotiator and avoid imposing your point of view on others.

● Share the glory. If the coalition is successful, give it some credit.

Identifying Community Power Structures

School administrators who reach into the community for support should do so with an understanding of where the power and the influence really lie. It is a rare community indeed where the real influentials also hold the authority of elective office. In most cases, the actual power structure is hidden from public view, but it is no less real when the decisions that count are made in the local bank or in a local coffee shop instead of in City Hall.

Of the several methods for identifying community power structures, the most famous was developed by E. Hunter in 1953. This method, called the "reputational technique," has been adapted by public relations practitioners to set up neighbor-hood networks of "key communicators." Hunters's approach requires four steps:

1. Influentials who appear to be at the center of community activities are asked to provide names of those in other spheres of the community who are powerful.

2. A panel of knowledgeable community people is asked to narrow the list to the most influential.

3. In-depth interviews are conducted with the most influential persons, dealing with formal and informal ties with other leaders.

4. A picture of the power structure is pieced together from all of the data gathered.[17]

The process of identifying community power structures need not be as formal, but neither can it be overlooked. Without a clear understanding of where the real influence resides, a school administrator could be guilty of spinning wheels when he or she could be making hay.

Public relations campaigns often start by establishing "key communicator" networks based on admittedly unscientific, but sufficiently reliable, information about informal community opinion leaders. This information can be gathered by staff members or volunteers who go into the various neighborhoods and ask citizens at random," Whose opinions do you respect?" In most cases, there is surprising consensus. Community influentials can be a cosmetologist or a barten-der, a banker or realtor, a homemaker active in civic affairs, or a teacher.

Those people whose names appear most frequently in the responses are wooed to join an elite group of education supporters who are then asked to relay infor-mation about the schools to the citizens in their community. Just as important, they are also asked to serve as a source of feedback from the community to the school administration.

This has been a relatively simple and effective technique of targeting messages from the schools to where they will do the most good. Whether the "key com-municators" found this way in local neighborhoods actually represent the "com-munity power structure" sought by sociologists is a matter for debate. Neverthe-less, it makes good sense to communicate directly with the grass roots than to waste time and money cultivating people with apparent status but little influence outside a very small and select circle.

Winning at the Polls

At no time are political skills more obvious—and necessary—than when a school district must ask the voters for money. Even though financing of public education is becoming more a function of state legislatures, the ability to get such a referendum passed is still a test of administrative leadership.

We have already discussed the need to understand community power structures. School administrators who bypass those structures, either through ignorance or error, often pay heavily for their mistakes. The development of political strategies to pass bond, tax, and other referenda has at its core accurate information about any power structures operating within the school district.

There is nothing outrageous about schools' developing political strategies consistent with community power structures. It would, in fact, be dereliction of duty if the school administration did not do everything in its power—within the legal restrictions governing political campaigns—to obtain adequate funding for its educational programs.

Those school administrators who work in districts where funding comes directly from another political body, rather than directly from the voters, are spared one form of political pressure. They would hardly agree, however, that persuading the city council or county supervisors to raise the tax rate is a simple matter. Very often, knowledgeable public officials are more difficult to convince than the average voter, especially when they are the product of an invisible power structure of their own.

Nevertheless, going before the voters is the ultimate political act and it calls for the ultimate in political acumen and public relations skills. In the 1970s, when tax revenues began to shrink dramatically, many school districts were surprised to find their routine funding requests defeated soundly at the polls. It was bad enough that money for education was denied. It was just as bad that school authorities were surprised that it happened.

That decade was one of political education for school administrators. Many of them had taken the electorate for granted for too long. After all, they reasoned, we are educating their children and they should be willing to pay. What they failed to notice is that most of the electorate no longer had children in the schools. They had not kept their fingers on the pulse of the community.

It was a rude awakening for many school superintendents. Some threatened to close the schools if the next referendum didn't pass, but the public voted no anyway. It was not until some schools actually were closed (whether by necessity or to make the point) that the voting public realized how critical the situation really was.

It became obvious in the 1970s that, to survive, school administrators had to become politically astute. Many, of course, declined the challenge and retired from careers that had spanned decades. But the young firebrands who took their place were a breed apart—educators who mingled with the community power structures, learned to play the political game, and began to win.

Nowhere was their success more evident than in the growing approval rate of local referenda. By understanding the local political structure, these school administrators were able to gather support where it counted. And by applying the best techniques of public relations to their finance campaigns — including, when necessary, the building of coalitions—they were able to persuade voters that a vote for public education was a vote for their community in general.

Tips for Winning at the Polls

Since laws governing finance campaigns vary so widely from state to state, these suggestions can be taken only as generalizations that may be adapted to specific situations. They represent the best thinking of political and public relations experts in this critical area.

Many of these suggestions are adapted from an extensive kit prepared by the National School Public Relations Association titled, "You Can Win at the Polls, [18] which surveyed 50 successful bond issues and operating fund elections and came up with ten characteristics that winning campaigns have in common. To improve your school's chances of winning at the polls, you should:

- *Develop a strong year-round public relations program.* People's attitudes are developed throughout the year. A last-minute campaign blitz is not going to change their minds. Keeping the voters informed about the good things in the schools, and especially the needs, will make them more receptive when election details are announced. It stands to reason that a school district will not succeed if it ignores the taxpayers 11 months of the year and then asks for their money in the twelfth.

- *Study and analyze long in advance.* This critical part of a campaign can begin almost a year ahead of time. It should involve advisory committees and citizens groups so that the public has a chance to contribute its priorities. Without early community support, the eventual campaign could be doomed easily.

- *Study district historical data.* By examining the voting results of past elections precinct by precinct, a district can figure out what worked and what didn't, and who helped and who didn't. This way, campaign planners can assign precinct quotas and identify areas that need special attention.

- *Survey the community.* The same kind of poll vital to any kind of public relations program can tell a school district exactly what the public's attitude might be toward money appeal. Never base your campaign on the narrow frame of reference of individual staff members. By plugging in some hypothetical tax questions, planners will be able to project potential "yes" voters and know who to go after when the campaign actually begins.

- *Develop campaign strategy.* Start drawing up the timeline for the announcement as well as the campaign itself. Appoint election coordinators representing the diversity of the district, along with a manageable-sized steering committee (10 to 15 members at most). Know who will be responsible for providing a continuous stream of information to campaign workers, voters, and the media.

- *Conduct a special voter registration.* If the law permits a special registration day, go after those voters who are most likely to support school elections, like parents of young children and new voters. These registrants then become an ideal audience for future informational activities and get-out-the-vote efforts on election day.

- *Develop the materials, tools, and techniques.* Fact sheets, brochures, and sample ballots help people understand the issues. But mass communications materials rarely change attitudes. Face-to-face communicating changes attitudes: coffees, open houses, meetings with neighborhood influentials, and the support of opinion leaders in the community.

- *Identify your "yes" voters and go after them*. The study of historical data early in the campaign should have revealed what precincts are most likely to produce favorable votes; so it's time to come up with techniques to reach those voters and get them to the polls. At this point, ignore the negative voters because such people are rarely reached by short-term efforts.

- *Get out the vote on election day*. The campaign plan should have been designed to peak on election day, when a combination of efforts focus on getting "yes" voters to the polls. This could mean arranging babysitting and transportation. And, experts insist, keep the campaign team working right up to the last minute. It develops an esprit de corps that even in defeat will serve the district well the next time around.

- *Evaluate the results carefully and promptly*. The final step in every public relations campaign is evaluation. This debriefing should be held immediately after an election, win or lose, while everything is fresh in people's minds. Not only does this reveal strengths and weaknesses of the campaign, it also identifies people who should be thanked for their help so they will be willing to help again.

School administrators who orchestrate winning referendum campaigns have, to all intents and purposes, made a successful entry into the world of politics. The strategies and techniques used to identify favorable voters and get them to the polls are not unlike those used by politicians in running for office. There remains, however, yet another challenge for school administrators that will thoroughly test all they have learned so far in the political arena.

The Art of Lobbying

It has already been noted how vulnerable school districts are becoming to the actions of political bodies. This is especially true where state governments responded to the fiscal plight of local districts by assuming some of the funding responsibilities and some of the control.

While many educators deplore the gradual removal of policy making from the local citizenry, that does not relieve them of the obligation to go where the power is and make their influence felt. When the state government is drafting regulations, local districts should have their input. Education financing is being determined by people in state legislatures who do not have to be responsive to all the districts. Because of this, educators must develop members' knowledge of the subject, the process, and the people in their districts. If the governor and state legislature are allocating funds for private education, local districts should be there to press for enough. As an AASA Critical Issues Report warned:

> The budgeting process had expanded far beyond local boundaries, and failure by school districts to enter the state legislative arena could be devastating to local education. In the not-too-distant future, moreover, the success of a school district may be measured by the skills of its lobbyists.[19]

Lobbying, like public relations and politics, used to be a dirty word to many educators. They sat in their ivory towers while teacher unions earned collective bargaining and agency shop, and senior citizens or fishermen or truckers obtained larger shares of thte state budget. And while these educators shunned state politics as something dirty, their local districts became saddled with growing mandates and shrinking resources.

Only the largest of school districts could ever afford to have a full-time lobbyist stationed in the state capitol, but they are well aware of the conflicting demands on the state government. Teacher unions are always well represented, as are many advocacy groups promoting increased services for special populations. Legislators respond first to visible pressures. Thus the absence of counterpressures, in other words, the absence of reliable sources of information about the potential impact of proposals on a state's school districts, could be fatal. A growing trend has been the formation of coalitions of school districts and private organizations to share the cost of legislative watchdog for education. More about that later.

Effective lobbying requires the skills of political game-playing and an under-standing of the arts of compromise and consensus. In this game, neither point of view is right or wrong—a concept that is completely unfamiliar to the average school administrator who was never told in graduate school that you take some steps not because they're correct, but because they'll fly.

For many reasons, therefore, a school superintendent may not be the ideal person to prowl the halls of the state capitol, collaring legislators and demanding their support. There are people who make their living in that environment. Still, the message from everybody who has been successful in taking the local school's message to the state is this: Lobbying should be a full-time effort:

> The most effective lobbying comes from developing a long-term, personal relationship with the legislator whose influence you need. If the legislator has gotten to know you personally, your viewpoint will be valued far more than if your only contact is the day before a crucial school aid vote. As one experienced lobbyist pointed out, "You can get to know legislators personally just as you can get to know anyone personally, over a long period of time. They *are* people."[20]

Understanding politics will lead school administrators to understand that remaining aloof from campaigns is not the way to develop a positive relationship with local representatives. Members of the school staff should be encouraged to take an active role in the campaigns of candidates who are supporters of education (and even their opponents, some experts advise, in case *they* win).

And while the local representatives may vote in the capital, they often make up their minds back home. Experts recommend that local delegates be cultivated during the time they spend in their home district—invited to visit schools and participate in school activities to meet parents and teachers. Like two-thirds of all American adults, these legislators may not have children in the schools either. Bringing them into direct contact with the educational process—and the product— is the best way to enlist them as allies.

Finally, when legislative decisions are imminent and local school districts must spring into action, successful lobbyists offer these tips:

● Encourage a letter-writing campaign from local constituents, but make sure that all letters are personally written and signed. While legislators are impressed by spontaneous reactions of voters, they resent being bombarded by hundreds of identical form letters bearing different signatures. These, they say, indicate a low level of commitment:

● A visit to the local delegation in the capital may be necessary at times, but don't try to impress the legislators with how expert you are. It's important to point out what these decisions will mean to the children back home and, of course, they are certainly committed to the welfare of children in their district.

● While you can imply gently that the parents and schools staffs of the district are watching what happens, don't make it sound like a threat.

● Always tell the truth; don't ever lie. Your credibility is your greatest asset. Don't suggest that you would "go broke" if a certain bill fails, because that just isn't so.

● Don't take any more of a legislator's time than is absolutely necessary. Time is very limited during a legislative session. Instead, leave a brief and simply written position paper outlining the points you are trying to make.

● After the session is over, write some quick notes to the local delegates. Thank those who voted with you. Invite those who voted against you to visit the schools to see for themselves what you were trying to tell them.

A Few Words About Coalitions

The formation of lobbying coalitions involves more than simply sharing the cost of representation in the state capital.

In the first place, legislators welcome the fact that a single voice will be heard promoting the cause of local school districts. If that voice is informed and reasonable, it can have a better impact and certainly makes a better impression than a parade of repetitious speakers and stacks of identical materials.

But more important, the person who speaks for the coalition can become a strong force for education in the capital by virtue of the broad base of power he or she represents. In the past, veteran legislators point out, different voices spoke for different facets of education and in essence cancelled each other out. The legislators, therefore, could avoid making decisions.

We learned in the 1980s that the institution of public education was more important than the narrow biases of each group. When the futures of local school districts were on the line as funding bills were debated in the capital, administrator and school board associations, teacher unions and citizen groups found they had a great deal in common. Their common front, in many cases, gained for the public schools the transfusions they desperately needed.

These coalitions, moreover, remain in force in many states, maintaining informational networks between school districts and, in some cases, creating mini-power structures within them. Members of this network can be selected because of their reputation in their neighborhoods — and their influence over the local legislator. They can be mobilized into action whenever an issue demands it because politically enlightened school leaders have learned the hard way the importance of taking the offensive and not leaving the legislative process to chance — or to politics.

What about the lifespan of a coalition? That depends on its function. Some coalitions build in a sunset provision. If they have work to do after three years, they decide to continue. It is always better for continuation to be a conscious decision. Experience shows that many coalitions cease to be effective if there is no longer a cause.

Collective Bargaining

The rise of teacher unions and collective bargaining have severely blunted the traditional power sources of school administrators. Very rarely can a teacher be fired—or rewarded—for other than the most extraordinary actions. An interminable string of grievance hearings and court cases will follow the former action, while automatic advancement on a standard salary schedule replaces the latter.

There were, in days gone by, four conceptions of leadership possible for a superintendent, according to Larry Cuban in his penetrating analysis of three big city superintendents: teacher-scholar, negotiator-statesman, corporate administrator, and rational school chief.[21] With the growing politicization of education and the conflict it represents and the growth of collective bargaining, only one of those concepts is now attainable: that of the negotiator-statesman. As Cuban left his post as superintendent of the Arlington, Virginia, public schools a few years ago, he observed in an interview in *The Washington Post*, "The times, the local political context, and the dominant conception of leadership may well determine whether a schoolman can do an effective job or not. There are fall, summer, spring, and winter superintendents — but none for all seasons."

Collective bargaining, of course, has replaced in many states the process of leadership that had been the foundation of public education from its beginning. No longer can the wise and powerful superintendent make pronouncements from on high. Now salary and working conditions — the latter phrase meaning virtually anything else not prohibited by law — must be hammered out through a structured process of negotiations.

Rules for successful negotiations could fill many volumes this size and still not apply directly to any given situation. As many experienced negotiators have observed, "A good technique is one that works."

The process of negotiation should be one of give-and-take, with each side working sincerely to reach agreement on the issues. Either side entering the process vowing to "break" the other is looking for long-term trouble. Teacher strikes harm the children, and while their settlement may show union or school board strength, it is usually a hollow victory as far as individual teachers are concerned. Negotiations should be conducted on a "win-win" basis, not "win-lose."

Furthermore, the period of financial crisis alluded to earlier put teachers' unions on the defensive in many parts of the country as their demands were seen as reponsible for "breaking the bank." As tax dollars became tighter, many unions switched their emphasis to non-budgetary demands such as planning time and job security. While school boards were happy to earn settlements without huge price tags attached to them, these concessions eroded even further the authority of the school administration over its staff. Lower teacher salaries also created other problems as many teachers left the profession.

Today's superintendent has learned to live with collective bargaining and with the type of contract administration it requires. The successful school leader must be, as Cuban observed, a statesman, because authoritarianism has no place in the negotiations process.

Generally, a superintendent does not take part in the actual negotiations. A staff person skilled in group dynamics, often with a specialist background in labor negotiations, represents the school district, presenting proposals, reporting back the counterproposals, and speaking for the board and administration up the moment agreement, or impasse, is reached. The superintendent, however, can serve as the spokesperson for the district in informing the media and the public of progress. So while a superintendent does not take part directly in the negotiating, he or she must be briefed and consulted after each session.

Finally, the way a contract is administered after it has been adopted can have a serious impact on employee relations and can influence the strength of the school district's position during the next round of bargaining. Although parts of a contract may not be applauded by individual supervisors, they must be accepted with good grace. The school district should conduct training sessions to familiarize all managers with the contract language and with the proper way of handling grievances.

The success of the collective bargaining process is predicated on respect for the other party and consistency of representation. It has nothing to do with liking the other side personally or agreeing with its point of view. Collective bargaining can be the most trying and frustrating challenge facing school superintendents today, but those who are skilled in the areas of compromise and public relations, and who have mastered the art of politics will find the same skills carrying the day for them both in negotiating and in maintaining equilibrium within the school district after agreement is reached.

Those experienced in contract negotiations say that in many cases strikes or near-strikes are won or lost in the public arena. "They say teachers are less likely to walk a picket line if they think the public is opposed to their position," said an AASA Critical Issues Report in 1981. "The best defense for a school district is credibility in the community. This credibility cannot be built in the weeks or

Conflict and Its Mediation

M.B. Nicholson noted that "a conflict arises when two or more people or groups endeavor to pursue goals which are mutually inconsistent." Conflict is mediated when the parties resolve differences so their goals are compatible or they accept a compromise position temporarily or permanently.[29]

Effective school leaders strive to know and understand their staff members, community members, students, school board members, and others and to understand their needs or what they expect of the schools. If administrators do this effectively, they can avoid a "conflict" situation most of the time. There are times, though, when conflict is unavoidable.

School leaders should be familiar with the three basic sources of intergroup conflict that can occur in a school system:

• **Philosophical/ideological conflicts** are caused by differences in values between people or groups (such as various conservative or liberal philosophies).

• **Personality/stylistic conflicts** occur when two persons or a person and a group operate differently (for example, differing management styles).

• **Territorial/jurisdictional conflicts** occur over power and resources (such as school decentralization battles).

The three major procedures that can be used to resolve the conflict are:

• **Role negotiation**—When a conflict is caused by parties being unsure of who is to do what, role negotiation can be effective in clarifying the sources of conflicts and helps both sides understand the problems. It usually involves writing down the things that need to be changed on both sides and the things that do not need changing. This usually leads to a solution.

•**Third party consultants**—People trained in handling conflict resolution can help two parties come to terms with one another.

• **Changes in organizational structure**—If the conflict is due to inappropriate clustering of jobs or duties, a change in structure can help resolve differences.

---

months prior to negotiations. It must be earned, instead, by the year-round practice of being open with the media and keeping the public informed."[22]

In a few areas of the country, negotiating sessions are open to the public or the press. In most cases, the information to be made public at various stages of the process is determined at the bargaining table. Both sides, however, have an interest in keeping their constituents informed about the issues under discussion and the progress of negotiations.

School districts that publish internal "negotiations bulletins" avoid the possibility of distortions from the other side making an impact on uninformed staff members. And sending the same information to the district's "key communicators" keeps the community updated on progress and avoids rumors.

It should be evident by now that as in so many other areas of school district governance, information is an administrator's most powerful tool. Suspicion and distortion can easily sabotage a district's position and undercut its negotiator's ability to act. And just as surely, in the case of a strike, a steady flow of accurate, understandable information, both to staff and public, will head off emotional reactions that often distort the real issues. Once again, the credibility of a school district and its leadership will carry the day.

Communicating and Projecting an Articulate Position for Education

There is one thing a school administrator must understand and be willing to accept: In that community, whether large or small, he or she *is* education.

Accepting the mantle of authority also means accepting the obligation to speak authoritatively and articulately for the local school district as well as for education in general. "Shrinking violets" do their profession a disservice because the community that puts its trust and its dollars behind a person wants to respect that person as an expert without peers. That is human nature.

The ivory tower of yore, therefore, can now be outfitted with a television camera and microphone so that the administrator will be able to communicate via all available media to the community. Better yet, that ivory tower is equipped with a picture window that lets the sunshine in, plus a swinging door the community uses to get inside and the superintendent uses to get out, to listen, and to take the message of education far and wide.

This means that administrators must be well read about the issues surrounding education today. Educational leaders don't "find time to read," they "make time to read." They read the hometown newspaper and the *Readers Digest*, and publications such as *The New York Times* and *Saturday Review*. Contemporary education journals like AASA's *The School Administrator*, *Education Week* or *Education USA* are useful to get briefings on current issues, thinking or practices, and *Educational Leadership* and the *Phi Delta Kappan* offer a more detailed examination of the same issues, and so on.

This also means that armed with this knowledge and information, a superintendent is willing to go on the stump for education — to speak at Rotary luncheons and Kiwanis dinners, to address community associations, and to appear on radio and television panel shows. And when the local newspaper asks for a contribution for the editorial page, that same superintendent should be ready and able to move to the keyboard and put the equivalent of a rousing speech on paper.

In the past, all a superintendent had to do was educate children. That, of course, is still the bottom line, but school administration has had to go public — and the person who represents it has had to become a public figure.

Those unwilling or unable to cope with that requirement are fading fast. Today's superintendent accepts the role of spokesperson for education with grace and wit. That is because he or she understands that spreading education's message in the community is the surest way to build support for all the wonderful things today's schools can do. Two recent AASA publications, titled *Home, School, Community*

Involvement and *Partnerships: Connecting School and Community,* offer key sources to assist school leaders in building coalitions using proven strategies.

Skill Accomplishment Checklist for Chapter Three

Competency and Skills	Reading and Activities for Mastery

Competency: Understanding internal and external communications and political skills and using them to build local, state, and national support for education.	Readings: See resources 1, 2, 3, 4, 5, 15, 23, 24, 25, 29, 30, 31
	Activities:
	1. Learner identifies an issue facing education nationally.
	2. Learner identifies an issue facing education locally.
	  a. A statement describing the issue.
	  b. A summary of background information that will make it possible for anyone studying the brief to understand quickly the development of the issue to date.
	  c. A designation of the issue as critical, ongoing, or emerging.
	  d. A designation of the political impact of the issue on education: high, medium, or low.
	  e. A listing of upcoming events that could have an impact on the issue.
	  f. A statement describing a preferred or actual position on the issue.

Skill A: School/community public relations, coalition building, and related activities.	Readings: See resources 4, 5, 11, 12, 16, 29, 30, 31
	Activities:
	1. Learner does an analysis of his/her own district's public program.
	  a. Identify internal and external publics.
	  b. Select two internal and external publics of great importance to the district's success and list what members of those individual publics need to understand if the district is to be successful.
	  c. Identify for each of those publics the communications channels and involvement activities that will lead to understanding and support.
	2. Learner does an analysis to identify key members of the community power or leadership structure and any other "major influentials" in the community. Briefly describe why each of these members is influential.

Skill B: Politics of school governance and operations.	Readings: See resources 12, 13, 17, 22, 23, 24 Activities: 1. Learner constructs a chart showing the structure of educational influence at the state level. Learners should indicate how their school districts or other districts fit into that structure, if at all.

Skill C: Strategies to pass bond, tax, and referenda.	Readings: See resources 11, 18, 24, 25
	Activities:
	    1. Construct an analysis of trends financing a school district's operations. If possible, relate the analysis to referenda, charting patterns in at least ten precincts and providing districtwide election results.
	
	    2. Discuss patterns that emerge from your analysis.
	    3. Learner might wish to obtain at least two census reports to determine what demographic changes have occurred that have had an impact on voter turnout and school finance or other election results during the same period covered by the trend analysis.

Skill D: Lobbying, negotiating, collective bargaining, power, policy development, and policy maintenance skills to ensure successful educational programs.	Readings: See resources 11, 12, 13, 17, 18, 19, 22, 23, 24, 25
	Activities:
	    1. Learner obtains copies of the past three to five contracts with the teachers union/associations and checks key passages for distinct language changes.
	    2. Learner describes any perceived shifts in "power." From whom to whom? Has the quality of communication or the spirit of cooperation improved or deteriorated? How? Describe.
	    3. Learner reviews the school district's policies. What process is used for their review and updating? Who is or should be involved? How could the process be improved? Describe.

Skill E: Communicating and projecting an articulate position for education.	Readings: See resources 2, 3, 4, 5, 8, 14, 31 Activities: 1. Learner has a person critique the delivery of a speech he or she makes on the future of education. 2. Learner makes a list of professional journals he or she will read regularly to improve understanding of major educational issues. 3. Learner critiques major national reports on education, placing special emphasis on content, persuasiveness, and style. Which of the reports communicates most effectively to professional educators? To laypersons?
Skill F: Role and function of mass media in shaping and forming opinions.	Readings: See resources 4, 8, 10, 31 Activities: 1. Learner analyzes coverage and editorial stands of local media on a major issue that has come before the local school board. What does the analysis reveal in terms of accuracy, bias, openness, and general school system-news media relations? 2. Meet, possibly over lunch, with a local reporter who covers the education beat. What does the reporter feel school administrators are doing well in working with the media? What does the reporter feel they could do better? 3. Construct a suggested board policy for set of procedures for working with the news media.
Skill G: Conflict mediation and the skills to accept and cope with inherent controversies.	Readings: See resources 26, 27, 28, 29 Activities: 1. Learner identifies three to five recent internal conflicts or communications problems in the school district and determines the causes of those difficulties. How were they mediated or solved, if at all? What should have been done? Describe. 2. Learner designs a budget development process that provides for extensive involvement and reduces competition for resources.

Resources

. *Public Relations for America's Schools*, Twenty-eighth Yearbook, American Association of School Administrators (Washington, D.C.: 1950), p. 14.

2. *Education Public Relations Standards for Programs and for Professionals*, National School Public Relations Association (Washington, D.C.: 1968).

3. Leslie W. Kindred, Don Bagin, and Donald R. Gallagher, *The School and Community Relations* (Englewood CLiffs, N.J.: Prentice-Hall, Inc., 1976).

4. Don Bagin, Don Ferguson, and Gary Marx, *Public Relations for Administrators*, (Arlington, Va.: American Association of School Administrators, 1985).

5. *Learn from the Winners: School PR Programs that Work*, National School Public Relations Association (Arlington, Va.: 1983), p. 5.

6. *Building Morale...Motivating Staff: Problems and Solutions*, American Association of School Administrators (Arlington, Va.: 1983).

7. Paul L. Ford, ed., *The Writings of Thomas Jefferson, Vol. 2* (New York: G.P. Putnam's Sons, 1892-1899), p. 69.

8. F. Fraser Bond, *An Introduction to Journalism, Second Edition* (New York: The Macmillan Company, 1961), p. 78.

9. Walter Cronkite as quoted in B. Rowes (ed.), *The Book of Quotes* (New York: Ballantine Books, 1979), p. 113.

10. William L. Rivers, *The Mass Media* (New York: Harper and Row, 1962), p. 11.

11. R. F. Campbell and T. L. Mazzoni, Jr., *State Policy Making for the Public Schools*, (Berkeley, Calif.: McCutchan Publishing, 1976), p. 275.

12. R. F. Campbell, L. L. Cunningham, R. O. Nystrand, and M. D. Usdan, *The Organization and Control of American Schools* (Columbus, Ohio: Charles E. Merrill Publishing Company, 1965), p. 94.

13. For a review of these forces, see E. L. and M. Useem, editors, *The Education Establishment*, (Englewood Cliffs, N.J.: Prentice-Hall, 1974).

14. D. Mann, "Some Cheerful Prospects for Schooling and Public Involvement," paper prepared for the National Forum of Leaders of Educational Organizations (Washington, D.C., November 6, 1978).

15. *Educating Americans for the 21st Century*, report prepared for the National Science Foundation by the National Science Board Commission on Precollege Education in Mathematics, Science and Technology, 1983.

16. *Business and Industry: Partners in Education* (Arlington, Va.: American Association of School Administrators, 1984).

17. F. Hunter, *Community Power Structure* (Chapel Hill, N.C.: University of North Carolina Press, 1953).

18. *You Can Win at the Polls*, multimedia kit (Arlington, Va.: National School Public Relations Association, 1981).

19. *School Budgeting: Problems and Solutions* (Arlington, Va.: American Association of School Administrators, 1982).

20. Larry Cuban, *Urban School Chiefs Under Fire* (Chicago,: University of Chicago Press, 1976), p. 170.

21. *Collective Bargaining: Problems and Solutions* (Arlington, Va.: American Association of School Administrators, 1981.)

22. See P. J. Cistone, "The Politics of Education: Some Main Themes and Issues," in P.J. Cistone (ed.) *School Boards and the Political Fact* (Ontario, Canada: The Ontario Institute for Studies in Education, 1982) p. 2.

23. M.Y. Nunnery and R.B. Kimbrough, *Politics, Power, Polls, and School Elections*, (Berkeley, Calif.: McCutchan Publishing Corporation, 1971), p. 3.

24. H.L. Summerfield, *The Neighborhood-based Politics of Education* (Columbus, Ohio: Charles E. Merrill Publishing Company, 1971) pp. 98-100.

25. P.W. Hersey, "Preparation is the Key to Effective Negotiations With Teachers--But Where is the Principal?" in J.D. Herring and J.A. Sarthory (eds.), *Collective Bargaining Techniques in Education* (Austin, Texas: MESA Publications, 1980) pp. 103-110.

26. W.C. Miller and D.N. Newberry, *Teacher Negotiations: A Guide for Bargaining Teams* (West Nyack, New York: Parker Publishing Company, Inc, 1970) pp. 25-28.

27. See J. Luft, *Group Processes: An Introduction to Group Dynamics* (Palo Alto, Calif.: The National Press, 1963).

28. See R. Wynn, *Collective Gaining: An Alternative to Conventional Bargaining* (Bloomington, Ind.: Phi Delta Kappa, 1983).

29. L. E. Decker and V. A. Decker, *Home, School, Community Involvement*, (Arlington, Va: American Association of School Administrators, 1988).

30. A. C. Lewis, *Partnerships: Connecting School and Community,* (Arlington, Va: American Association of School Administrators, 1986).

31. P. West, *Educational Public Relations,* (Beverly Hills, Calif.: Sage Publications, 1985).

CHAPTER FOUR

SKILLS IN DEVELOPING SCHOOL CURRICULUM

It is assumed that school leaders must possess or acquire the ability to develop a systematic curriculum that provides for mastery of the fundamentals as well as extensive cultural enrichment activities. Administrators are especially concerned with control of the curriculum throughout the system. The curriculum is seen as the means to the end of improved performance and the accomplishment of education's mission. For this reason, administrators must approach curriculum development with the *entire school system* in mind. A new book, titled *Curriculum Auditing*, can assist school leaders in their search for systematic school improvement. According to Fenwick English, the curriculum audit is system oriented. He states that auditing is a technology to evaluate how well system-wide goals and objectives are being met.[106] Modern-day administrators doubtless hold a more humanitarian view of a school's mission and the nature of learners, but they are the inheritors of a management orientation based on the work of Franklin Bobbitt, who conceptualized curriculum as a means of producing the skills needed by society — in his time a "scientific" industrial society.[6, 7, 8]

Another pervasive influence on curriculum development since 1949 has been the Tyler Rationale.[24] Tyler assumed that (1) purposes exist apart from the school, (2) schools must be selective about which of these purposes to embrace and (3) some purposes appear to be more appropriate than others.

Tyler also dealt with curricular organizational problems because, "in order for educational experiences to produce a cumulative effective, they must be so organized as to reinforce each other."[25] This concern required school administrators to take up the issue of *continuity, sequence, and integration* of a curriculum. These were defined as follows:

• *Continuity* refers to the vertical repeat of the major curriculum elements for skills to be practiced and mastered.

• *Sequence* deals with the element of enhancing skills through repetitious but progressive development of those skills in a planned manner.

• *Integration* refers to the horizontal relationship of curricular experiences to assist the student to develop a unified view of subject matter or skills to be taught.

Skills of Systematic Curriculum Development

In this chapter we introduce six specific skills necessary to develop a systematic school curriculum. The emphasis on "systematic" is essential because:

- It ensures continuity of instruction within a school and among and between schools.

- Continuity of instruction ensures progressive skill development among and between schools.

- It maximizes the use of student time, avoids unnecessary instructional overlaps or gaps from occurring, thereby minimizing boredom and ensuring mastery of curriculum.

- It enables schools to reach their goals within school systems at the lowest possible cost without sacrificing educational quality in the process.

- It is the strongest barrier against the problem of concentrating upon one school or level of schools at the expense of the total system.

The skills of curriculum development are presented in Figure 1 by levels of the educational organization. Viewing the skills from these perspectives has a dual function. It reminds us of the need to take the systematic approach to curriculum development by integrating the three levels to maximize learning. It also introduces us to a rich literature about curriculum at each level.[26] Curriculum goals and objectives are more general at the system than at the school level and more general at the school level than at the classroom level. The classroom is, for the educational system, the operational level. It is at this level that curriculum is delivered on a daily basis. Here is where actual effectiveness of the curriculum may be assessed and evaluated.

Planning/Future Methods to Anticipate Occupational Trends

One important function of schooling is to prepare students to participate effectively in the economic environment in the future — the future of the students, not that of their administrators or teachers. This function demands two things of administrators. They must be able, somehow, to determine or anticipate occupational conditions in the future, and they must be able to design and implement a curriculum that enables students to survive and succeed in the occupations of the future.

Stanford University economists Russell Rumberger and Henry Levin compiled data that reveal the fastest growing occupations 1982 through 1995.[36] The fastest relative growth will be for computer service technicians and legal assistants. The greatest actual increase in new jobs is expected to occur in nursing, cashiers, and teaching.[29] Only nursing and teaching, of the nine occupations expected to have the largest actual increase in jobs, require education beyond high school. Awareness of trends in future occupations is necessary to permit educators sufficient lead time to design an appropriate curriculum and provide inservice and/or pre-service education to prepare teachers to implement curricula for the future.

Figure 1.
Skills of Systematic School Curriculum Development
At Three Administrative Levels.

The Six Skills of Systematic School Curriculum Development

Level	Planning/ Futures Methods	Taxonomies of Objectives	Theories of Cognitive Development	Valid/ Reliable Performance Indicators	Use of Computers and Other Tech. Aids	Use of Cultural Resources
System	long term planning horizon 15-25 years	goals based on system processes or character- istics	districtwide scope and sequence based on outcomes	global goals with some performance indicators	define computer literacy in goal state- ments	organize school community workshops; identify resources
School	intermediate planning horizon 1-5 years	program goals by discipline within the school	program or course design and development based on district	some performance indicators with specific objectives	define computer literacy in performance terms with other objectives	focus pro- gram goals on available resouces
Classroom	current year planning horizon	individual pupil goals within a discipline and a grade level	lesson plans or learning modules based on school program	specific pupil performance objectives	apply concept of computer literacy in planned instructional contexts	use community resources such as speakers field trips

The Administrative Level Involved (vertical label, left side)

In using various forecasting techniques, James McNamara cites the Institute of the Future's six indicators that serve as guidelines to assess the general quality of forecasts. They are:

● *Specificity* — the statements about the future should be clear enough to know whether or not they have transpired.

● *Uncertainty* — a forecast should be stated in terms of probability of occurrence or a range of possible dates.

● *Time relatedness* — a forecast should reflect stages of change and concurrent events

● *Intrafield relatedness* — any forecast must reflect knowledge of competitive and complementary developments in the same field as the event

● *Interfield relatedness* — knowledge of developments in other fields should be reflected in a forecast.

● *Costs and benefits* — forecasts should reflect judgments about economic and social costs and benefits.[38]

The skills involved in moving from trends to curriculum development and then implementation are listed in Figure 2.

Figure 2.
Ten Steps To
Using Labor Trend Data In Curriculum
Management.

Step	What the Curriculum Administrator Does
1. Obtain labor trend data	Develops labor trend data from U. S. Census, state and local labor publications on job needs.[40]
2. Analyze trend data for content, knowledge, and skill requirements	Takes jobs estimated to be in availability exceeding existing labor pool and lists the "core" skill areas required to successfully perform each job. The "core" is sometimes known as a "cluster."
3. Locate "clusters" in existing curriculum	Locate the "clusters" in the existing curriculum and course offerings to know if skills are now included to be taught.[41]
4. Perform a discrepancy analysis	This is a process of "match-match." Take the "clusters" that are not included to be taught and list them.[25]
5. Determine priorities	Develop a list of priority "clusters" based upon criticality of need (short and long term) in the labor pool, complexity of the skills required to be taught compared to existing skills of the staff, costs of machinery acquisition, and time required to implement a new course.
6. Perform cost/benefit analysis	Develop a list of costs required to implement a new course, how long it would have to operate to be considered successful, cost per pupil based on step 5 criteria.[42]

7. Develop high priority curriculum	Develop new curriculum/courses that yield best benefits compared to costs.
8. Implement new curriculum	Implement the new curriculum and with it a plan for evaluation based on feedback regarding numbers of graduates who have succeeded in the occupation.[43]
9. Evaluate the curriculum	Gather evaluative data, relate to critical decisions that must be made about the effectiveness of the curriculum.[44]
10. Revise the curriculum	From evaluative data make revisions in the curriculum or instruction that appear to be required or desired.[45]

The concept of a planning horizon shows dramatically the need for different skills and procedures at each of the three levels introduced in Figure 1.[38] A long term planning horizon may span 15 to 25 years. It would stretch into the future as far as the administration dared to go. This type of planning would occur at the central or system level. It would be strategic rather than tactical in nature.[39] These administrative differences in curriculum planning are shown in Figure 3.

Figure 3.
Curriculum Development Continuum.[31]

	Strategy	**Tactic**
Scope	Systemwide, all levels	Program, school, or classroom specific
Specificity	Low level of detail	Higher level of detail
Delineation of Instructional Methods	Broad or nonexistent	Embedded and more specific, closer to the classroom
Organization, Location of Decision	Highest levels of management/policy	Much lower level, building, classroom
Risk Involved	High risk, more uncertainty	Lower risk, much less uncertainty
Assessment	Broadly indicated as a requirement upon which to make decisions and re-examine policy	Specifically delineated by objective, type, expected standards of achievement for groups of students
Consideration of Alternatives	Broad, conceptual	Narrow, operational

Various types of futures methodologies can be employed by school administrators in anticipating and preparing for future events. These include contextual mapping, force field analysis, scenario writing, or the use of the Delphi Technique.[39] Using futuristic data is more than "crystal ball gazing" or using high powered statistical procedures. It is not only a careful consideration of emergent trends, but understanding where one might end up if those trends persist.[40]

The purpose of engaging in futures planning is to move from a reactive to a proactive position. In the past, too many educational planners merely documented trends and did not assume responsibility for initiating action based on what those trends might mean for the educational enterprise. Taking their cues from planning models in the private sector, educational administrators are now seeing that assuming a proactive role in planning means either (1) encouraging trends deemed to be positive, or (2) engaging in activities that will negate or detract from trends considered harmful.[44, 40] Inevitably this involves political action of various types that may be overt, covert, or both.[43]

The Taxonomies of Instructional Objectives

The second skill for school administrators is the use of the taxonomies of instructional objectives and the validation procedures for curricular/units and sequences. Perhaps the best known taxonomies are the cognitive domain by Benjamin Bloom, affective domain by David Krathwohl, and a widely used work of application by Robert Mager.[44, 45, 46] These works were aimed primarily at developing individual classroom or program objectives for pupils, but proved ineffective for system-level administrative purposes.

The major contribution of the taxonomies was to create a more precise vocabulary with which school administrators could describe the outcomes of instruction. The necessity for outcome statements was underscored by the accountability movement which demanded more clarity in terms of relating inputs to outputs in the then dominant approach toward examining and improving schooling operations.[47]

The "behavioral objectives" approach came under fire from at least two perspectives. The first was that some educational goals or purposes cannot be observed or tested directly, and the second was that learner goals are not necessarily appropriate as system goals because it is not always clear what systems do collectively to produce the desired individual learning results.[49] In-other-words, *clarity of ends* does not necessarily lead to *clarity of means*[49]

School administrators must think of what goals or objectives are appropriate for the system or district level, school or program level, and the classroom level. The classroom goal/objective is an instructional goal firmly couched in student behaviors.[50] Program goals are appropriate for groups of classrooms and schools. They may be framed in terms of group test gains on a variety of instruments. They may also be conceived as activities or processes within academic disciplines.[50] School system goals/objectives may cut across many programs and be interdisciplinary in nature. School system goals/objectives therefore may be *ver-*

tical (academic discipline centered) or *lateral* (interdisciplinary). This relationship is shown in Figure 4.

Figure 4.
System/Program Goals/Objectives As Vertically and Laterally Directed.

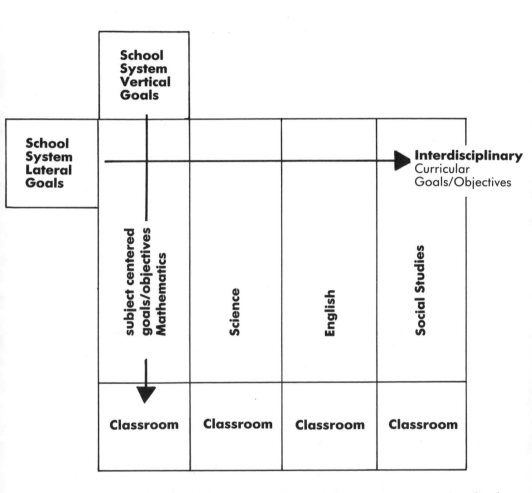

The subject centered curriculum has been dominant for many decades in school curriculum development/management.[52] It does not appear that any plan now available will seriously challenge that dominance in the future.[53] One reason is that the subject-centered curriculum is closely linked to the control/authoritative structure of school systems, schools, and classroom. Whether vertical or lateral, system goals are statements of policy based on a set of values intended to shape or control system behavior at all three levels of organization and operations.[54]

Curricular content may be validated from a variety of approaches. Tyler's classic model indicates that goals should consider the nature of society, the nature of knowledge, and the nature of the learner.[25] With these foci, administrators can use a needs assessment process to arrive at consensus on what goals should be selected at each of the three levels of a school system in a more modern framework as advanced by Roger Kaufman.[55]

The goals and objectives are used to build the curriculum in ways known to all educators. We sometimes speak of models, sometimes units. Units are organized in different ways, sometimes by subjects, sometimes by skills, sometimes by centers of interest, often by combinations of organizing elements.

The essential elements of a curricular unit were characterized as possessing three types of objectives: learner acceptance of the objectives; statements of situations and experiences to be encountered by learners; and evaluation or testing.[58] While this list of essential elements has been embellished somewhat in more contemporary context, it still contains the rudimentary outline of a curriculum unit.[59]

The arrangement of modules or units within a curriculum is guided by concepts of continuity, sequence, and integration defined in the Tyler Rationale. To this we must add the term *scope*, which indicates how much time should be spent on a unit or module, and how thoroughly it should be studied. Monitoring these organizing units of the curriculum can be accomplished with curriculum mapping.

Curriculum Mapping

One of the emerging skills in relating taught curriculum, its scope and sequence, to developed curriculum, is curriculum mapping. Developed in 1978, mapping has been used in a variety of school systems to:

> "carefully examine an existing configuration instead of assuming that the guidelines represent the curriculum and the curriculum should be changed by developing new guidelines. The actual or real curriculum may never be touched in the cycle of updating curriculum guidelines."[104]

Curriculum mapping can reveal what was taught, in what order, and for how long a period of time. It presents a picture of the actual "live" curriculum in classrooms on a day to day or week to week basis. From such data, school administrators may "adjust" the curriculum by issuing directions to the instructional staff as to change in subject matter content, the presentation of sequence of that content, or the amount of instructional time devoted to the content.[60]

Figure 5 shows a typical format for mapping a secondary school course, "Introduction to Physical Science."

Figure 5.
Sample: Secondary School Mapping Format.

Type: Checklist by Course

Teacher's Name: _____

School: _____

Grade: _____No. of Students: _____

Course: Intro. Phys. Science

Enter class periods or
portions thereof, i.e.,
.25 - .50 - .75 - 1.00 -
1.25 - etc.

Weekly data gathering (Complete by Friday of each week) Account for total class time each week						
Pupil contact days in week	week days					

Discipline					
Clerical/Announcements					
Testing					
Equipment set-up time (within class period)					
Other Activities (Assemblies, field trips, etc.)					

Strands/Objectives

1. Follow data collection procedures.					
2. Use reference material to gain information.					
3. Construct line graph from data.					
4. Identify qualitative relationships between variables.					
5. Interpret values from a graph.					
6. Identify the problem in an investigation.					
7. Identify common laboratory equipment.					
8. Perform mathematical operations with decimals.					
9. Convert SI and metric values.					
10. Make observations of phenomena.					
11. Propose conclusions based on data.					
12. Identify sources of error in experiments.					
13. Determine mass using a balance.					
14. Measure metric dimensions of solid objects.					
15. Apply formula V = LxWxH to solid objects.					
16. Determine liquid volumes with graduated cylinder.					
17. Determine liquid volumes by displacement.					
18. Determine density of regularly shaped objects.					
19. Determine density of irregularly shaped objects.					
20. Classify substances by density.					
21. Measure temperature using Celsius thermometer.					
22. Measure thermal expansion of solids, gases.					

Figure 6 illustrates a typical format for use of curriculum mapping at the elementary school level.[61]

Figure 6.
Sample: Elementary School Mapping Format.

Instructions: Record each day the total minutes spent in each curricular area and noncurricular area. Compute totals in minutes by week for each line. Total vertically by day for curricular area (line 17) and noncurricular each day (line 28). Compute total time per week (line 29). Do not count any activity twice (in more than one category). Total instructional time per day cannot exceed 265 for kindergarten, 265 for grades 1-2, 275 for grade 3, or 310 for grades 4-6. For total maximum time, add noninstructional time for your school.

Time Distribution (in minutes)

May

Curriculum Area/Topic/Skill/Subject	24	25	26	27	28	Weekly Total
1. Reading (formal reading instruction, follow-up)						
2. Spelling						
3. Oral Language						
4. Written Language						
5. Handwriting (formal instruction, drill only)						
6. Mathematics (formal instruction, follow-up)						
7. Science (formal instruction)						
8. Health Education (formal instruction)						
9. Art (formal instruction and follow-up)						
10. Music (formal instruction, listening)						
11. Physical Education (instruction plus play)						
12. Social Studies (history, geography, gov.)						
13. Career Education (nonduplicative time)						
14. Multicultural Education (formal instruction)						
15.						
16.						
17. Total Minutes on All Curricular Areas (lines 1-16)						
18. Attendance						
19. Assemblies						
20. Classroom Discipline						
21. Testing						
22. Collections, Drives						
23. Announcements						
24. Recess						
25. Lunch						
26. Other (Specify)						
27. Total Time on Noncurricular (18-26)						
28. Total Time Minutes per Day (17+27)						
29. Total Time per Week (17+27)						

(Lines 18-26 labeled vertically: NonCurricular Time)

Noncurricular Time

Figure 7 shows mapping data after they have been compiled across a school direct with seven elementary schools (K-5) in the area of science. The areas mapped within science are 13 topics.

Figure 7.
Using Mapping Data
To Diagnose Scope and Sequence
Problems Within A School District.

Topic/Area	Kindergarten	First	Second	Third	Fourth	Fifth	Total
Science							
01- Material objects	418	602	55	5		12	1092
02- Organisms	18	269					287
03- Interaction and Systems		52	413	82	8	12	567
04- Life cycles		57	229			61	347
05- Systems and Variables			53	304	25	20	402
06- Populations			42	340	6		388
07- Relative, position/ motion			1	7	596	65	669
08- Environments			2	5	98	88	193
09- Energy Sources			2		176	566	744
010- Communities					36	381	345
011- Models, Electricity, Magnets						12	12
012- Ecosystems				5			5
013- Nature study	72	91	56	85	11	77	392
Total Minutes	508	1071	853	833	956	1258	5479

The data show that there are areas of little emphasis in science at the elementary level in the district. For example, Topics 11 and 12 have little if any time spent on them. The topics with the greatest percentage of total time spent on science K-12 are numbers one (20 percent), nine (14 percent), seven (12 percent) and three (10 percent).

Apparently the curriculum was designed to be sequential (for example, delivered from numbers 1 through 13 across the grade levels). This can be discerned by noticing the "stairsteps" of the curriculum across and down the chart.

For example, these topics and numbers when circled would show the "stairsteps" of the delivered or taught curriculum in the district. Stairsteps in delivered or taught curriculum are referred to as the "spiral" or planned level of expansion and repetition that many curriculum guides attempt to develop. A curriculum administrator could use these data to locate breakdowns in the spiral and take corrective action by either directing instructional staff to make adjustments in the curriculum they teach, or revising the curriculum if there is too little time to teach the planned curriculum effectively. The skills involved in employing curriculum mapping in a school or school system are described in Figure 8.

Curriculum mapping is a powerful tool to ascertain what the actual curriculum is within schools and to determine whether the curriculum is being followed. It is both an instrument and procedure to discern what the curriculum is and to monitor the planned curriculum.[62]

Theories of Cognitive Development and Curriculum

For some time the ordering of school curriculum was chronological sequencing of material to be taught, a primitive linearity that assumed levels of difficulty, or was established by leading thinkers in education.[63] Then in 1902 John Dewey wrote *The Child and the Curriculum*, which challenged a priori schemes of organizing curriculum content that were outside of the learner and that did not take into account a student's prior experiences. Dewey argued there was a difference between the *logical* ordering of curriculum and the *psychological* ordering of curriculum. What was logical to an adult was not necessarily logical to a child because of the potentially vast difference in life experiences and maturity.

According to Dewey:

> "Abandon the notion of subject-matter as something fixed and ready-made in itself, outside the child's experience; cease thinking of the child's experience as also something hard and fast; see it as something fluent, embryonic, vital; and we realize that the child and the curriculum are simply two limits which define a single process."[64]

Theories of cognitive development range from the traditional stimulus response theories of the Skinnerians to schema theories.[65, 66] On a continuum, what is known about cognitive development tends to be far more *descriptive* than *prescriptive*, for example, it is difficult to move from various models and studies about how humans learn to fashioning a curriculum that is always prescriptive in nature.

Points of view about organizing curriculum content range from selecting curricular content based on a "fit" to the learner following some type of model such as Jean Piaget's, to simply allowing learners to supply their own order to sequencing content as they encounter it or are "ready" for it.[67]

In describing the potential value of a theory of instruction, Jerome Bruner indicated that a theory would be able to specify at least four things:

Figure 8.
Skills Involved in Curriculum Mapping.

Step	What the School Administrator Does
1. Determine curricular areas to map.	Based on poor test scores, observation, survey data or staff/student/parental complaints designate specific curricular areas to map.
2. Determine level of specificity to employ.	Based on the desirability of matching test data to map data, determine the level of specificity required to develop maps and decisions to be made with the data.
3. Decide how often mapping is to occur.	Relate the types of decisions to be made with the mapping data to the necessary frequency of mapping (daily, weekly, monthly, semester, or yearly).
4. Determine how mapping data will be consolidated.	Decide who and how mapping data will be gathered and collated. Will automation be part of the collation process? Develop computer software if necessary.
5. Determine how the data will be interpreted and reported?	What does the data mean? Decisions will have to be interpreted in light of what the numbers really mean about the "taught" curriculum. What will be done with the data?
6. Determine the benefits of mapping to the school/system.	Analyze the major anticipated benefits of engaging in mapping. Who specifically benefits? Do students and teachers benefit? How?
7. Determine the costs of mapping.	Determine the costs involved in conducting mapping. Include staff training, use of consultants, development of a computer program teacher time, changes in curriculum guides, other changes that may be required. What are the sources of funds for mapping?
8. What follow-up activities are anticipated after mapping?	How will it be known if mapping was a success or a failure? Who will decide? What has to happen after mapping? Determine the criteria by which you will have to answer the above questions.
9. Determine policy changes that may be required.	Based on analysis of existing board policies or administrative regulations, what may have to be altered to engage in mapping? Consider policies pertaining to teacher evaluation, use of data, reporting of data, public review of the data, and so on. Develop new policies that will facilitate mapping.

- The experiences that most effectively implant an individual toward a predisposition for learning.

- The ways to structure a body of knowledge so that it can be grasped most readily by the learner.

- The most effective sequences for presenting materials to be learned.

- The nature and pacing of rewards and punishments in learning and teaching.[68]

The fact that this is not easily done with prevailing cognitive theories even today suggests that we are far away indeed from moving from normative studies to adequate curriculum design schemes that use learning as the sole base for sequencing content.

Development/Application of Valid and Reliable Performance Indicators

A perennial problem for school administrators is how to move from global statements to performance requirements. The *connectors* are usually hard to discern. It is a process that is more of an art than a science. It is akin to making specific daily decisions about actions you might or should take after reading your horoscope in the newspaper. Usually such astrological offerings are global enough to encompass almost anything or everything.

For organizations to be effective the people in them must be able to translate organizational goals into concrete work tasks.[69] Once a board of education adopts global statements in any form, the demand for translation is immediate. Board statements may be in the form of student results desired as:

- Students will learn the essential basic skills.

- Students will acquire the necessary knowledge and attitudes to participate effectively in a democratic society.

- Students will come to appreciate the role of the fine arts in improving the quality of life.[70]

The board may adopt statements regarding *the processes* that should be going on within the school system such as:

- The district will incorporate the best forms of financial management practices to optimize taxpayer resources.[71]

- The district will take steps to attain a balanced curriculum to optimize a comprehensive educational program.[92]

- The district will use personnel practices that ensure the consistent growth and development of the total organization and the professional staff.[73]

The administrative staff is faced with the problem of translating such general aspirations into specific things to be done. The development of a performance indicator creates a kind of "middle ground" between a goal and a performance objective.

Since an educational goal is a kind of non-time bound global statement of intent (either stated as a work result or as a process), a performance indicator begins to define more precisely what is meant.

For example, regarding the global statement, "Students will learn the basic skills," some performance indicators might be:

● Students will acquire the communication skills via reading, writing, speaking, and listening.

● Students will acquire necessary computation skills through use of microcomputers.

● Students will learn to think logically via problem solving exercises.

The *validity* of a performance indicator is determined by consensual techniques, from poll taking to "Q" sort methods.[6] In essence the approach is asking those who set goals, "Is this what you meant?"

The *reliability* of a performance indicator is a determination that the measurement of it represents consistent attainment of the goal and that it is internally consistent. Reliability takes into account measurement itself and a goal or sub part thereof. It is an acceptance that the data gathered will stand for a representation of the consistent attainment (or lack thereof) of the goal.

To put the question of validity and reliability back into the real world, if a board of education adopted the "basic skill" goal cited, it would then have to agree that reading is a valid performance indicator of learning a basic skill. For example, reading will be allowed to be a representation of the goal. Next, a reading test (or some other means of assessment) would have to be acceptable to the board as evidence of learning to read. Such data would have to be gathered each year and be related to the goal. The board may adopt the Stanford Acheivement Test as the basis for determining whether or not the goal was met based on technical information it has received about the test from the administration, and whether it is a consistent measurement of reading. The latter considerations are those of reliability.

The Matter of Curriculum Quality Control

Determining the link between goals and performance indicators is part of a larger process of putting quality control into a school system concerning the curriculum and educational program.[75] Quality control refers to the internal linkage between three elements shown in Figure 9.

The relationship between the three elements consists of internal system alignments between the written curriculum in whatever form it exists, the taught curriculum as it is being delivered by classroom teachers, and the congruence to the total testing program. Disjointedness between any of the elements causes a

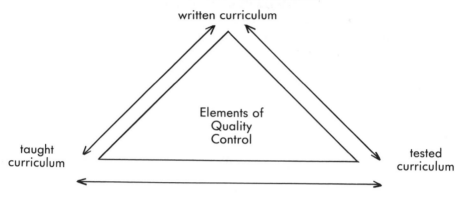

Figure 9.
The Elements of Quality Control of the School Curriculum.

breakdown among all three. The result of incongruence is normally lower test performance on the part of students, particularly if the test has been selected because it was congruent with the written curriculum.[76]

Some common causes of breakdowns between the three elements are these:

● Board policy goals for curriculum are nonexistent or too vague.

● The written curriculum as it has been developed in school system guides is vague and not keyed to available textbooks in use nor adopted tests employed.

● Teachers ignore district curriculum guides, and teaching is an independent activity, apart from the district testing/assessment program and the district's curriculum guides.

● School administrators are ineffective in monitoring the delivery of the adopted curriculum of the district.

Breakdowns in quality control that are caused by poor planning and lack of inclusion of all three elements in curricular guides are *design problems*; for example, disjointedness is caused by an absence of connecting the elements at the outset.

Breakdowns caused by lack of attention to making sure the elements are occurring as planned are called *delivery problems*.[77] Knowing the difference between the two is a matter of some concern to school administrators such as principals and central level staff in charge of curriculum development and systemwide implementation.[78]

Figure 10 is a sample questionnaire that can be used to assess the adequacy of a district's curriculum guides to ensure quality control. It assesses whether or not locally produced curricular materials contain the necessary elements of quality control to ensure that there will be no design problems in curriculum management. It has been used in many national educational performance audits.[79]

Figure 10.
Survey to Check for Quality Control Elements Present in Locally Developed Curriculum Guides.

Criteria	3	2	1	0	Points

Clarity and Validity of Objectives   __ __ __ __ _____
    0. No goals/objectives present
    1. Vague delineation of goals/objectives
    2. States tasks to be performed or skills
to be learned
    3. What, when, how, actual standard of
performance, and amount of time to be
spent learning each objective.

**Congruity of the Curriculum to the
Testing/Evaluation Program**   __ __ __ __ _____
    0. No evaluation approach stated
    1. Some approach of evaluation stated
    2. Skill, knowledge, concepts that will
be assessed
    3. Objective is keyed to performance
evaluation and district tests in use

**Delineation by Grade of the Essential
Skills, Knowledges, and Attitudes**   __ __ __ __ _____
    0. No mention of required skills
    1. Prior general experience needed
    2. Prior general experience needed
in grade level
    3. Specific documented prerequisite or
description of discrete skills required

**Delineation of the Major Instructional
Tools**   __ __ __ __ _____
    0. No mention of textbook in instructional
tools
    1. Must name the textbook used
    2. Basic text and supplementary materials to
be used
    3. "Match" between the textbook and
curriculum objective-by-objective

Clear Linkages for Classroom Use   __ __ __ __ _____
    0. No linkage cited for classroom use
    1. Overall, vague statement on linkage for
approaching subject
    2. General suggestions on approach
    3. Specific examples on how to approach
key concepts/skills in the classroom

                                          Totals __ __ __ __ **Total**___

Of critical importance in determining the linkage between the instructional program as it is being delivered by teachers and the written and tested curricula is the textbook. Textbooks continue to exert a powerful influence on actual classroom teaching and learning time. Therefore, their selection should ensure effective curricular congruence to a school system's adopted objectives.[80]

Use of Computers and Other Technologies

Computers. The infusion of computers into U.S. school systems has been swift and relentless. According to a telephone survey of all 15,442 school districts in the country in 1981, some 19 percent of all schools in those districts (16,000) were using computers for instruction. By 1990 that number is expected to be between 85 and 95 percent.[83]

A national survey in 1982 by the Educational Research Service revealed that 89 percent of all school districts sampled were using computers for administrative purposes (accounting, operations and maintenance, transportation, student scheduling), and 77 percent were using them for instructional purposes.[82]

The New York Association of Mathematics Teachers has developed a list of eight inclusive uses of computers in the classroom. These are:

Curriculum Area/Topics Activity	Expected
1. Learning about computers	computer history, organization and operation, careers in computing
2. Computer Assisted Instruction (CAI)	for use in instructional delivery such as tutorials, practice programs
3. Computer Managed Instruction (CMI)	diagnosis and testing, recordkeeping, instructional materials generation
4. Drill and practice	questions, student response, feedback, new questions
5. Simulation	create real events or situations, games, economic or business problems, or even experiments
6. Demonstration	concepts and ideas can be graphically displayed
7. Problem solving	using the computer as a high speed calculator
8. Programming	defining and analyzing programs, debugging programs[83]

Computer literacy is a term that encompasses many areas in curriculum development. If computer literacy becomes an educational goal, it can mean anything from simply understanding computers and their impact (computer awareness) to knowing the various computer languages and being able to solve problems with them.[84]

While use of computers portends a possible revolution in the schools, bringing with it the real potential of a science of individualized instruction, the disadvantage is that computers force upon the curriculum a very rigid type of thinking and problem-solving capability. Computer programs are linear by design. The computer is an overwhelming convergent force in developing thinking skills in students.[85] It is possible to use computers creatively, but so far we have little or no evidence of such creative applications. A veteran classroom teacher summed up her feelings about it when she said, "I'd be a little relieved if I knew the computer could laugh at itself." At the present that capability represents something beyond a technological breakthrough.

Other Technological Aids. Other technological and instructional aids include motion pictures, television, tape recordings, puppets and props, voice slide presentations, lectures with posters, slide projectors, programmed instructional devices, live demonstrations, exhibits, field trips, radio broadcasts or recordings, still pictures, or dramatized experiences. A model of media selection and prescription has been developed by Robert Gagne and Leslie Briggs on how to select and use the varied technology available for use in the schools. The ten-step process includes these activities:

1. Develop statement of lesson objectives.
2. Classify the objectives.
3. Select the type of instructional events desired.
4. Determine the type of stimuli required for each event.
5. List the potential media for each event.
6. List the best media for each event.
7. Make media choice.
8. Write a rationale for the decisions made.
9. Write a prescription for each event.
10. Write a script for all of the prescriptions.[86]

An excellent media flow chart and selection process has been developed by Reiser and Gagne that is highly recommended for use by school administrators.[87]

Development and Use of Available Cultural Resources

The use of available cultural resources has two dimensions for the school administrator. The first is forming closer relationships with the community the schools serve. This brings the community "in." The second is reaching out into the community to tap resources not available to students otherwise. This extends the school *into* the community.

Community Schools and Community Education. In the beginnings of American public education, citizens had direct and often daily contact with their schools. Gradually, as schools became larger, staffs more professional, and operations more complex, schools became more removed from their communities. The consequences of this removal became apparent in the lack of support for schools in terms of taxes and approved bond referenda. The 1965 ESEA Act made public participation mandatory in the form of citizen advisory groups in order to forge new links with communities and to reduce school isolation.

The trend toward public participation has not been enough, however, in the minds of many thoughtful educators. Authorities in school finance Walter Garms and James Guthrie commented:

> "We believe that the trend toward professional control of education has gone too far in the United States. The tension between expertise and popular control that underlies many areas of public policy in a democracy has become unbalanced in favor of professional educators. The balance needs to be restored by reasserting the right of the public to control its schools."[71]

A broader form of public participation in the governance of schools and regular influential participation in school activities, through a full-blown community education program are two ways to restore the imbalance identified by Garms and Guthrie. The major elements of a community education program are:

● Maximum use of community resources to provide a comprehensive educational program for the entire community.

● Coordination and cooperation among individuals, groups, and organizations to avoid unnecessary duplication.

● Increased opportunities for lay and professional people to assume leadership roles.

● Social interaction and improved human relationships among people with differing cultural backgrounds.

● Assessing and evaluating the extent to which the goals of community education are met by the program and process.[88]

The checklist in Figure 11 represents a means for assessing the extent to which citizens in the community are involved in various facets of school programs and activities.[89]

Use of cultural resources has another dimension as well. School administrators must consider the broadest use of cultural resources in curriculum development because the major instructional resources have not always presented all sides to

Figure 11.
Checklist for Community Involvement in the Schools.

Type of Involvement	Yes	No	Pending
1. Service on school building advisory councils	___	___	_____
2. Service on board advisory councils/committees	___	___	_____
3. Service on special program advisory committtees (Chapter 1, gifted and talented, etc.)	___	___	_____
4. Participation in goal-setting exercises	___	___	_____
5. Participation in developing the annual budget	___	___	_____
6. Service on special committees to assist administration on such things as purchase of computers	___	___	_____
7. Involvement and input as it pertains to school desegregation or redistricting due to declining enrollment	___	___	_____
8. Involvement in groups/committees regarding school closings	___	___	_____
9. Input/involvement as it regards collective bargaining	___	___	_____
10. Service on special committees to evaluate schools or programs	___	___	_____
11. Service on committees to select/evaluate curriculum content	___	___	_____
12. Participation in the development of new board policies	___	___	_____

current issues. School textbooks have historically presented a somewhat biased picture of social issues within the country as well as the role and motivations of our nation in the world to U.S. students.[90] A detailed examination of some 63 textbooks on history, geography, and economics by the Hudson Institute noted that there was incorrect information on population trends, magnified statistics regarding malnutrition and hunger, an overheated view of pollution trends, shallow explanations of running out of resources, and an incorrect use of some countries of the Third World to characterize the entire Third World.[91]

Educators have come to terms with the understanding that a great many forces outside the schools educate. The American culture at large has a profound influence on the young and their social attitudes. While some of the forces represent merely passing fads, the impact of soap operas, rock groups, attitudes toward life and issues by the Archie Bunkers of the world, and other long running media sitcoms become part and parcel of the everyday idiom of thinking and perceiving. The media culture itself is pervasive but not well understood.

Typically, cultural resources are seen as historical sites, museums, student attendance at operas, plays, musicals, quality movies, or field trips to historical areas in foreign countries. The use of such cultural resources may not be without conflict.

Conclusion

The development of a systematic school curriculum is undeniably managerial in scope with an emphasis on defining the direction for the school system and ensuring that available resources are marshalled to sustain that direction. Curriculum development is a part of curriculum management, but development per se will not ensure the adequate implementation of curriculum. Curriculum development also does not answer questions posed by requirements for systemwide curricular continuity nor the necessity for economies of scale that are only possible within school systems.

Curriculum as a set of operational procedures must fit within the existing managerial structure or it will be changed so that it does become congruent with the structure. Those who would argue for a different curriculum must therefore change the management structure prior to changing the curriculum.

Skill Accomplishment Checklist for Chapter Four

Competency and Skills	Reading and Activities for Mastery

Competency: Developing systematic school curriculum that ensures both extensive cultural enrichment activities and mastery of fundamental as well as progressive, more complex skills required in advanced problem solving, creative, and technological activities.	Readings: See resources 1, 3, 4, 5, 6, 21, 22, 22, 25, 27, 31, 59, 77, 80, 85, 88, 94, 96, 94, 96, 97, 100
	Activities:
	  1. Using Figure 10, rate and rank each of the curriculum guides currently in your school/district.
	  2. Using the criteria for community involvement in the schools, estimate the extent to which your community is actively involved in the schools.
	  3. Examine existing board policies to ascertain the extent to which the strategic development of curriculum is controlled by the board.
	  4. Critique existing curriculum guides using *Bloom's Taxonomy of Objectives* to determine in which category most fall. Are they higher or lower order cognitive objectives?

Skill A: Planning/futures methods to anticipate occupational trends and their implications.	Readings: See references 21, 28, 29, 32 Activities: 1. Contact local office of Labor and gather statistics on available job openings, areas in short supply to note job possibilities. Identify the skills required to be in the curriculum as shown in the ten steps in the chapter. Are the costs worth the potential benefits?

Skill B: Taxonomies of Instructional Objectives and validation procedures for curricular units/ sequences.	Readings: See references 60, 61, 62, 103, 104 for mapping. Taxonomies 44, 45
	Activities:
	  1. Using curriculum mapping as a technique, ascertain which objectives or areas of the curriculum are most frequently taught in the written curriculum.
	  2. By applying Glatthorn's unit criteria (reference 74) perform a critique of typical curricular units in your school's or district's guides. Where are they congruent? Where not and why?

Skill C: Theories of cognitive development and the sequencing/structuring of curricula.	Readings: See references 64, 65, 66, 67, 68
	Activities:
	   1. Examine the existing scope and sequence chart. What assumptions have been made about cognitive learning? What is the apparent base for the sequencing of content? Develop an alternative scope and sequence chart using a different set of assumptions.
	   2. Develop a scope and sequence chart based on a continuum of skill/cognitive development rather than grade levels.

Skill D: Develop valid and reliable performance for instructional outcomes.	Readings: See references 6, 74, 75,
	Activities:
	   1. Take one instructional goal and develop as many indicators for its outcome as possible. What criteria might be employed to limit the number of indicators?
	   2. Determine the number of ways that consensus can be reached on selecting performance indicators.
	   3. Estimate whether instructional breakdowns in your situation are more the result of design or delivery problems.

Skill E: Use of computers and other technologies as instructional aids.	Readings: See references 81, 82, 83, 84, 85, 85, 86, 87
	Activities:
	   1. Perform a survey of the use of various technologies in the current school system as to frequency of use and purpose.
	   2. Determine the difference between computer managed instruction and computer assisted instruction. Which should be preferred in your situation?

Skill F: Development/use of available cultural resources.	Readings: See references 88, 89 See also R. S. Brandt (ed.) *Partners: Parents and Schools* (Alexandria, Va.: ASCD, 1979).
	Activities:
	   1. Develop a list of resources in your own community that includes museums and work places such as newspaper, court houses, fire departments and link them to specific curricular units and/or objectives. Publish the list for classroom teachers.
	   2. Examine the current list of texts in use. Do any contain cultural biases or stereotypes?

Resources

1. P. Drucker, *Management* (New York: Harper & Row, 1973), p. 508.

2. R. J. Murnane, *The Impact of School Resources on the Learning of Inner City Children* (Cambridge, Mass.: Ballinger Publishing Company, 1975).

3. J. I. Goodlad, *A Place Called School* (New York: McGraw-Hill Book Company, 1984).

4. See K. E. Weick, "Educational Organizations as Loosely Coupled Systems," *Administrative Science Quarterly* 23 (December 1978), pp. 541-52.

5. D. B. Tyack, *The One Best System* (Cambridge, Mass.: Harvard University Press, 1974).

6. F. W. English and R. A. Kaufman, *Needs Assessment: A Focus for Curriculum Development* (Washington, D.C.: Association for Supervision and Curriculum Development, 1975).

7. W. H. Schubert, *Curriculum Books: The First Eighty Years* (Washington, D.C.: University Press of America, 1980), pp. 32.

8. R. E. Callahan, *Education and the Cult of Efficiency* (Chicago: University of Chicago Press, 1962), pp. 79-94.

9. W. H. Newman, C. E. Summer, and E. K. Warren, *The Process of Management* (Englewood Cliffs, N.J.: Prentice-Hall, Inc., 1961), p. 495.

10. F. P. Hunkins, *Curriculum Development* (Columbus, Ohio: Charles E. Merrill Publishing Company, 1980), pp. 220-243.

11. G. A. Beauchamp, *Curriculum Theory* (Wilmette, Ill.: The Kagg Press, 1975), pp. 109-110.

12. A. R. King Jr. and J. A. Brownell, *The Curriculum and The Disciplines of Knowledge* (New York: John Wiley and Sons, Inc., 1966).

13. See P. H. Phenix, *Realms of Meaning* (New York: McGraw-Hill Book Company, 1964).

14. D. Pratt, *Curriculum* (New York: Harcourt Brace Jovanovich, Inc., 1980), p. 4.

15. W. B. Ragan and G. D. Shepherd, *Modern Elementary Curriculum*, Fourth Edition (New York: Holt, Rinehart & Winston, 1974), pp. 109-121.

16. W. F. Zenger and S. K. Zenger, *Curriculum Planning: A Ten Step Process* (Palo Alto, Calif.: R and E Research Associates, Inc., 1982).

17. A. D. Hauenstein, *Curriculum Planning for Behavioral Development* (Worthington, Ohio: Charles A. Jones Publishing Company, 1972).

18. J. D. McNeil, *Curriculum: A Comprehensive Introduction* (Boston: Little, Brown and Company, 1977), pp. 157-205.

19. P. M. Halverson (ed.), *Balance in the Curriculum* (Washington, D.C.: Association for Supervision and Curriculum Development, 1961).

20. H. Taba, *Curriculum Development* (New York: Harcourt, Brace and World, Inc. 1962), p. 374.

21. F. L. Steeves and F. W. English, *Secondary Curriculum for a Changing World* (Columbus, Ohio: Charles E. Merrill Publishing Company, 1978), pp. 296-306.

22. R. S. Brandt (ed.), *Applied Strategies for Curriculum Evaluation* (Alexandria, Va.: Association for Supervision and Curriculum Development, 1981).

23. F. A. Rogers, "Curriculum Research and Evaluation," in F. W. English (ed.), *Fundamental Curriculum Decisions* (Alexandria, Va.: Association for Supervision and Curriculum Development, 1983), pp. 142-153.

24. H.M. Kliebard, "Reappraisal: The Tyler Rationale," *School Review* (February 1970), pp. 259-272, as cited in W. Pinar (ed.), *Curriculum Theorizing* (Berkeley, Calif: McCutchan Publishing, 1975), pp. 70-83.

25. R. Tyler, *Basic Principles of Curriculum and Instruction* (Chicago: University of Chicago Press, 1949).

26. See D.F. Walker, "A Barnstorming Tour of Writing on Curriculum," in A.W. Foshay (ed.), *Considered Action for Curriculum Improvement* (Alexandria, Va.: Association for Supervision and Curriculum Development, 1980), pp. 71-80.

27. F.W. English and B.E. Steffy, "Curriculum Mapping: An Aid to School Curriculum Management," *Spectrum, Journal of School Research and Information* 1, 3 (Fall 1983), pp. 17-26.

28. R.W. Rumberger and H.M. Levin, "Forecasting the Impact of New Technologies on the Future Job Market," (Stanford, Calif.: Institute for Finance and Governance, 1984) as cited in "Service Areas to Exceed High-Tech in Job Growth," *Education Week* 3, 34 (May 16, 1984), p. 11.

29. Source of the data is G.T. Silvestri, J.M. Lukasiewicz, and M.E. Einstein, "Occupational Employment Projections Through 1995," *Monthly Labor Review* 106 (November 1983); Figure 2 is based on the 1980 Public Use Sample, U.S. Census Bureau, as cited in *Education Week*.

30. D.L. Bates and D.L. Eldredge, *Strategy and Policy* (Dubuque, Iowa: William C. Brown Company Publishers, 1980), pp. 46-48.

31. F.W. English and B.E. Steffy, "Curriculum as a Strategic Management Tool," *Educational Leadership* 39, 4 (January 1982) pp. 276-284.

32. L.J. Bailey, "Curriculum for Career Development Education," in J. Schaffarzick and D.H. Hampson (eds.), *Strategies for Curriculum Development* (Berkeley, Calif.: McCutchan Publishing, 1975) pp. 185-210.

33. M. Provus, *Discrepancy Evaluation* (Berkeley, Calif.: McCutchan Publishing, 1971).

34. See "Cost Considerations and Economic Analysis," in S.B. Anderson, S. Ball, and R.T. Murphy (eds.), *Encyclopedia of Educational Evaluation* (San Francisco: Jossey-Bass Publishers, 1973), pp. 92-98.

35. See E.J. Webb, D.T. Campbell, R.D. Schwartz, and L. Sechrest, *Unobtrusive Measures* (Chicago: Rand McNally and Company, 1966).

36. See "Decision-Management Strategies," in B.R. Worthen and J.R. Sanders, *Educational Evaluation: Theory and Practice* (Worthington, Ohio: Charles A. Jones Publishing Company, 1973), pp. 128-209.

37. For a complete review of the process from curriculum through instruction see W. Dick and L. Carey, *The Systematic Design of Instruction* (Glenview, Ill.:

Scott, Foresman and Company, 1978).

38. J.F. McNamara, "The Design of Technological Forecasting Studies," in S.P. Hencley and J.R. Yates (eds.), *Futurism in Education: Methodologies* (Berkeley, Calif.: McCutchan Publishing, 1975) pp. 375-405.

39. H.G. Shane, *The Educational Significance of the Future* (Bloomington, Ind.: Phi Delta Kappa, 1973).

40. K. Cirincione-Coles (ed.), *The Future of Education* (Beverly Hills, Calif.: Sage Publications, 1981).

41. L. Reinhart, H.J. Shapiro, and E.A. Kallman, *The Practice of Planning* (New York: Van Nostrand Reinhold Company, 1981).

42. H.I. Ansoff, *Strategic Management* (New York: John Wiley and Sons, 1979).

43. T. Deal and M. Wise, "Planning, Plotting, and Playing in Education's Era of Decline," in J.V. Baldridge and T. Deal (eds.), *The Dynamics of Organizational Change in Education* (Berkeley, Calif.: McCutchan Publishing, 1983) pp. 451-472.

44. B.S. Bloom (ed.), *Taxonomy of Educational Objectives: Handbook I: Cognitive Domain* (New York: David McKay Company, Inc. 1956).

45. D.R. Krathwohl, B.S. Bloom, and B.B. Masia (eds.), *Taxonomy of Educational Objectives: Handbook II: Affective Domain* (New York: David McKay Company, Inc. 1956).

46. R.F. Mager, *Preparing Instructional Objectives* (Palo Alto, Calif.: Fearon Publishers, 1962).

47. See M.W. Apple, Chapter Six, "Systems Management and the Ideology of Control," in *Ideology and Curriculum* (London: Routledge and Kegan Paul, 1979), pp. 105-122.

48. E.W. Eisner, *The Education Imagination* (New York: Macmillan Publishing Company, Inc., 1979).

49. R. Kaufman and B. Stone, *Planning for Organizational Success* (New York: John Wiley and Sons, 1983).

50. L.S. Hannah and J. U. Michaelis, *A Comprehensive Framework For Instructional Objectives* (Reading, Mass.: Addison-Wesley Publishing Company, 1977).

51. B.O. Smith, W.O. Stanley, and J.H. Shores, *Fundamentals of Curriculum Development* (Yonkers-on-Hudson, New York: World Book Company, 1950), pp. 412-461.

52. See Part Five, "The Curriculum as Academic Rationalism," in E.W. Eisner and E. Vallance (eds.), *Conflicting Conceptions of Curriculum* (Berkeley, Calif.: McCutchan Publishing, 1974) pp. 162-200.

53. D.F. Walker, "What Curriculum Research?" *Journal of Curriculum Studies* 5 (January 1973) pp. 58-72, as cited in H.A. Giroux, A.N. Penna, and W.F. Pinar, *Curriculum and Instruction* (Berkeley, Calif.: McCutchan Publishing Corporation, 1981) pp. 281-296.

54. See M.W. Apple, Chapter Five, "Curricular Form and the Logic of Technical Control: Commodification Returns," in *Education and Power* (Boston: Routledge and Kegan Paul, 1982) pp. 135-164.

55. R.A. Kaufman, *Educational System Planning* (Englewood Cliffs, N.J., Prentice-Hall, Inc. 1972).

56. H.C. Morrison, *The Practice of Teaching in the Secondary School* (Chicago: University of Chicago Press, 1931), pp. 24-25.

57. A.J. Jones, E.D. Grizzell, and W.J. Grinstead, *Principles of Unit Construction* (New York: McGraw-Hill Book Company, Inc. 1939), p. 19.

58. See A.A. Glatthorn, *A Guide for Developing an English Curriculum for the Eighties* (Urbana, Ill.: National Council of Teachers of English, 1980) pp. 121-122 and pp. 127-129.

59. See M.J. Weiss, "A Thematic Interdisciplinary Approach to Basic Skills in the Secondary School," in D.G. Wallace (ed.) *Developing Basic Skills Programs in Secondary Schools* (Alexandria, Va.: Association for Supervision and Curriculum Development (n.d.) pp. 85-96.

60. See D.F. Weinstein, "Curriculum Mapping: Results of a Large-Scale Automated Program," in *Spectrum, Journal of School Research and Information* 1, 3 (Fall 1983), pp. 27-32.

61. For an example of the use of this mapping format and the data gathered from the process see F.W. English, "Pull-Outs: How Much Do They Erode Whole-Class Teaching?" *Principal*, 63:5 (May 1984) pp. 32-36.

62. P.J. O'Malley, "Learn the Truth About Curriculum" *The Executive Educator* 4 (August 1982), pp. 14 and 26.

63. M.J. Adler, *The Paideia Proposal: An Educational Manifesto* (New York: Macmillan Publishing Company, Inc., 1982).

64. J. Dewey, *The Child and the Curriculum* (Chicago: University of Chicago Press, 1902), p. 11.

65. B.F. Skinner, "Teaching Machines," in J.P. DeCecco, *Human Learning in the School* (New York: Holt, Rinehart, & Winston, Inc., 1964), pp. 164-182.

66. R.C. Anderson, "The Notion of Schemata and the Educational Enterprise," in *Schooling and the Acquisition of Knowledge* (New York: Erlbau, 1977), pp. 415-431.

67. J.H. Flavell, *The Development Psychology of Jean Piaget* (Princeton, N.J.: D. Van Nostrand Company, Inc. 1963).

68. J. Bruner, *Toward a Theory of Instruction* (Cambridge, Mass.: The Belknap Press of the Harvard University Press, 1966), pp. 40-41.

69. For public sector organizations like schools this is a hard process because of the risks involved in alienating specific constitutencies; see P.F. Drucker, "Managing the Public Service Institution," in F.S. Lane (ed.) *Current Issues in Public Administration* (New York: St. Martin's Press, 1978), pp. 376-387.

70. See D.W. Johnson, "Affective Outcomes," in H.J. Walberg (ed.) *Evaluating Educational Performance* (Berkeley, Calif.: McCutchan Publishing Corporation, 1974) pp. 99-112.

71. See Chapter Eleven, "Reforming Public School Management and Budgeting," in W.I. Garms, J.W. Guthrie, and L.C. Pierce, *School Finance: The Economics and Politics of Public Education* (Englewood Cliffs, N.J.: Prentice-Hall, Inc., 1978) pp. 262-294.

72. See J.P. DeCecco and A.K. Richards, *Growing Pains: Uses of School*

Conflict (New York: Aberdeen Press, 1974).

73. See E.G. Bogue and R.L. Saunders, *The Educational Manager: Artist and Practitioner* (Worthington, Ohio: Charles A. Jones Publishing Company, 1976).

74. R.F. Mager, *Goal Analysis* (Belmont, Calif.: Fearon Publishers, 1972).

75. J.M. Juran, "Basic Concepts," in J.M. Juran, F.M. Gryna, Jr. and R.S. Bingham, Jr. (eds.) *Quality Control Handbook* (New York: McGraw-Hill Book Company, 1974) pp. 2-1.

76. See W.H. Hannum and L.J. Briggs, "How Does Instructional Systems Design Differ from Traditional Instruction?" *Educational Technology*, 12 (January 1982) pp. 9-14.

77. See F.W. English and B.E. Steffy, "Differentiating Between Design and Delivery Problems in Achieving Quality Control in School Curriculum Management," *Educational Technology*, 13 (February 1983) pp. 29-32.

78. See D.D. Christensen, "Curriculum Development: A Function of Design and Leadership," *The Executive Review* 1, 3 (December 1980) Institute for School Executives, The University of Iowa.

79. F.W. English, R.M. Oppenheim, and C. Robertson, "Management Planning Pinpoints Schools' Problems," *Management Focus* 28, 5 (September-October 1981) Peat, Marwick, Mitchell & Co., pp. 31-36.

80. See D.J. Freeman, T.M. Kuhs, A.C. Porter, R.E. Floden, W.H. Schmidt, and J.R. Schwille, "Do Textbooks and Tests Define a National Curriculum in Elementary School Mathematics?" *The Elementary School Journal* 83, 5 (May 1984) pp. 501-513.

81. J. Lindelow, *Administrator's Guide to Computers in the Classroom* (Eugene, Oregon: Clearinghouse on Educational Management, 1983) p. 7.

82. Educational Research Sevice, "School District Uses of Computer Technology," (Arlington, Virginia: ERS, 1982).

83. New York State Association of Mathematics Teachers, "Guidelines for Computers in Education," July 1982.

84. M.T. Grady and J.D. Gawronski (eds.) *Computers in Curriculum and Instruction* (Alexandria, Va.: Association for Supervision and Curriculum Development, 1983).

85. S. Papert, *Mindstorms* (New York: Basic Books, Inc., 1980).

86. R.M. Gagne and L.J. Briggs, *Principles of Instructional Design* (New York: Holt, Rinehart & Winston, 1979) p.195 .

87. R.A. Reiser and R.M. Gagne, *Selecting Media for Instruction* (Englewood Cliffs, N. J.: Educational Technology Publications, 1983).

88. C.B. Epstein and American Association of School Administrators, *Community Education: Managing for Success* (Washington, D.C.: U.S. Government Printing Office, 1980) p. 10.

89. P.O. Gonder and National School Public Relations Association, *Linking Schools and the Community* (Arlington, Va.: NSPRA, 1977) p. 21.

90. See F. Fitzgerald, *America Revised* (Boston: Little Brown and Company, 1979).

91. The Hudson Institute, "Visions of the Future: The Treatment of Limits-to-

Growth Issues in U.S. High School Textbooks," (Croton-on-Hudson, New York: 1984).

92. See A. L. Ayars and C. Bovee, "How to Plan a Community Resources Workshop," (Buffalo, New York: National Association for Industry-Education Cooperation, 1975).

93. See H. C. Perkinson, *The Imperfect Panacea: American Faith in Education, 1865-1965* (New York: Random House, 1968).

Other resources by F. W. English on this or related topics:

94. "Management Practice as a Key to Curriculum Leadership," *Educational Leadership* 36,6 (March 1979) pp. 408-413.

95. "Untying the Knots in Public School Curricula," *Management Focus* (May-June 1979), pp. 32-38.

96. *Improving Curriculum Management in the Schools* (Washington, D.C.: Council for Basic Education, 1980), pp. 220-243.

97. "Curriculum Mapping," *Educational Leadership* 37,7 (April 1980), pp. 558-559.

98. "What's Ahead in Curriculum?" *The School Administrator* 35, 11 (December 1978), pp. 18-19.

100. "Contemporary Curriculum Circumstances," in F.W. English (ed.), *Fundamental Curriculum Decisions* (Alexandria, Va.: Association for Supervision and Curriculum Development, 1983), pp. 14-15.

101. "Re-tooling Curriculum Within On-Going School Systems," *Educational Technology* 19, 5 (May 1979), pp. 7-13.

102. "Curriculum Development Within the School System," in A. W. Foshay (ed.), *Considered Action for Curriculum Improvement* (Alexandria, Va.: Association for Supervision and Curriculum Development, 1980), pp. 145-157

103. "Curriculum Mapping," *The Professional Educator* 3, 1 (Spring 1980), pp. 8-12.

104. *Quality Control in Curriculum Development* (Arlington, Va.: American Association of School Administrators, 1978), p. 26.

105. "The Politics of Needs Assessment," *Educational Technology* 17, 11 (November 1977), pp. 18-23.

106. *Curriculum Auditing* (Lancaster, Pa.: Technomic Pub. Co. Inc., 1988).

CHAPTER FIVE

SKILLS IN INSTRUCTIONAL MANAGEMENT

In this chapter we build on the foundation laid in chapter four. We assume that now the administrator has a curriculum. The task, then, is to implement that curriculum — to deliver it effectively to the intended recipients. Managing this task is an administrator's responsibility. To succeed in implementing the curriculum, administrators must acquire these skills in instructional management:

- Curriculum design and instructional delivery strategies.
- Instructional and motivational psychology.
- Alternative methods of monitoring and evaluating student achievement.
- Management of change to enhance the mastery of educational goals.
- Applications of computer management to the instructional program.
- Use of instructional time and resources.
- Cost effectiveness and program budgeting.

These seven skills will be applied in the context of an instructional management system. We begin with a consideration of that system followed by a consideration of each of the instructional management skills in the order listed.

The instructional management system and the requisite skills to implement curriculum are professional construct and professional competencies applied to a purpose. That purpose should be identified in a clearly defined mission statement. Without constant orientation to the mission, the system's energy may be different and misdirected. The mission of a school provides focus for its system's energy. Edmonds and others have stated that the goals and objectives of an organization must be written down, understood by faculty, and serve as a guide to instructional planning.[3] These goals and objectives are directed toward the school mission. The mission provides the overarching goal toward which the resources of the system are directed.[4]

A Model of an Instructional Management System

The focal point of the instructional system does not lie within the domain of an administrator. The true decision-making power resides with the classroom teachers. Pre-instructional decisions, instructional decisions, and post-instructional decisions are all made by classroom teachers with little or no direction from administrators. Decisions about what content to cover, how much time to spend on instruction, how to group students, how to monitor and evaluate student work, the amount of academic learning time to be assigned to a particular activity, and the instructional strategies to be used are generally all teacher decisions. In other words, administrators must often orchestrate and manipulate the system without the power base to do it.

To compound the problem, variables affecting the instructional management system are multifaceted and complex. Figure 1 is a graphic representation of an instructional management system. Curriculum design and instructional delivery strategies are the core of the system. Skills in these areas are surrounded and affected by the use of instructional time and resources. These skills are clearly under the control of the teacher. While administrators have control over the peripheral skills of cost effectiveness and program budgeting, applications of computer management to the instructional program, and the management of change; the skills of instructional and motivational psychology and alternative methods of monitoring and evaluating student achievement are largely within a teacher's domain. Clearly, success in instructional management requires more than the acquisition of knowledge; it demands the ability to accomplish the mission through others with skills in human interaction. Four recent textbooks have clearly reinforced this notion of human interaction and school improvement.[51, 52, 53, 54]

Curriculum Design and Instructional Delivery Strategies

The first skill of instructional management speaks to an administrator's ability to assess the match between the curriculum as it is written to the curriculum as it is taught. We assume that the curriculum as written is the appropriate curriculum for the community, the system, the school, the students, and the teachers within the system. Assuming this is true, the administrator must be able to determine if that curriculum is being experienced by students. Further, the administrator must determine if the curriculum is being implemented in the most effective way. And, if the curriculum is not effectively implemented, the administrator must know why it is not. To do this, administrators must be able to assess the students, their needs, and learning styles; and to assess the teachers, their strengths, preferred teaching styles, and their areas of weakness. The school administrator, proficient in curriculum design and instructional development, will be able to answer questions such as the following:

- What tests are given?
- Are pre-tests given?
- Who developed the pre-tests?
- How are the results used?

Figure 1.
Instructional Management System Skill Integration.

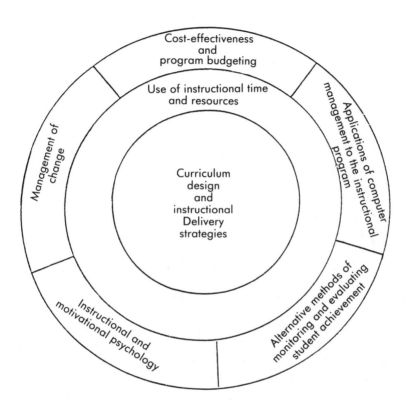

- What placement procedures are used in the district?
- What grouping practices are used in the classroom?
- Is the concept of mastery learning employed?
- Is mastery learning carried out effectively?
- What is the repertory of instructional strategies employed by the teaching staff?
- How does a teacher decide which instructional strategy to use?
- Are the strategies used appropriate for the student population?

Administrators cannot answer questions such as these without being familiar with all aspects of an instructional program. They obviously will not be spending an inordinate amount of time seated at their desks. Moreover, knowing the answers to the questions is merely a beginning. Although a myriad of instructional strategies are available to teachers, too often a teacher-directed method of presenting facts and testing are predominant. If this is the case, or if the answers to the questions delineated are not satisfactory, the challenge is for the administrator to help teachers change their behavior. This challenge leads directly to the next of the skills deemed necessary for success in instructional management.

Instructional and Motivational Psychology

Discussions in previous chapters have dealt with methods of viewing and working with individuals and organizations. We know that situational differences make some approaches to leadership and motivation more effective than others. Most of us will probaby err on the side of democratic-participative leadership styles when unsure of the best approaches, but we soon learn to discriminate between situations requiring strong directive leadership and those dictating a consensus resolution reached by full participation of all. And in dealing with individuals we come to understand comedian Flip Wilson's law of administration: "Different strokes for different folks." On the group or organizational level we reluctantly agree with Sergiovanni and Elliott that sometimes Theory X behavior is appropriate.[5] Whatever organizational theories or leadership styles we espouse, we are faced with the challenge of influencing or changing teacher behavior.

Altering teacher behavior is difficult and to change patterned response is to make the environment less secure. When administrators ask teachers to learn and implement new teaching methods, they are asking the teachers to make the environment more dangerous. A significant request for a competent professional, it may be almost impossible for an insecure, marginally competent teacher.

Learning the technique of a new teaching strategy is not necessarily the problem. Facilitating the risk-taking behavior on the part of staff is. People tend to take risks when they feel safe and secure within themselves. They hide behind familiarity when they are not comfortable with themselves.

Three conditions are necessary before a teacher will accept a new teaching strategy:

● The new strategy must be explained in such a way that the teacher clearly understands what the procedure entails.

● The procedure must be consistent with the teacher's present teaching style.

● The procedure must be cost effective in terms of time and energy.[7]

Benjamin Bloom has suggested that when teachers can identify the skills and knowledge necessary for new learning and when teachers promote the appropriate attitude, interests, and positive self-concept of students, then students can achieve at rates commonly reserved for the academically gifted.[8] This is the basis for his concept of mastery learning. It seems to suggest that before instructional strategies and curriculum design can be addressed, teachers and administrators need to be well grounded in motivational and instructional psychology.

How teachers go about facilitating meaningful change may depend on their perceptions of:

- What people are like.
- The goals and purposes of education in our society.
- The adequacy of the teacher's own personality.
- Effective methods of encouraging learning.

The administrators' roles require that they be able to answer these questions from the perspective of the teaching staff. If they cannot, then they cannot be effective in helping teachers grow and improve. Just as the teacher must take the students from where they are to the next level, so the administrator must take the classroom teachers from where they are to the next plateau. To be persuasive in changing teachers' behavior, it is important that administrators work toward the goal of improving student achievement. To that end, they need to acquire or possess skills in monitoring and evaluating student achievement.

Alternative Methods of Monitoring and Evaluating Student Achievement

School principals rely heavily on classroom observation data and other indirect indicators they gather to evaluate the effectiveness of teachers. The public, who cannot by law see teacher evaluations, tends to rely more heavily, if not exclusively, on standardized achievement information to acquire some notion of the effectiveness of an instructional program.

Whereas many principals are suspicious of standardized tests because of their inherent limitations and narrowness in assessing the full scope of a school's program, the public wants to be able to compare results statewide and nationally and finds such data credible and useful because it does just that. Test data are, therefore, probably under-used by professionals but overvalued by the public.

The effective school research movement has relied heavily on standardized achievement data to determine sound and operationally healthy educational programs.Despite some overextended use of research in this area(reviewed in chapter nine), functional schools appear to have characteristics not possessed in the same quality or quantity as those deemed not so functional.

Schools labeled effective tend to have carefully developed systems for short range and longitudinal evaluation. These evaluation systems permit early identification of students who fall below expected levels of achievement and the development of intervention strategies to remedy identified deficiencies.[14] Closely aligned with characteristics of effective schools is the behavior of a school administrator who makes it clear that student achievement is a concern of the entire system.

Student achievement can be assessed both formally and informally. Informal evaluation involves greater subjectivity. As such, it is less reliable and carries a greater risk of misinterpretation of the relationship and of the variables being assessed. In an informal evaluation a judgment is made explicit.[15] Research documents that effective schools "regularly employed achievement and diagnostic test results in monitoring student's progress" that greater weight is given to standardized test results than to criterion referenced tests, and that effective schools are more likely to require that low achieving students repeat a grade.

A myriad of alternative methods exist for evaluating student progress directly through assessing student achievement and indirectly through program evaluation. Some of these techniques include classroom observations, the use of rating scales, student questionnaires, content analysis, and self-evaluation.

As mentioned in chapter two, *Mirrors for Behavior*, is an anthology of observation instruments designed to assess attitudes, self-concepts, aptitude, opinion, and values in addition to achievement.[16] Published in 1967 it remains a premier resource for the practitioner. Of course, Buros' *Eighth Mental Measurements Yearbook* is a more available reference, found in any library.[17]

Observation instruments can be categorized as sign systems or category systems.[15] Sign systems typically describe events in an instructional setting. Category systems are generally more limited in the number of items addressed and provide a more continuous record of events within the broadly stated areas. The use of an overhead projector may be an item on a sign observation instrument. The area of "off-task" behavior may be a designation on a category observation instrument. Classroom observation instruments are the most typical means of collecting process-type data in the classroom. This is what teachers are actually "doing" in the act of "teaching." The current "time on task" emphasis largely resulted from classroom observation data.

Rating scales, student questionnaires, and self-evaluations are less commonly used methods of student and program evaluation. Content analysis is seldom attempted. A scholarly review of evaluation methods including naturalistic approaches is now available.[18]

There are at least five steps to developing a curriculum design that will deal with instructional programs. Alternatives can be developed by following these procedures:

1. Identify the audience that will receive the data:

2. Determine the critical outcomes.

3. Identify the data sources.

4. Determine the techniques for collecting the data.

5. Specify techniques for establishing standards.[19]

Robert Stake prepared a summary of nine major approaches to educational evaluation.[20] Alternatives to assessing student achievement will be either one of these nine approaches or a derivative. The nine approaches are shown in Figure 2.

Figure 2.
Alternative Methods of Assessing Student and Program Effectiveness.

Type	Description	Protagonists
Student Gain by Testing	To measure student performance and progress. Goal statements need to be specified; test score analysis of discrepancy between goal and actuality	Ralph Tyler Benjamin Bloom James Popham Mal Provus
Institutional Self-study by Staff	To review and increase staff effectiveness. Committee work; standards set by staff; discussion	National Study of School Evaluation Dressel
Blue Ribbon Panel	To resolve crises and preserve the institution. Prestigious panel; the visit; review of existing data and documents	James Conant Clark Kerr David Henry
Transaction Observation	To provide understanding of activities and values	Louis Smith Parlett-Hamilton Robert Rippey Robert Stake
Management Analysis	To increase rationality in day-to-day decisions. Lists of options; estimates; feedback loops; costs; efficiency	Leon Lassinger Daniel Stufflebeam Marvin Alkin Alan Thomas
Instructional Research	To generate explanations and tactics of instruction. Controlled conditions, multivariate analysis; bases for generalization	Lee Cronbach Julian Stanley Donald Campbell
Social Policy Analysis	To aid development of institutional policies. Measures of social conditions and administrative implementation	James Coleman David Cohen Carol Weiss Mosteller-Moynihan

Whatever alternative approach to evaluation is employed, school leaders must be able to supply answers to these questions:

- How is the effectiveness of the program monitored?
- What is the system for evaluating each content area?
- What are the various means for assessing program effectiveness?
- How are data collected?

- What decisions are made based on the data?

- Are both formal and informal means used?

- How are data shared with the community, parents, teachers, students?

- What means of evaluation are most effective to use the data at various grade levels?

- What means of evaluation are most effective for gifted, learning-disabled, or language-impaired students?

- What is the best use of parent conferences? Report cards? Newsletters?

Perhaps the area that provides more anxious moments for school leaders than any other is how to report such data to the public. School administrators are faced with the task of reporting data that will almost certainly be misinterpreted. Reporting and explaining test results represents a difficult problem.

The National School Public Relations Association in *Building Public Confidence for Your Schools* has some suggestions about reporting to the public. First, develop an adequate understanding of what the tests measure and do not measure with the teaching staff. Parents who have questions will lean on teachers to provide cues as to the meaning of a particular score. The teaching staff should be extremely well versed in handling parents' questions. Their training should be provided by school principals who are even more well versed.

The media have become more important in building public confidence in education. The following has been developed from the experience of the authors in reporting test data to the public with some success.

Use simple charts and graphs to explain results of test and show trends. Experience has shown that simple, straightforward, and uncomplicated reporting remains the best, even when the testing experts would be cautious about such things as using percentiles or grade equivalents scores as possibly distorted. What the public wants to know is whether the scores, are up or down, and what the district is going to do about areas that show need for improvement.

Have all the data available and avoid being defensive. Show all the results, whatever they may be. Avoid being put on the defensive. Take the occasion to present the information. After all, it is your data, not the media's. Explain what it means.

Share your action plan with the media on what you intend to do in the future. Present a list of things you are going to do about areas that show a trend in score decline or areas not up to par. Make specific responses such as:

- We will examine the textbooks in math at the sixth grade level to determine if they match the test in use of fractions and division of fractions.

- We intend to put more time on place geography to improve our test performance in the future.

● We are going to have to switch some of our science units in sequence to prepare our students more adequately for the science section of the test.

● We will place less emphasis on certain aspects of grammar and more emphasis on critical writing to correct an apparent imbalance in the program at grades 7-8.

● The test scores show our curriculum is out-of-date. Costs for the overhauling of the curriculum will be in next year's budget.

Don't treat the data casually as if it didn't matter. This may seem patronizing and breeds suspicion. If the data don't matter, the public will wonder why the tests were performed. Test data are important. Since they have limitations, define the importance of data within those limitations.

It is patently self-serving to blame state or federal governments for poor test scores. Educators are well advised to be candid and to credit the public with the ability to draw appropriate conclusions when data are properly prepared and presented.

Management of Change to Enhance the Mastery of Educational Goals

We have set the stage for a discussion of change in our consideration of instructional and motivational psychology. In this section we build on the concepts of motivation and situational differences presented previously. It should be emphasized that our set of skills in instructional management is neither exhaustive nor discrete.

To begin, we acknowledge that not all change is for the better. We also are aware that there is invariably some cost associated with change. That is why administrators pause before pursuing a change strategy and ask who will be affected by the change, who will have to work harder, and who may be hurt by the change.

Even with administrative support, there may be a great deal of resistance to change. For any system to function, a firm pattern of repetitive behavior must be established. Understanding and following these patterns is one of the reasons our public schools function as well as they do. Given the fluid nature of a school system, the constantly changing mix of student needs, content, and resources, there would be chaos without some repetitive behaviors. Consequently, classroom teachers resist changes in the status quo. Teacher isolation and insularity reinforce their inflexibility.[23] Conformity is valued, and educational practices and tradition lock people and organizations into the past. This apparent resistance to change is often taken as proof that education is a closed system. It would be more reasonable to explain that the education system is quite open to influence, and the power of that influence is directed at maintaining things just as they are.

Organizational change can be conceptualized as three processes: unfreezing the present, moving, and refreezing.[26, 27] The institutionalization of change incorporates these three processes.[28] There are five steps in institutionalization. They are:

1. Knowledge of the desired behavior.

2. The ability to perform the behavior.

3. Preference for the behavior.

4. Consensus that the new model is the best one to use.

5. The new model becomes valued and is held in high regard. [28]

The pioneering works of Chris Argyris, Rensis Likert, and Douglas McGregor all address the need for participative decision making in the change process. [29,30,31] Lawler has gone beyond the need for participative organizations by outlining a model to produce a high quality of work life (Quality of Work Life or QWL). [32]

The three main components of operating effectiveness in Lawler's model are motivation for organizational effectiveness; individual performance capability; and communication, coordination and control.

Elements included in the QWL model are:

- Flat, lean, team-based organizational structure

- Open, decentralized, team-based information system.

- Participatively set goals and standards.

- Heavy commitment to peer training.

- An open reward system.

- Skill based with egalitarian prerequisites.

- Stability of employment and participatively established personal policies.

Effective administrators must be able to improve the quality of work life within the schools. Changes perceived by the faculty as taking away from the quality of work-life will not succeed. It is up to administrators to show faculty members that suggested changes will make their work easier, not more difficult.

A change-minded administrator must know the characteristics of the change process, who to involve, what decision-making processes to use, whether to involve outsiders, and must also have a sense for how much change the school can tolerate successfully. George Odiorne suggests that administrators solve the problems of change by anticipating and avoiding them. He advocates a strategic approach that requires changes in the way administrators typically view their roles. The steps in Odiorne's model for management by anticipation are:

1. Keep your range of vision higher than you do now.

2. Get a bigger picture of the world than you now hold.

3. Do not stare at the world, scan it.

4. Make yourself visible to others and make your opinions known.

5. Always have alternative plans.

6. Practice your skill in managing your timing, for timing and positioning are the keys to survival.[21]

Whether administrators seek change or not, it will be thrust upon them by events beyond their control. An ideal example of this is found in the next skill of instructional management — dealing with the computer revolution.

Application of Computer Management to the Instructional Program

Computers will become invaluable tools in the management of an instructional program. The exact form and use of the particular computer to achieve this end is difficult to identify as the technical sophistication of the equipment seems to expand daily. What can be stated with assurance, though, is that every administrator employed in the public schools will be using some form of this equipment daily. The problem is not going to be the capability of the equipment. The problem will be finding the time necessary to learn how to use the programs already available and to design new programs to meet the special needs of administrators.

Computers can be used for skill reinforcement, computer assisted instruction, computer managed instruction, and the development of computer literacy. Figure 3 outlines the meaning of these uses and describes the steps necessary to implement them in schools.[4]

Figure 3.
Preparation For Computer Use in Education.

Use of Computer	Steps to Get There
Skill Reinforcement - After a student has learned a particular skill, the computer is used to provide practices. For example, the computer may generate a number of division problems for the student to solve after the student has learned how to divide.	Selected staff should be trained to select quality software. Equipment compatible with the software should be purchased. Software should be purchased and staff trained in the most effective way to use this guided practice material.

Computer Assisted Instruction (CAI) - When computer software actually teaches the skill, provides skill reinforcement tests for mastery, and then moves on to another skill. This is one of the most popular uses of the computer. Finding well-developed software has been a problem with CAI although the quality of the software is improving continuously.

Train staff in the selection process

Identify the objectives to be achieved with CAI. Focus on skills that most often need reteaching, for instance the concept of borrowing when subtracting.

Use software review services to assist in the selected process.

Train staff in the use of the software.

Design evaluation process to measure effectiveness of software.

Computer Managed Instruction - (CMI) - This is an extension of skill reinforcement and CAI. CMI not only teaches the skill and provides skill reinforcement, it records where the student is and automatically starts the student at that point when the students begins again. This use of the computer is often found in Special Education and Compensatory Education.

Train staff in the use of this type of teaching tool.

Select programs that match the curriculum

Train aides in the use of the equipment.

Select computers that are compatible with the software and printers to supply the teacher and the student with a record of what was accomplished.

Computer Literacy - This term may have a variety of definitions. One theme that can be found refers to the notion of being "comfortable" with the computer, or having a general understanding of it. Another theme is the ability to program in a particular computer language. It may be useful to conceive of "Computer Literacy" as a continuum of knowledge beginning with elementary concepts and continuing through advanced programming techinques. Given this conceptualization, computer literacy can be considered as a sequence of skills and concepts that form the backbone of a curriculum.

Appoint a coordinator of the computer education program.

Develop a mission statement for the district program.

Identify program objectives for three to five years based on the mission statement.

Train staff in the use of the equipment and the programs that will be used with students. These could include Basic, Logo, and word processing.

Budget necessary funds to support the project.

Budget necessary funds to support the project.

Provide teachers with modeled lessons and then supportive coaching.

In addition to these applications, computers are also being used as tools for intellectual and creative expression in the fine and practical arts. Many school libraries now use computers to access resource materials. Videodisc use can also extend an experience and reinforce the concepts presented.

Before school administrators jump into the computer age with both feet, five deliberate steps are recommended:

1. Do preliminary research.

2. Form a steering committee.

3. Attend conferences about the subject.

4. Define the objectives to be attained.

5. Launch the program.

These procedures will be augmented using the change tactics advocated in the preceding discussion. All personnel need to be carefully brought to a condition of computer literacy.

Use of Instructional Time and Resources

Educators often mean different things when talking about instructional time. William Spady has clarified the different types of time in schools in AASA's pamphlet *Time on Task*.[49a] These are shown in Figure 4 below:

Figure 4.
Types of Instructional Time in Schools.

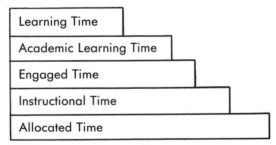

Allocated time refers to the total time scheduled for schooling to occur, most often the school day. *Instructional time* refers to classroom teaching time and excludes such things as passing periods, lunch time, recess, assemblies, and so on. *Engaged time*, the time a student is actually involved in learning, may vary from class to class by the day, week, semester, or year. *Academic learning time* (ALT) is the actual success a student encounters within engaged time.

The amount of total time available, no matter how defined, is finite. While educators have found many ways to expand the curricular offerings within the school day, they have not found ways to add to the total amount of instructional time available to achieve the ever-increasing demands placed on the schools by legislators and school boards.

The average school day for most students begins at about 8:30 a.m. and ends about 3 p.m., with 45 minutes devoted to lunch. Determining the actual allocated time is simply a matter of knowing the length of the school year, subtracting vacations and multiplying the number of hours per day. Normally, this would be

180 days x 6 hours per day = 1080 hours
OR for 13 years (K-12) = 14,040 hours
OR for 13 years = 2,340 days (six hours per day)
OR for actual 24 hour days = 585 days

From these data it can be seen that it is a myth that a student is educated for 13 years. Assuming 24-hour days, a student is only educated for 1.6 years or for six-hour days, 6.4 years! Considering that this is only raw allocated time and not even real instructional time, schools have less than 10 percent of a student's actual time within the 13 years they are "in school."

The most limited resource in the schooling process is time. Decisions about how instructional time is spent are made most often by teachers.[5]   Differences in allotted time for instruction to meet specific objectives can be dramatic, especially at the elementary level. All aspects of time use become critical to the school effectiveness issue. To make the best use of this most precious resource, school administrators must become guardians of how instructional time is spent. Some questions that administrators will wish to answer include these:

• How much control do I have over how instructional time will be spent?

• What is the amount of instructional time, engaged time, available for each content area of the curriculum?

• Has any assessment been made regarding the amount of engaged time devoted to each content area?

• What is my degree of competence in assessing engaged time? What instruments can I use? Are they reliable? How are the data interpreted?

• How much time is used for pull-out programs?

• Am I able to modify the amount of instructional time available for various content areas based on program evaluation, or am I limited by the district schedule?

• Is the amount of instructional time modified based on the needs of the students?

The amount of allotted instructional time available to a school in a given calendar year does not seem to differ significantly from school to school.[38] According to research, there does seem to be a relationship between student academic achievement and the amount of time students are actively engaged in the learning process.[39,40,41,42] However, there appears to be conflicting evidence about the impact of increased engaged time. Simply increasing engaged time may not be enough to improve achievement. Other factors of far more significance may be the nature of the instruction going on. That is, the time must be spent on doing the right things in the right way.

Instructional materials are seen too often as an end and not a means or vehicle used to achieve an end. Textbooks and teacher's manuals become the curriculum. For many teachers, getting to the end of the book is the objective for the year. Some have been heard to comment, "This is a good group, we finished the book in May." Used appropriately, text and supplementary materials serve as a vehicle to help teachers achieve specified goals. The text is a tool, not a product.

The administrator needs to be certain that sufficient learning materials are available, designed for a variety of instructional modalities and geared for instruction at a variety of learning levels. There is little research that relates materials to achievement. There seems to be a greater relationship between achievement and how the materials are used.[46] In addition, there is little evidence to show that the size of a library collection or the number of textbooks secured relate significantly to the achievement of students.[47] We also lack evidence that expenditures for materials and supplementary aids affect student achievement.

Despite these gaps in the research about relationships between materials and achievement, we maintain that appropriate resources are of great importance, especially in the implementation of a new program. None of us would endeavor to implement a computer literacy program without computers, monitors, discs, and the necessary software.

Administrators must orchestrate the materials selection process to ensure that the resources acquired fit the objectives of the program. Quite often, materials are purchased and then a program is designed. This has been especially true with the acquisition of microcomputer hardware. Before resources are purchased, the revised or newly designed program should be written. Selection of materials should not depend on the sales ability of the publisher's representative; rather, the selection should be made of the best available materials to meet the needs of the students and the demands of the curriculum.

Cost Effectiveness and Program Budgeting

Cost effectiveness and program budgeting should refer to more than the budgeting of financial support for an instructional program. The resources of the system, namely time, materials, and people all need to be considered in effective program budgeting. This means that administrators must be able to identify the organizational units in the school and also list the goals and objectives of each of these units in terms of people, material, and time. Few school districts can do this. Effective school research, however, suggests that where people, materials, and time have been used to achieve specific, behaviorally stated objectives, success has been achieved.

The concept of quality control is useful for the administrator wanting to ensure program effectiveness. Quality control refers to the internal capability of a system to manage itself.[49] When applied to instructional management, it refers to the relationship among the stated goals and objectives of a content area, K-12, the instruction in the classroom, and the evaluation of student achievement. Stated another way, it is the relationships among the written, taught, and tested curriculum.[50]

To determine whether a program is cost effective, administrators must know first what the program is. This requires not only a general goal statement for each content area, K-12, but also demands that specific objectives be established for each grade level within the program. Goals stated must be achievable in the amount of instructional time available, and appropriate materials and resources must be secured to support instruction.

The administrator must then determine whether there is any means currently used to assess the degree to which the stated goals have been achieved. Finally, the administrator should be able to determine whether or not the objectives as stated and assessed are being taught. Only after both design and delivery problems relative to quality control have been corrected can a true assessment of program effectiveness be made.[50] This assessment is rarely made in most systems today.

True program budgeting demands major changes in organizational behavior and in the decision-making structure of a school.[48] To implement program budgeting, these are the recommended steps:

- A goal statement is prepared for each program, expressing the purpose it serves in the school.

- Administrators and department chairmen determine what available data best describes service levels and program achievement.

- Budget guidelines are prepared that state areas to be stressed.

- Past cost information is assembled to guide budget estimates.

- Program budget instructions and worksheets are developed.

- Workshops are held to explain how the budget is to be prepared.

- Each program leader defines the resources required to meet stated goals within the budget guidelines.

- Departments prepare financial and other data that support budget documentation.

- Budgets are submitted for approval.

- Cost effectiveness is determined based on the degree to which the stated goals and objectives are attained.[48]

While program budgeting in the strictest sense of the word may be difficult to attain in the school setting, administrators should strive to relate the effective use of the school's resources to program success. The administrator might begin by asking these questions:

- How are decisions made about the acquisition of materials?

- Are these decisions made based on program effectiveness data?

- How are they related to budget building?
- How is cost effectiveness determined?
- What are the various ways to build a budget?
- What are the benefits of each way? The problems?
- How should staff be involved in the budget-building process?

Conclusion

This concludes our presentation of the skills of instructional management. We have identified seven skills and shown their relationships in a model (Figure 1). Each skill was then considered and, when available, insights from research were brought to bear. It was noted that administrators cannot directly accomplish the successful application of the skills to the mission of their institutions. The interaction between teachers and students, between students and the curriculum is the essence of schooling. Administrators must work through others to provide the resources and facilitate success by others closer to classrooms, where learning occurs or does not occur. Legislators and board members define the mission. Administrators and specialists arrange personnel, facilities, materials, and other resources, but teachers and students are the raison d'etre of all this.

Skill Accomplishment Checklist for Chapter Five

Competency and Skills	Reading and Activities for Mastery
Competency: Planning and implementing an instructional management system that includes learning objectives, curriculum design, and instructional strategies and techniques that encourage high levels of achievement.	Readings: See resources 1, 2, 3, 4 Activities: 1. Review the learning objectives identified in each curriculum guide to be sure the objectives are behaviorally stated, sequential, and achievable in the alloted amount of instructional time. 2. Compare the curriculum implementation procedures used in a variety of school districts. Trace the process from the planning stage to full implementation. 3. Develop a matrix of instructional strategies for each major content area. Develop an inservice training model for staff to expand their competence with two new models.

Skill A: Curriculum design and instructional delivery strategies.	Readings: See resources 6, 7, 8
	Activities:
	    1. Develop an observation instrument with the cooperation of staff representation designed to evaluate the effectiveness of teaching strategies in the following areas: information processing, social interaction, stimulus-response, and personal development.
	    2. Design a format for the written curriculum that helps promote the concept of quality control.
	    3. Develop a reading list for each content area that includes state of the art information regarding curriculum design and instructional strategies.

Skill B: Instructional and motivational psychology.	Readings: See resources 9, 10, 11, 12, 13, 14
	Activities:
	    1. Develop an annotated bibliography of learning theory from the early 1900s to present.
	    2. Complete a list of motivational techniques for elementary, middle school, and high school students.
	    3. Prepare a videotape dramatizing various motivational techniques.

Skill C: Alternative methods of monitoring and evaluating student achievement.	Readings: See resources 14, 15, 16, 19, 20
	Activities:
	    1. Develop an evaluation system for use with learning disabled students.
	    2. Develop a program evaluation designed for a gifted program that includes feedback from students, parents, regular teachers, administrators, and board members.
	    3. Design a report card for the middle school that addresses the affective development of students.
	    4. Design a K-12 district testing program, using both norm referenced and criterion referenced tests.

Skill D: Management of change to enhance the mastery of educational goals.	Readings: See resources 21, 22, 23, 24, 25, 26, 27, 28, 29, 30, 31, 32 Activities: 1. Identify a change you would like to accomplish. Develop a plan to produce the change detailing pre-implementation activities, training needs, consultation and reinforcement plans, monitoring and evaluation activities, and plans for internal and external communication regarding the change.

	2. Develop an inservice program for a school district wanting to implement a computer literacy program K-12. Specify the inservice courses to be given, who would teach them, follow-up, equipment needs, and course design.
Skill E: Application of computer management to the instructional program.	Readings: See resources 34, 35, 36, 37 Activities: 1. Develop a computer program to record and update instructional objectives in each content area. 2. Develop a program to record the instructional materials used in each inventory course (primary) and keep a running inventory. 3. Develop a computer software review form to evaluate computer management programs. 4. Identify types of reports needed from a computer personnel package, an attendance package, and a budget package.
Skill F: Use of instructional time and resources.	Readings: See resources 38, 39, 40, 41, 42, 43, 44, 45, 46, 47 1. Develop an instrument to collect total amount of instructional time allocated for each content area of the curriculum at the elementary level. Outline how the data will be analyzed and the type of reports that will be developed from the data. 2. Become proficient in the use of two instruments to collect data of engaged learning time. Use one of the instruments to assess the amount of engaged time in three classrooms in two different content areas. Develop a report using the data and share the report with the teachers observed. Make recommendations for improvement in the amount of engaged time available for instruction in each class.
Skill G: Cost-effective and program budgeting.	Readings: See resources 48, 49, 50 Activities: 1. Review the budget summaries from six school districts. Compare format, categories, and costs. 2. Interview the business managers from three districts. Write a report summarizing the budget development process in each. 3. Assume you were the business manager for a school district and wanted to institute a program budgeting process. Design a plan to implement the process. Develop the forms, design the inservice necessary to initiate the process, and design the budget summary brochure.

Resources

1. T. Mulliken, "Approaching the Research on Effective Schools and Effective Classrooms," Pennsylvania Department of Education, 1982.

2. *Effective Schools: A Summary of Research* (Arlington, Va.: Educational Research Service, Inc., 1983).

3. R. Edmonds, *A Discussion of the Literature and Issues Related to Effective Schooling*, Volume 6 (St. Louis: Cemrel, Inc., 1979).

4. F. English and B. Steffy, "Curriculum as a Strategic Management Tool," *Educational Leadership* 39, 4 (January 1982), pp. 276-284.

5. T. Sergiovanni and D. Elliot, *Educational and Organizational Leadership in Elementary Schools* (Englewood Cliffs, N.J.: Prentice-Hall, Inc. 1975), Chapter 7.

6. B. Joyce, R. Wald, and Marsha Weil, "Can Teachers Learn Repertoires of Models of Teaching," *Flexibility in Teaching: An Excursion into the Nature of Teaching and Training* (New York: Longman, Inc, 1981), pp. 141-156.

7. W. Doyle and G. Ponder, "The Practicality Ethic in Teacher Decision-Making," *Interchange* 8 (1977), pp 1-12.

8. B. Bloom, *Human Characteristics and School Learning* (New York: McGraw-Hill, 1976).

9. D. McGregor, *The Human Side of Enterprise* (New York: McGraw-Hill Book Company, 1960), pp. 33-57.

10. R. Owens, *Organizational Behavior in Schools* (Englewood Cliffs, N .J.: Prentice-Hall, Inc., 1970), p. 25.

11. A. Maslow, *Motivation and Personality* (New York: Harper & Row, 1954).

12. F. Herzberg, *Work and the Nature of Man* (Cleveland: The World Publishing Company, 1966).

13. A. Combs and D. Snygg, *Individual Behavior: A Perceptual Approach to Behavior* (New York: Harper & Row, 1959).

14. *Effective Schools: A Summary of Research* (Educational Research Service, Inc., 1983), p. 41.

15. T. Levin and R. Long, *Effective Instruction* (Alexandria, Va.: Association for Supervision and Curriculum Development, 1981), pp. 38-53.

16. A. Simon and E. G. Boyer, *Mirrors for Behavior: An Anthology of Classroom Observation Instruments* (Philadelphia: Research for Better Schools, 1967).

17. O. K. Buros (ed.), *The Eighth Mental Measurements Yearbook* (Highland Park, N.J.: Gryphon Press, 1980).

18. E. Guba and Y. Lincoln, *Effective Evaluation* (San Francisco: Jossey Bass Publishers, 1981).

19. F. Rogers, "Curriculum Research and Evaluation," *Fundamental Curriculum Decisions* (Alexandria, Va.: Association for Supervision and Curriculum Development, 1983), pp. 142-153.

20. R. Stake, *CIRCE*, September 1974.

21. G. Odiorne, *The Change Resisters: How They Prevent Progress and What*

Managers Can Do About Them (Englewood Cliffs, N.J.: Prentice-Hall, Inc., 1981), p. ix.

22. H. Brickell, "State Organization for Educational Change: A Case Study and a Proposal," *Innovation in Education*, M. Miles (ed.) (New York: Bureau of Publications Teachers College, Columbia University, 1964), p. 504.

23. H. Kaufman, *The Limits of Organizational Change* (University, Ala.: The University of Alabama Press, 1971).

24. S. Robbins, *Managing Organizational Conflict* (Englewood Cliffs, N. J.: Prentice-Hall, Inc., 1974) p. 15.

25. L. Rico, "Organizational Conflict: A Framework for Reappraisal," *Industrial Management Review* (Fall 1964), p. 67.

26. P. Goodman and Associates, *Change in Organizations* (Washington: Jossey-Bass Publishers, 1982).

27. K. Lewin, *Field Theory in Social Science* (New York: Harper, 1951).

28. P. Goodman and J. Dean Jr. "Creating Long-Term Organizational Change," *Change in Organizations* (Washington: Jossey-Bass Publishers, 1982), pp. 226-279.

29. C. Argyris, *Personality and Organization* (New York: Harper & Row, 1957).

30. R. Likert, *New Patterns of Management* (New York: McGraw-Hill, 1961).

31. D. McGregor, *The Human Side of Enterprise* (New York: McGraw-Hill, 1961).

32. E. Lawler III, "Increasing Worker Involvement to Enhance Organizational Effectiveness," *Change in Organizations* (Washington, D.C.: Jossey-Bass Publishers, 1982), pp. 280-325.

33. W. Brosnan, *Microcomputer Based Learning: A Proposal* (unpublished report, 1982).

34. S. Papert, *Mindstorms* (New York: Basic Books, Inc., Publishers, 1980).

35. J. Licklider, "Social and Economic Impacts of Information Technology of Education" (Information Technology in Education, Joint Hearings before the Subcommittee of Science, Research, and Technology, 96th Congress, No. 134, April 2, 3, 1980) Washington, D.C.: U.S. Government Printing Office, 1980.

36. R. Hughes, "Before You Leap into the Computer Age with Both Feet, Take These Five Deliberate Steps," *The American School Board Journal* (March 1983), pp. 28-29.

37. A. Bork, "Interactive Learning" in R. Taylor, (ed.), *The Computer in the School: Tutor, Tool, Tutee* (New York: Teachers College Press, 1980), p. 59.

38. W. Grant and L. Eiden, *Digest of Education Statistics 1982* (Washington, D.C.: National Center for Education Statistics, 1982).

39. J. Stallings and D. Kaskowitz, *Follow-Through Classroom Observation Evaluation*, 1972-73 (Menlo Park, Calif.: Stanford Research Institute, 1974).

40. S. Samuels and J. Turnure, "Attention and Reading Achievement in First-Grade Boys and Girls," *Journal of Educational Psychology* (1974), pp. 29-32.

41. T. Good and T. Beckerman, "Time on Task: A Naturalistic Study in Sixth-Grade Classrooms," *The Elementary School Journal* (1978), pp. 193-201.

42. C. Evertson, *Differences in Instructional Activities in High and Low Achiev-*

ing Junior High Classes, R&D Rep. No. 6106. (Austin, Texas: Research and Development Center for Teacher Education, University of Texas at Austin, March 1980), p. 47.

43. D. Berliner, "The Half-Full Glass: A Review of Research on Teaching," *Using What We Know About Teaching 1984 Yearbook* (Alexandria, Va.: Association for Supervision and Curriculum Development, 1984), pp. 51-70.

44. F. English and B. Steffy, "Curriculum Mapping: An Aid to School Curriculum Management," *Spectrum Journal of School Research and Information* (Arlington, Va.: Educational Research Service, Inc., Vol. 1., No. 3 Fall 1983), pp. 17-26.

45. T. Levin and R. Long, *Effective Instruction* (Alexandria, Va.: Association for Supervision and Curriculum Development, 1981), pp. 1-13.

46. C. Denham and A. Lieberman, editors, *Time to Learn* (Washington, D.C., U. S. Department of Education, National Institute of Education, 1980).

47. *School Facts Influencing Reading Achievement: A Case Study of Two Inner City Schools*, (Albany, N.Y.: State of New York Office of Education Performance Review, March 1974).

48. B. Mundt, R. Olsen, and H. Steinberg, *Managing Public Resources* (United States: Peat Marwick International, 1982), p. 39.

49. L. Lessinger, "Quality Control and Quality Assurance in Education," *Journal of Education Finance* 1 (Spring 1976) pp. 505-515.

50. F. English and B. Steffy, "Differentiating Between Design and Delivery Problems in Achieving Quality Control in School Curriculum Management," *Educational Technology* 23 (February 1983), pp. 29-33.

51. D. Duke, *School Leadership and Instructional Improvement,* (New York,: Random House, 1987)

52. R.A. Gorton, *School Leadership and Administration* (Dubuque, Iowa, Wm.C. Brown Publishers, 1987), chap. 1-7.

53. L.L. Lyman, A.P. Wilson, C.K. Gerhart, M.O. Heim, and W.O. Winn, *Clinical Instruction and Supervision for Accountability,* (Dubuque, Iowa, Kendall, Hunt Publishers, 1986).

54. K.J. Snyder and R.H. Anderson, *Managing Productive Schools*, (Orlando, Fla.: Academic Press, Harcourt Brace Jovanovich Publishers, 1986).

CHAPTER SIX
SKILLS IN STAFF EVALUATION

Staff evaluation, more art than science, may draw critical reviews from some researchers, but leading educators view staff evaluation as a process to improve the performance of individuals and the entire educational system.[1] Knowing this and with public pressure to improve administrator and teacher evaluation processes, school leaders should have skills in designing and implementing staff evaluation programs that include:

- Evaluating administrator and supervisor performance.
- Evaluating teacher performance.
- Evaluating other staff members.

Few educational personnel question the need for appraising individual performance. The majority of personnel are committed to an equitable and educationally sound evaluation process, but they also feel they have a right to ask these questions:

- What are the standards of the evaluation?
- Who will do the evaluating?
- What type/s of instrument will be used?
- How will the evaluation results be used?
- How many times will I be evaluated?
- What are the appeal procedures if I disagree with the evaluation results?

Administrators and teachers are vitally interested in the improvement of the quality of education and in the improvement of student outcomes. The hard problem is to develop and improve appraisal procedures and to create greater understanding of the purposes and limitations. What is good evaluation? What is effective evaluation? These questions greatly influence the ways in which teachers, administrators, and taxpayers view the schools and their effectiveness.

For effective evaluations, the process should be conducted by competent professionals who employ thorough and open methods. This type of evaluation promotes ongoing communication and mutual support. Candor and openness create a climate of trust. The Educational Policy Service of the National School Boards Association feels that school board policy governing staff evaluation can establish a climate of trust if it includes the 11 cardinal principles of evaluation. We have adapted the 11 principles to apply to administrator and teacher performance evaluations:

1. The criteria used in evaluation are based on the stated [district] goals and objectives and relate to staff members' job descriptions.

2. Evaluation procedures, forms, job descriptions, guides, and criteria are developed cooperatively by the (board), administration, and instructional staff.

3. Evaluative criteria are explicit, encourage objective judgments, and relate as much as possible to behaviors that bear directly on the performance of administrators, teachers, and students.

4. The evaluative process is carried out on a regular, continuing basis and includes opportunities for both formal and informal evaluations.

5. The process employs a variety of techniques for assessing performance.

6. The process encourages continuing self-evaluation and self-improvement in job performance.

7. Each observation and evaluation includes follow-up consultations between the staff member and his or her evaluator, and the staff member then receives a signed copy of any written evaluation of his or her job performance.

8. Staff members are aware of their right to appeal unfavorable evaluations through channels to the superintendent and, ultimately, to the school board.

9. Evaluators (school board members and administrators) are trained in the techniques and skills of evaluation.

10. The evaluation program includes reliable measures for evaluating the performance of the evaluators.

11. The information gained will be applied in the planning of professional staff development and inservice training activities.[2]

The staff evaluation process that applies these 11 cardinal principles of evaluation will have a stronger chance of success and acceptance by educational personnel.

Evaluating Administrators and Supervisors

Why evaluate administrators and supervisors? The major purpose is to improve district management and leadership. Iowa State University researchers believe that the evaluation should be based on an analysis of progress made toward accomplishment of predetermined objectives through the use of "good practice." They ask the following questions:

- What do we expect each administrator to accomplish?

- How do we expect each administrator to perform?

- What changes in behavior do we want?
- How does his/her performance interrelate with that of others?[3]

The problems faced in answering these questions seem unsolvable when we consider the volumes of research on leadership styles and organizational performance. Most research suggests unclear relationships among management training, work, and organizational effectiveness.[4, 5, 6, 7] We may know what school administrators do each day, hour, and minute, but we have little hard evidence about what impact these activities have on school organization and specifically on student outcomes or achievement.

But most social systems theories present the compelling notion that productive organizations are lead by individuals who place high emphasis on both production and concern for people in the organization.[8] Consequently, conventional wisdom about administrator evaluation taught in university graduate courses and in inservice academies or workshops stresses the production and human dimensions. This is not to imply that the complexities of administrator evaluation can be limited to two dimensions. Schools are complex, loosely coupled institutions interrelated with a larger society. A California research project verifies a "loose coupling" theory and that the three levels of local educational organizations—district, school, and classroom—operate independently. Educational administrators may be charged to become instructional leaders, but the organizational structure defies rather than encourages their efforts.[9]

Until researchers can provide specifics, we must continue efforts to identify the best practices of administrative performance and to use those practices as a basis for assessing and improving performance. Max Abbott of the University of Oregon, a noted authority on administrator evaluation, reminds us of the difference between the role of an administrator and the roles of other personnel in the school. Teachers, counselors, nurses, and therapists work directly with students and, thus, are intended to affect them directly.[10] Administrative performance relates only indirectly to student behavior and performance. Administrators must create the proper school climate in which teaching and learning occur. Thus, says Abbott, "It is the effects of the administrators' performance upon teachers and other functionaries as a group—upon the organization—that provide the basis for determining effectiveness."[8]

Leadership by Objectives and Results (LBO/R) Model. The model in Figure 1 incorporates the best thinking about administrator and supervisor behavior and describes distinctive administrative roles found in most school districts.

Figure 1.
Leadership by Objectives and Results (LBO/R) Cycle.

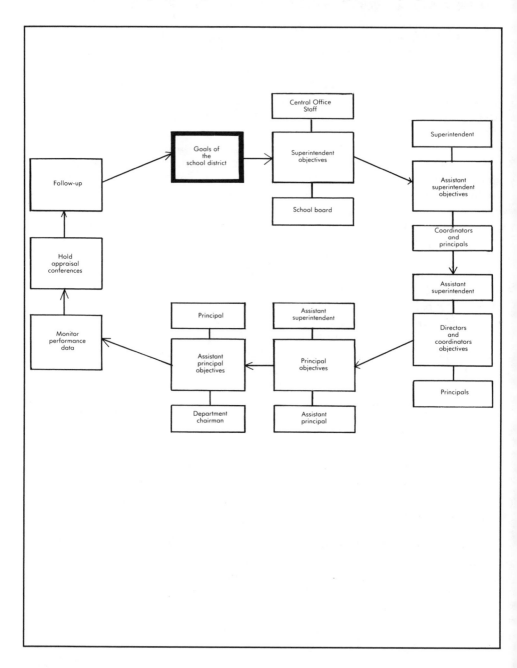

The LBO/R Model, an adaption of the management-by-objectives (MBO) model from business, is also similar to models established by George Redfern, Richard Manatt, and Dale Bolton.[11, 12, 13] Based on "best practice" drawn from the literature, we can make these six assumptions about LBO/R:

1. Staff members are goal oriented and wish to improve their administrative performances.

2. Teachers teach more, learners learn more if administrators promote a program that is goal and performance oriented.

3. Administrators in the district, within limits, desire to understand what is expected of them.

4. General responsibilities should be stated in written form, and administrators should know to whom to look for direction and supervision.

5. General performance objectives related to standards of excellence should be designed to achieve the objectives and the results should be monitored and evaluated systematically.

6. The school board, superintendent, central office and building administrators must be sold on the program, or else it will fail.

We recommend that school leaders planning to overhaul an old staff evaluation system or to initiate a new one should strongly consider suggesting self evaluations by the board first, then initiate an administrator evaluation plan. The administrator evaluation plan should include a well designed self evaluation as well as evaluations by supervisors and subordinates. If school board members, superintendents and other members of the administrative team are evaluated, then teachers and other staff members will be more open to being evaluated themselves. The LBO/R model can be expanded for use in teacher, counselor, and other staff performance evaluation programs.

Steps to implementing the LBO/R administrator evaluation cycle are as follows:

Step 1: The superintendent and a planning committee composed of administrators at all levels, including department heads, plan a "retreat" to establish or renew the LBO/R cycle.

Step 2: All administrators including directors, coordinators, and board members should attend the opening session and should be encouraged to stay the entire time.

Step 3: Each administrator should review the mission statement and goals for the district one week before the retreat.

Step 4: Administrators and board members, if they wish to establish an evaluation program, should bring to the retreat four or five objectives, not necessarily in behavioral form, that relate directly to the district goals. Three or four more objectives should be prepared that relate to the specific job description or role leading to personal and professional improvement.

Step 5: The superintendent or a consultant delivers an opening address about school improvement and the goals of the district, each school, and the use of LBO/R cycle to accomplish the goals.

Step 6: Each staff member presents his or her objectives to supervisors and to those who report to him or her. Individuals most closely affected by the objectives will discuss the value of the objectives and the likelihood of their accomplishment. Once the objectives are approved by the group, the evaluatee will suggest processes and activities to be used to accomplish the objectives. The group should agree on the process of monitoring the evaluation data and the dates for evaluation observations and/or conferences.

Step 7: Staff members who report directly to the superintendent will present in writing their objectives, data monitoring processes, and conference dates with the superintendent for approval. The number of people reporting directly to the superintendent will vary with size of the district.

Step 8: The retreat should end with remarks by the superintendent and board president reassuring all that evaluations will be done "with" and not "to" the administrators. Also, the "rules of the game" should be clearly understood by each board member and administrator. Copies of the objectives should be prepared in triplicate — one copy for the central personnel file, one for the evaluator, and one for the evaluatee.

Evaluating Principals

Since the success or failure of schools seems often to be credited to principals, care must be taken in developing a principal evaluation program that it is timely and assistance for improvement available. Also, it is important to design a step-by-step process indicating what is to be done, when it is to be done, how it is to be done, where it is to be done, and who is to do it.

Among the basic indicators of the principal evaluation program are:

- Instructional management.
- Community, staff, and student relationships.
- Building and staff management systems.
- Student and teacher performance.
- Staff evaluation and assistance.

An assessment team composed of at least two, no more than three, evaluators will meet with each principal and assess progress on each of the five indicators. Information about the principal's performance in the five areas should be gathered from the principal's self evaluation, from teachers, and from data gathered by the assessment team. Each evaluator will assign a "1" to "5" rating on each of the indicators within the five components, with "1" representing poor performance and a "5" indicating outstanding performance. Ratings of "1" or "2" by an assessor must be accompanied by a supporting statement describing the weakness.

Growth Plan

All principals regardless of level of performance should be guided by a growth improvement plan. This is especially important for a principal who receives a "1" or "2" on any of the five indicators. Based on the growth plan, pre- and post-assessment conferences should be planned by an assistant superintendent or member of the central office evaluation team. These conferences should be supportive and should assist the principal in making improvements. [24]

The LBO/R model or cycle can simplify the administrator evaluation process. Management-by-objectives systems can become too long and consume too much time if they are used to evaluate items generally included in detailed job descriptions. In other words, routine duties should not be included in the items unless there is a problem with a specific item. All administrators are expected to handle routine duties. True school leaders reach beyond expected performance and set higher goals. The LBO/R Model combines research with common sense to streamline the administrator evaluation process for a district.

Almost all levels of school administration require a common set of skills; therefore, evaluation should be based on the eight skill areas mentioned earlier. The degree of importance of each area varies with the administrative position. Many textbooks, articles, and monographs include comprehensive checklists, responsibilities, tasks, and functions for administrative roles. [10, 14]

While these indicators for principal evaluations contribute to specificity and to the design of job descriptions, most items can be placed into one of the eight skill areas in the AASA *Guidelines*. We recommend that administrator evaluation programs build evaluation forms around the eight skill areas because they include the administrative knowledge upon which "best practice" should be based. Regardless of the model, system, or forms employed and the number of skills, tasks, or functions included, an administrator evaluation program, should be well planned involving those being evaluated, and based on the belief that people who are goal oriented will take risks without fear from "on high" and will want to improve.

Evaluating Teacher Performance

School leaders, especially principals, are under great pressure to ensure high levels of teacher competence. A new publication, titled *Assessment of Teaching: Purposes, Practices, and Implications for the Profession*, is the most comprehensive work to help administrators assess teacher competence. One chapter especially helpful to the school leader addresses "Teaching Assessment: The Administrator's Perspective." The author presents the problems and workable solutions in assessing teacher performance. [23]

In his article "How to Evaluate the Teacher — Let me Count the Ways" Donald Haefele, a researcher from The Ohio State University, summarizes 12 approaches to teacher evaluation. [15] He also points out the strengths and weaknesses of each approach. The approaches to teacher evaluation include:

- Use of standardized test scores of students.
- Informal observations.

- Systematic observations by administrators and peers.
- Use of the Teacher Perceiver Interview (TPI).
- Job-target mutual goal setting approach.

Haefele concludes that a goal-setting approach that includes growth plans is preferable, though demanding, to instructional improvement since it is based on mutual trust.

Why have many teacher evaluation plans been faulty? In a study by the Rand Corporation, a researcher concludes that "teacher performance evaluation is underconceptualized and underdeveloped at present and that few school organizations have a true system."[16] Some of the major problems, which have plagued teacher evaluation for years, are:

1. Principals' attitudes, competence, and ability to assume the role due to their conflicting roles as colleagues and evaluators.

2. Perceptions of teacher evaluation as another added chore.

3. Teacher apathy and resistance.

4. Lack of uniformity and consistency among school buildings (too much room for taste or predisposition of principal to enter into rankings).

Two of the best reviews of the literature and current practice are titled "Teacher Evaluation in the Organizational Context: A Review of the Literature" by Hammond, Wise, and Pease[17] and *Evaluating Educational Personnel* by Ann C. Lewis.[18] "Teacher Evaluation...," which includes more than 166 references, states that:

> Teacher evaluation is an activity that must satisfy competing individual and organizational needs. The imperative of uniform treatment for personnel decisions may result in standardized definitions of acceptable teaching behavior. However, research on teacher performance and teaching effectiveness does not lead to a stable list of measurable teaching behaviors effective in all teaching contexts. Moreover, research in individual and organizational behavior indicates the need for context specific strategies for improving teaching rather than systemwide hierarchical efforts. If teacher evaluation is to be a useful tool for teacher improvement, the process must strike a careful balance between standardized, centrally administered performance expectations and teacher-specific approaches to evaluation and professional development.[17]

These researchers indicate that rigid teacher evaluation systems equally applied to all teachers in all situations are of little benefit to teachers or students. The central office staff, building principals, and teachers must work out a delicate balance between common centrally administered performance expectations and those specific to each building, classroom, and in some cases, each child.

Whereas Lewis agrees that many educational evaluators are highly critical of the state-of-the-art in teacher evaluation she says that everyone does it. The reason is two-fold: (1) the public demands assurance and evidence that teachers can teach children to learn; (2) state legislators, and other political figures activated by national reports on education are demanding teacher evaluation to reward merit or master teachers, to weed those found incompetent and to help select students who wish to enter the teaching profession.[18]

Governors, legislators, and state education boards express deep concern about public schools facing the prospect of fewer and less-qualified teaching candidates in universities. These concerns are causing them to enact legislation that stiffen requirements for entrance and promotion. Bright young people viewing these test hurdles and other evaluation requirements wonder why salaries stay embarrassingly low.

But in spite of the low salaries, many dedicated, bright young people still enter teaching and stay. It is obvious that personnel evaluation systems work better with better personnel. A bright, enthusiastic teacher is more enjoyable to evaluate than one who is having serious problems. Perhaps some legislators and administrators may see the purpose of teacher evaluation as establishing a basis for firing incompetent teachers and rewarding outstanding ones, but most educational leaders realize that teacher evaluation has a greater value than this. *The challenge facing school leaders is how to use teacher evaluation successfully to improve teaching and student outcomes.* Lewis reports that of the more than 400 school administrators replying to a survey about teacher evaluations, the overwhelming concern was "how to convey that evaluations are for improvement...how to relate evaluation to learning improvement of students...how to develop a personal improvement plan for each teacher."[18]

Characteristics for Any Teacher Evaluation System

According to the late Harold McNally, a staff evaluation specialist and professor at the University of Wisconsin, Milwaukee, 11 characteristics should be part of any teacher evaluation system.

1. The purposes must be clearly stated in writing and well known to the evaluators and those who are to be evaluated.

2. The policy and procedures must reflect knowledge of extensive research related to teacher evaluation.

3. Teachers should know and understand the criteria by which they are to be evaluated.

4. The evaluation program should be cooperatively planned, carried out, and evaluated by teachers, supervisors, and administrators.

5. The evaluations should be as valid and as reliable as possible.

6. Evaluations should be more diagnostic than judgmental.

7. Self-evaluation should be an important objective of the program.

8. The self-image and self-respect of teachers should be maintained and enhanced.

9. The nature of the evaluation should encourage teacher creativity and experimentation in planning and guiding the teaching-learning experiences provided to children.

10. The program should make ample provision for clear, personalized, and constructive feedback.

11. Teacher evaluation should be an integral part of the instructional leadership role of the superintendent or central office instructional personnel and principal and of the program for inservice teacher development.[18]

Several reputable teacher evaluation systems strive to include these and other important characteristics. Two of the most widely discussed are Richard Manatt's "Mutual Benefit Evaluation" and George Redfern's "Management by Objectives Evaluation."[19,20] Variations of the programs used throughout the nation are characterized by (1) good setting, (2) teacher involvement in the evaluation process, and (3) centralized teaching standards and criteria.[17] Ben Harris and Jane Hill of the University of Texas and developers of the DeTek teacher evaluation system maintain that clinical supervision and management by objectives models have brought meaningful improvement to the field of teacher evaluation but are themselves lacking in systematic, developmental judgments derived from an appropriate analysis of data.[21]

Obviously no one system encompasses all elements and possibilities faced by evaluators. Each writer on the subject adapts to his or her interests and experiences. One such adaption is the Leadership by Objectives and Results Model (LBO/R) mentioned earlier.

The LBO/R model may be expanded to include teacher evaluation. The same six assumptions about LBO/R listed earlier hold for teacher evaluation by substituting the word "teacher" for "administrator." The model includes the underlying assumption of similar efforts and emphasizes the major components of clinical supervision (see Figure 2).

Developing LBO/R Teacher Evaluation Forms

These are the procedures that could be followed to develop an LBO/R teacher evaluation procedure.

Step 1: A committee composed of eight elected teachers from elementary, junior high, and senior high schools and an administrator from each level plus the director of personnel and a consultant should be charged to develop the evaluation instruments and supporting rationale.

Step 2: The committee should study research and information about teacher evaluation and examples of evaluation forms and instruments.

Figure 2.
LBO/R Teacher Evaluation Model.

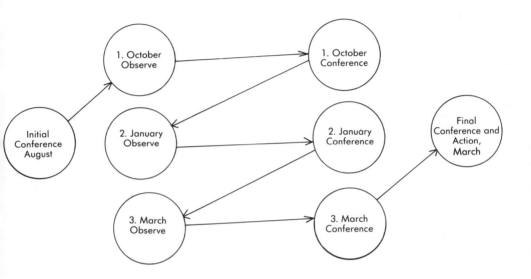

1. Each person to be evaluated meets with the evaluator. Together, a few specific areas of the job that relate to the goals of the system are selected. Teacher and evaluator agree on specific objectives for the teacher and on dates for classroom visits.

2. Evaluators concentrate on observable skills during classroom visitation. At least two different observers visit at least three times for a 50-minute period. Master teachers may need a formal evaluation every other year.

3. Teacher is given a copy of evaluator's comments at the performance follow-up conference following each visit. Both help write new objectives and growth plans. Both sign the evaluation form and indicate agreement or disagreement with the assessment.

4. The final evaluation conference informs teacher of recommendations concerning employment and new growth targets are mutually identified.[22]

Step 3: The instruments should be developed with three parts:

- Part I should be designed to include the evaluation of those "best practice" professional skills and activities that are observable in the classroom.

- Part II should include other teacher responsibilities on which the principal or other evaluators will make summary judgments prior to making teacher recommendations.

- Part III should be a form to record growth targets and specific action to be taken by assessor and assessee to reach the targets.

Step 4: A rationale statement should be written by the committee to explain their reasons for including each component in the three parts of the instrument.

Step 5: The three instruments and the rationale should be submitted to teachers and administrators in the district for their suggestions or additions, which are then returned to the committee.

Step 6: The committee should include the suggestions and return enough copies to each campus to ensure access to all teachers who wish to review the forms a second time.

Step 7: A copy of the final forms along with the rationale and LBO/R cycle information is given to each teacher and administrator.

Step 8: Begin LBO/R cycle.

Step 9: Committee reviews the LBO/R cycle at the end of the year.

The LBO/R model, which has proved to be less subjective than most previous evaluation systems has proponents in New York, Ohio, Oklahoma, Pennsylvania, and Texas school systems. Properly employed, the LBO/R model is aimed at:

- Improving performance through improving supervision.

- Planning for individual growth and development.

- Providing information to assist in marginal performance.

- Identification of special talent and skills.

- Providing means of protecting both individual and school district rights in determining dismissals due to substandard performance.

Indicators of Teaching Effectiveness

In Figure 2 of the LBO/R teacher evaluation model, step 2 suggests that at least two different observers visit *at least three times for 50-minute periods.* The primary observer is, of course, the principal; the second could be an instructional supervisor, associate superintendent, or assistant principal. Each administrator must be trained to do these things:

- Identify the teacher's strengths and weaknesses and provide assistance.
- Recognize "best practice" teaching performance.
- Use the vocabulary of staff evaluation and instructional management.
- Use motivation skills to inspire teachers to do their best.

Current research shows that students are more attentive in classrooms that are businesslike and task oriented. A key to this businesslike classroom is not time-on-task alone but "academic learning time" (ALT). ALT is the amount of time students actually spend on an appropriate learning activity in which they are achieving at a high rate of success (90 percent or better). Researchers have found that in more effective schools teachers waste less time in starting and ending instructional activities, and they select appropriate curricular materials that match the students' abilities. Also, these teachers build high expectations for the learners and themselves. Therefore, any teacher evaluation form should include the following indicators:

- Motivates students to achieve.
- Uses academic learning time effectively.
- Demonstrates proficiency in subject areas.
- Demonstrates command of the language.
- Promotes student academic growth.
- Establishes clear learning objectives.
- Bases learning strategies on objectives.
- Bases testing on objectives.

Obviously, there are other important observable and nonobservable behaviors that contribute to any overall assessment of a teacher's peformance. However, if the above indicators are not measured or present then the other factors hold little value in determining a teacher's ability.

The LBO/R or any other approach to teacher evaluation is only as effective as the administrators and teachers involved. If administrators are protecting images of total authority over their teachers, then the best evaluation models and instruments are useless. Likewise, if teachers feel they do not need supervision, choose to ignore school policy, and view the principal or supervisors as the enemy, then any system regardless of its claims of a "mutual approach" is of little help.

Ghosts of Principals Past

It is unfortunate that principals today are fighting the "ghosts of principals past." It is difficult to assure teachers that the "newer breed" principals may have better preparation in instructional supervision and want to help each teacher and student in the building improve. Because of past experiences, many teachers fear that asking a principal or supervisor for help may be viewed as a sign of weakness that may be held against them at contract renewal or merit consideration time. Thus, the principal and other evaluators must work to establish trust among their staff.

To be successful in the personal facets of evaluation, evaluators have to be open. An open system maintains equilibrium and allows individuals to have a say in the direction and purpose of the organization. Teachers will not reject the idea of having an administrator or supervisor who offers constructive help. They welcome open people who will support them and help them and give them the kind of environment, material, and psychological support that they need. Most teachers want to improve, and the more responsibility given them to improve, the greater support they will give an administrator.

Creating a New Image

If teachers have problems relating to the authority role of the evaluators, it is up to the evaluator to change that image. To create a new image try this approach:

1. Trust yourself and teachers. Ask teachers for help. By asking for help and using it, a leader/principal creates a dynamic activity that tends to urge initiative and constructive effort among teachers.

Most research findings from studies in organizational behavior clearly indicate that when individuals are given more responsibility to do their jobs, they become more deeply involved and are more willing to accept broader jobs and responsibilities.

2. Help teachers identify some job targets. Sit down with each teacher at the beginning of the school year. The process of helping each teacher set a few well-developed job targets primarily aimed at instructional improvement allows teachers to release tension.

Create a climate in the interview session that encourages conflict to emerge. It is more sound to bring conflict out into the open and candidly discuss problems that may block effective principal-teacher relationships and improved instruction. It is highly important to create an atmosphere in which attitudes can be expressed toward the actual objects. This reduces tension and almost surely changes perceptions and behaviors. Such an atmosphere promotes sound morale.

Evaluating Other Staff Members

Although we have chosen to emphasize rationale and strategies for evaluating administrators, supervisors, and teachers, we do recommend self evaluation by school boards also. A joint publication of the American Association of School Administrators and the National School Boards Association titled *Goal Setting and Self Evaluation of School Boards* is helpful in assisting board members in a self evaluation. Other staff members also need to be evaluated. The director of maintenance and operations, food services, and other support staff should have job descriptions that include duties, reporting responsibilities, and expected performance. The evaluation forms should be developed cooperatively to allow for open communication about each job function and the skills required. This openness can promote better public relations for the total school district. Supervisors and evaluators need training in management skills, evaluation processes, and contract procedures. These important staff members must be invited to work with their supervisor to develop specific written plans for improvement based on each staff member's identified needs. The purpose of any assessment is to advocate experiences that promote constructive changes in all staff members.

Conclusion

Staff evaluation systems stand at the crossroads. One road leads to a system created by legislators and special interest groups. The other road leads to a system created by educational researchers and practitioners working with legislators and state department personnel to improve administrator, teacher, and student performance by designing evaluation systems based on best practice derived from effective school research. This practice includes careful analysis of educational needs and the development of clear goals to meet the needs. A staff evaluation model must be based on the belief that school personnel will work cooperatively to improve district and individual performance and deserve to be viewed as competent professionals. No single evaluation is adequate to cover all elements of personnel performance. However, the most widely accepted models are based on mutual goal setting. The Leadership by Objectives and Results (LBO/R) is a mutual-goal-setting evaluation model and is presented as a vehicle upon which this other road can be traversed.

Skill Accomplishment Checklist for Chapter Six

Competency and Skills	Reading and Activities for Mastery
Competency: Design staff evaluation system to enhance effectiveness of educational personnel.	Readings: See resources 11, 12, 13, 14, 18 Activities: 1. Learner could collect staff evaluation forms and handbooks from several districts and then develop a model based on research and best practice. 2. Learner could interview school and business leaders to compare processes and rationale for staff evaluation.
Skill A: Evaluating administrator and supervisor performance.	Readings: See resources 3, 8, 9, 10, 11, 13, 14 Activities: 1. Learner could simulate an LBO/R retreat for administrators as a class or in-service project. District goals and job descriptions could be designed for each participant before the activity begins. Have participants present their goals for discussion.

149

2. Learner could observe an administrator for a designated time period and also administer and interpret the LBDQ or similar leadership self-report instrument — See chapter two.

3. Learner could meet with teacher groups to gather their perceptions about criteria for administrator evaluation.

4. Learners at the principalship level could go through an NASSP Assessment Center to determine level of skill in the 12 areas.

5. Learner should review all eight skill areas in this book to determine mastery level.

Skill B: Evaluating teacher performance.

Readings: See resources 1, 11, 12, 15, 18, 19, 21, 22

Activities:

1. After reviewing the suggested readings the learner could write a seven- to eight-page paper to provide the rationale for teacher evaluation.

2. The learners could accompany an authority on teacher evaluation and observe a variety of classroom teachers and compare the observations with best practice research.

3. Learners could observe videotapes of teachers and repeat suggestions in number two above.

4. Learner could simulate post observation conferences with teacher using best clinical supervision methods.

5. As part of the learners pre-service internship he/she could form a committee of teachers and administrators and develop a new teacher evaluation system using the LBO/R model as a guide.

Skill C: Evaluating other staff members.

Readings: See R. W. Rebore, *Personnel Administration in Education*, (Englewood Cliffs: N.J., 1982), pp. 178-180, 197-212; also see resources 3, 11, 13.

Activities:

1. Learners could develop an evaluation plan for classified personnel and identify the similarities and differences between the evaluation plan for administrators and teachers.

2. Learners could describe the value of staff development from a public relations perspective for all classified personnel.

3. Learner could develop a paper describing job enrichment for classified personnel.

Resources

1. R.S. Soar, D.M. Medley, and H. Coker, "Teacher Evaluation: A Critique of Currently Used Methods," *Phi Delta Kappan* 65, 4 (1983), p. 239; see also B. Harris and J. Hill, *The DeTek Handbook* (Austin, Texas: National Education Publishers, 1982).

2. T.A. Shannon, "Teacher Evaluation: Some Points to Ponder," *CEDR Quarterly* 15, 4 (1982), p. 18.

3. S. Stow and R. Manatt, "Administrator Evaluation Tailored to Your District or Independent School," *Educational Leadership* 39, 5 (1982), p. 353.

4. R. Stogdill, *Handbook of Leadership: A Survey of Theory and Research* (New York: The Free Press, 1974).

5. F.E. Fiedler, *A Theory of Leadership Effectiveness* (New York: McGraw-Hill, 1967).

6. Also see Silver, Part IV, "Leadership in Organizations," pp. 121-176; A.W. Halpin, "How Leaders Behave," *Theory and Research in Administration* (New York: MacMillan, 1966), pp. 81-130.

7. P. Hersey and K.H. Blanchard, *Management or Organizational Behavior: Utilizing Human Resources (3rd ed.)* (Englewood Cliffs, N.J.: Prentice-Hall, 1977).

8. Two instruments are used extensively to measure the two dimensions: *The Leadership Behavior Description Questionnaire LBDQ* (See Chapter 2) and *The Managerial Grid* by Blake and Mouton (Austin, Texas: Scientific Methods, Inc., 1964).

9. T.E. Deal and L.D. Celotti, "How Much Influence Do (And Can) Educational Administrators Have on Classrooms," *Kappan* (March 1970), pp. 471-473.

10. M. Abbott, "Evaluating School Administrators: The Scope and Nature of Administrative Performance," *The Evaluation of Administrative Performance: Parameters, Problems, and Practices*, W.J. Gephart and others, (eds.), (Bloomington, Indiana: Phi Delta Kappa, 1975), p. 52.

11. G.B. Redfern, *Evaluating Teachers and Administrators: A Performance Objective Approach* (Boulder, Colo.: Westview Press, 1980).

12. R.P. Manatt, "The School Improvement Model: A Scenario for Operational Status, 1983-84," The School Improvement Model Project, Iowa State University, College of Education; also AASA and the Association for Supervision and Curriculum Development have produced audio and videotape series by Manatt on the topic of staff evaluation (Arlington, Va.: AASA; Alexandria, Va.; ASCD, 1981).

13. D.L. Bolton, *Evaluating Administrative Personnel in School Systems* (New York: Teachers College Press, 1980).

14. AASA/NSBA *Selecting the Administrative Team* (Arlington, Va.: AASA, 1981); AASA *Administrative and Supervisory Behavior* (Arlington, Va.: 1977); AASA *Evaluating the Superintendent* (Arlington, Va.: 1980); A. Lewis, *Evaluating Educational Personnel*(Arlington, Va.: AASA, 1982); R. P. Manatt, *Evaluat-*

ing and Improving the Performance of School Administrators and Board Members (Arlington, Va.: AASA, 1981); Gephart, *The Evaluation of Administrative Performance: Parameters, Problems, and Practices*, (Bloomington, Ind.: Phi Delta Kappa, 1975); and Redfern, 1980.

15. D.L. Haefele, "How to Evaluate Thee, Teacher—Let Me Count the Ways," *Phi Delta Kappan* 61, 5 (1980), pp. 349-352.

16. M.W. McLaughlin, "A Preliminary Investigation of Teacher Evaluation Practice," A National study of 32 school districts in 24 states, conducted by the Rand Corporation, 1982.

17. L. Darling-Hammond, A.E. Wise, and S.R. Pease, "Teacher Evaluation in the Organizational Context: A Review of the Literature," *Review of Educational Research* 53, 3 (Fall 1983), p. 285.

18. A.C. Lewis, *Evaluating Educational Personnel* (Arlington, Va.: AASA, 1982).

19. R.P. Manatt, K.L. Palmer, and E. Hidlebaugh, "Evaluating Teacher Performance with Improved Rating Scales," *NASSP Bulletin* 60, 40 (1976).

20. G.B. Redfern, *Evaluating Teachers and Administrators: A Performance Objective Approach* (Boulder, Colo.: Westview Press, 1980).

21. B. Harris and J. Hill, 1982. The DeTek is a comprehensive system designed for instructional improvements of all teachers regardless of area of specialization or teaching experience. It is divided into four phases that include ten steps. Within the four phases, seven different instruments are used.

22. H.M. Crenshaw and J.R. Hoyle, "The Principal's Headache—Teacher Evaluation," *NASSP Bulletin* 65, 442 (February 1981), p.37.

23. J. Hoyle, "Teaching Assessment: The Administrator's Perspective," in B.S. Plake (ed.), *Assessment of Teaching: Purposes, Practices, and Implications for the Profession* (Lincoln, Neb.: Buros Institute of Mental Measurements, Publisher, 1989).

24. E. Manigold, *Management and Leadership Development for School Administrators* (Austin, Texas: Texas LEAD Center, Texas Association of School Administrators, 1988).

SKILLS IN STAFF DEVELOPMENT

Skills required for developing staff evaluation models are closely linked to skills required for staff development.[32] Leading a vital, growing, innovative, dynamic school system requires risk-taking, stretching, painful, exhilarating change. This change is accomplished through staff development. Real staff development is not confined to one or two inservice days when the faculty listens to a motivating speaker, attends a show and tell workshop, and chats with co-workers over coffee and danish. Staff development that promotes true school improvement demands thoughtful, long-term planning; commitment to specific goals; and the same tender nurturing from administration that is required in guiding a child through adolescence.

To do this, administrators need the ability to:

● Conduct system and staff needs assessment to identify areas for concentrated staff development and resource allocation for new personnel.

● Use clinical supervision as a staff improvement and evaluation strategy.

● Assess individual and institutional sources of stress and develop methods for reducing that stress.

Interaction of Staff Development with Organizational Development

Effective staff development is related to the development of an organization. It merges the personal growth needs of individuals in an organization and the formal institutional needs of the system.[1] Without the linkage, systemwide improvement in an organization does not take place.

Staff development and organization development have been defined as follows:

> *Staff Development:* Staff development is a process designed to foster personal and professional growth for individuals within a respectful, supportive, positive organizational climate having as its ultimate aim better learning for students, and continuous, responsible self-renewal for educators and schools.

> *Organization Development:* Organization development is the process undertaken by an organization, or part of an organization, to define and meet changing self-improvement objectives, while making it possible for the individuals in the organization to meet their personal and professional objectives.

Together the terms staff development and organization development form the "gestalt" of school improvement.[3] Both terms are relatively new to the literature of education. The overall purpose of organizational development is to enhance the ability of an organization to achieve its goals and to improve the "quality of life" within the organization.[33] In many ways the two terms have overlapping goals. Figure 1 summarizes the characteristics of successful staff development and organizational development programs.[3]

The term staff development has evolved from literature on inservice education and supervision. The current thrust of supervision is supervision as staff development.[4] To understand the evolution of staff development in schools, we should trace changes in supervision.[5] The 1900 - 1930 period of supervision has been labeled the *traditional scientific* era. During this period supervision was characterized as a directing, checking, judging activity. There was little preservice education and inservice as a term was yet to be heard.

From 1930 - 1960 the *human relations* label was attached to supervision. While supervision was described as democratic during this time, in reality teachers were treated kindly and manipulated into doing what supervisors wanted.

The 1960 - 1980 period, the *neo-scientific era*, actually began with Sputnik in 1957. The federal government's increased involvement in local school operations funded large curriculum projects to improve the quality of education, particularly in math and science. Supervisors were added to monitor the implementation of these projects. It was during this period that the supervisor's role became increasingly confused. Unions were growing in power, numbers, and involvement in the collective bargaining issue. Contact time with professional staff for the purpose of staff development or inservice was being negotiated out of contracts. Limitations on the length of afterschool meetings and use of "free" periods were frequent contract items.

Clinical supervision was born at Harvard University. Support for the educational community declined as the public became increasingly aware of the deficiencies of high school graduates. There was an explosion of electives at the high school level, and the country was beginning to experience high levels of inflation.

Figure 1.
Successful Staff Development and
Organizational Development Programs — A Summary.

Staff Development	Organizational Development
1. Long term commitment (3-5 yr.)	1. Long term commitment
2. Staff involvement in needs assessment and planning	2. Careful passage through three phases Entry and start-up Initial operation Maintenance or institutional-ization
3. Active participation of key central administrators and principals	3. Top management and central office commitment
4. Development of an in-house cadre of knowledgeable leaders to carry on training	4. Commitment and involvement of principals
5. Sufficient staff involvement to provide support system to main-tenance of change long enough for it to become institutionalized	5. Use of outside consultant
6. Provision for immediate application	6. Voluntary commitment of signifi-cant percentage of staff
7. Adequate economic support	7. Careful planning with early visible success
	8. Provision for funding

The 1980s and beyond have yet to receive their label — they may become the *school improvement* era. Whatever the label, educators are coping with the back to basics, competency based education, the technology explosion, and something being called the "Toyota Experience." Staff development is perceived as the nirvana to cure all the ills of education in only two inservice days while still meeting all contractual obligations of length of school day, prep time, free time, starting time, and ending time. The task is almost impossible. In addition, some state legislators are mandating school improvement and staff development through merit pay systems. Pointing out the futility of these efforts only seems to heighten the efforts of those intent on legislating the behavior of students and teachers.

With all of this, where does staff development really begin? In reality good staff development begins with a well designed needs assessment.

System and Staff Needs Assessment

What is a needs assessment? Essentially it is an assessment of the difference between what is and what should be. A needs assessment can deal with inputs, processes, products, outputs, and outcomes.[6] It can focus on elements within the system or external to the system, identify needed organization efforts, results or specify societal goals and objectives. In design, it can be simplistic or comprehensive. However constructed, it is the basic problem-solving tool for any organizaton or institution. Used effectively by school administrators, staff development will provide the foundation for long-term growth and self-renewal of the system.

This problem-solving process has six steps.

- Identify problem based on needs.
- Determine solution requirements and identify solution alternatives.
- Select solution strategy(ies) from among alternatives.
- Implement selected methods and means.
- Determine performance effectiveness.
- Revise as required. [6]

Figure 2 depicts graphically the Organizational Elements Model (OEM) that can assist in determining the type of needs assessment required for a particular problem. It also includes some educational examples of each of the elements.[7] The model can be used to determine if a gap exists between one element and another.

Most needs assessments focus on the elements of processes, products, and outputs. It is beneficial occasionally to conduct an outcome needs assessment. It deals with the questions of "What are we attempting to accomplish?," "Why do schools exist?", or "What type of educational program do we wish to offer,— classical, social utility, or humanistic?"[8] Outcome needs assessments deal with education's societal impact and are external to the school system. It tells a school system what's happening to their students after they graduate. How are they faring? When a district attempts to develop a mission statement, it involves dealing with some level of outcome needs assessment.

Needs assessments may be conducted for any of the five elements of the OEM model. A district needs assessment may focus entirely on analyzing the gap between the skill levels desired of students and the skill levels currently being achieved by students. Once a gap is recognized, an entire staff development program may be developed to reduce any discrepancies. (For a complete review of the needs assessment process we recommend the work of Roger Kaufman.)

Figure 3 provides an example of the planning processes that should be used once a needs assessment has been completed. If an analysis reveals a gap in

Figure 2.
The Organizational Elements Model (OEM) Including Some Educational Examples of Each
and the Relationship Between the Elements and the Internal and External Frames of Reference.

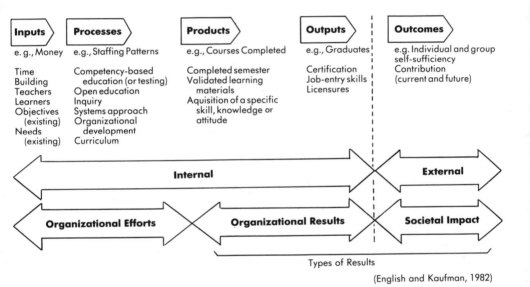

(English and Kaufman, 1982)

actual achievement and desired goals, the administrators must establish clear objectives to enable the district to achieve its desired goal. They must also identify available resources and develop and implement a program. Figure 4 outlines topics that should be addressed in designing and implementing a staff development plan.

Figure 3.
Curriculum Planning.

Current Status	Need	Goal
"What is"	Gap between "what is" and "what should be"	Ideal state of "what should be"

	Program	Objective
	Treatment to move from current status toward goal	Acceptable state of "what should be"

Resources
What is required for a program to function

The planning relationship using a reading example would be:

Planning for a specific reading need

Current Status	Need	Goal
Fifteen percent of third graders are reading below grade level. (This is an example of needs assessment data)	The number of third graders reading below grade level should be reduced.	One hundred percent of third graders should be reading at or above grade

	Program	Objective
	The XYZ Instructional System for Reading will be implemented	Ninety percent of third graders should be reading at or above grade level as shown on next year's testing results.

Resources
List of Performance Objectives; Instructional Guides; 60 minute per day study allocation per child; and so on.

Source: *Fundamental Curriculum Decisions ASCD Yearbook* (Alexandria, Va.: Association for Supervision and Curriculum development, 1983, p. 69).

Figure 4.
Considerations in Designing and
Implementing a Staff Development Plan.

Personnel

● Determine what staff will be involved in the actual implementation of the change effort.

● Identify the person or people who will train that staff.

● Assign specific personnel the responsibility for all direct communication with staff, the media, the board, and central office personnel.

● Plan for awareness activities that include secretarial and custodial staff in addition to professional staff.

● Decide how staff awareness for the project will be handled and to what extent it is necessary.

● Identify staff members who have expertise in needed areas and arrange to have them assist in the awareness session.

Organization for Change

● Establish job responsibilities and standards for success.

● Determine how often personnel will report progress and what format these reports will take.

● Establish a procedure for periodic reports to the board on the development and implementation of the plan.

● Determine how much administrative support is necessary to enable the accomplishment of the objectives.

Political Considerations

● Plan a strategy for informing and gaining the support of the school board and the taxpayers.

- Be sure that financial expectations for change are realistic and communicated to the necessary populations.

- Develop a system to process questions, inquiries, and criticism, both positive and negative.

- Determine if staff is willing to support the change effort.

- Develop a plan to identify and work with staff people who are openly negative to the proposed change.

Time

- Study time requirements for each phase of the plan.

- Develop a timeline that identifies key activities, and identifies who is responsible for completing the activity.

- Determine the total expected duration of the project.

Cost

- Specify the cost of each component of the change effort, not just the total cost.

- Develop a budget reporting system to ensure fiscal accountability during program implementation.

Source: Implementation Kit: *Differentiating Between Design/Delivery Problems in Improving Instructional Supervision*, B. Steffy, permission granted.

Using Clinical Supervision as a Staff Improvement and Evaluation Strategy

Clinical supervision is believed by some to be the most effective supervisory model in education.[10] Developed at Harvard in the late 1960s it combines a democratically humane approach to supervision with a methodologically sound process.[11] Successful implementation assumes that building principals will spend approximately one half of their time involved in:

- Curriculum planning.
- Clinical supervision.
- Staff development.
- Teacher evaluation.

While this is a desired and valued goal, current research does not document its actualization. A 1980 revision of Robert Goldhammer's *Clinical Supervision*, quotes Krajewski:

Conceived at Harvard University more than fifteen years ago, "clinical supervision," as it is commonly called, still remains primarily a latent force for the improvement of instruction. Written about, discussed, taught and sometimes attempted, clinical supervision has yet to be fully born to the world of public education, K-12. Scholars and practitioners alike have made valiant efforts to stimulate its birth, yet clinical supervision remains largely in the womb.[12, 13]

As originally conceived, the clinical supervision model is based on five stages:[14]

- Preobservation conference.

- Observation.

- Analysis and strategy.

- Supervision conference.

- Postconference analysis.

- In the *preobservation conference* the teacher and the administrator discuss the impending observation and the lesson objectives. They decide the observation's focus on specific items or problems. The techniques the administrator will use to collect the data are also discussed and agreed on. This conference not only serves as a communication link but it should also reduce the natural tension created by the observation process.

- During *observation* the administrator views the lesson as planned in the pre-observation conference. Since the method for collecting data was discussed prior to the observation, the time set in advance, and the lesson's purpose thoroughly discussed, the actual event should progress smoothly.

- The purpose of the *analysis and strategy* stage is to develop a plan for helping the teacher grow. It includes reviewing the events of the lesson in terms of the teacher's intent, the teacher's past history, the teaching techniques used, and the outcome. The administrator will have to determine the priorities to be discussed with the teacher since both the administrator and the teacher are limited in the amount of conference time available to them. Determining what behavior a teacher can change requires knowledge of the area of instruction and of personal dynamics. It is one thing to suggest that a teacher may need to adopt a new instructional strategy. It is quite another to assess whether the teacher has the competence and personal motivation necessary for that to happen. The success of the clinical supervision model depends on administrators' skills in this area more than any other stage. Even when there is enough time to conduct clinical supervision, it may still fail because an administrator lacks expertise with this stage.

- The *supervisory conference* provides a time to give the teacher feedback that will enable the teacher to improve the teaching act. Again, the success of this conference depends on the administrator. Responsibility for maintaining the pace of the conference, effectively communicating areas of success and weakness of the lesson, and making the conference a growth opportunity for the teacher rests with the administrator. This can be done by using the conferences as a time to:

- Provide adult awards and satisfactions.
- Define and authenticate issues in teaching.
- Offer didactic help (if appropriate).
- Train the teacher in techniques for self-supervision.
- Develop incentives for professional self-analysis.[14]

- The *postobservation analysis* stage offers both teachers and administrators a chance to reflect on the effectiveness of the process. It is at this stage where the supervisor gets feedback as to his/her effectiveness in carrying out the democratic, humane objectives of this time consuming, sophisticated, highly structured procedure. This stage is considered by the authors to be the second most important stage in the process, preceded only by an administrators' ability to analyze the lesson.

Few educators question the spirit of the clinical supervision model or its methodology. Unfortunately, it is not used that effectively in many situations. Its lack of success may be due to poor skills with stages three and five, but the issue most often raised is the question of the amount of time required to implement the process.

Too many teachers, as researchers have indicated, are unaware of their pedagogical behavior. Their lack of awareness impedes their ability to improve and grow professionally. If not a clinical supervision model, then what other staff development models are available?

Other Approaches to Staff Development

> Supervision is a process of facilitating the professional growth of a teacher, primarily by giving the teacher feedback about classroom interactions and helping the teacher make use of that feedback in order to make teaching more effective.[18]

Allen Glatthorn strongly supports a differentiated approach to staff development and believes that teachers should have a choice in the type of supervision they receive. He builds his case on three assumptions. First, that administrators often have poor supervisory skills. Second, because of the amount of time and expertise needed, clinical supervision is not feasible. Finally, teachers have varying growth needs and learning styles. All three of these assumptions are documented with research.[25, 26, 27, 28] Glatthorn's model of differentiated staff development provides the teacher with four types of staff development.[18]

- *Clinical supervision* — which is an intensive process designed to improve instruction by conferring with a teacher on lesson planning, observing the lesson, analyzing the observational data, and giving the teacher feedback about the observation.

● *Cooperative professional development* — which is a collegial process in which a small group of teachers agree to work together for their own professional growth.

● *Self-directed development* — which enables the individual teacher to work independently on professional growth concerns.

● *Administrative monitoring* — which, as the term implies, is a process in which an administrator monitors the work of the staff, making brief and unannounced visits simply to ensure that the staff are carrying out assignments and responsibilities in a professional manner.

Variations to clinical supervision have also emerged over the years. Most can be classified as scientific supervision, accountable supervision, artistic supervision, and learning-centered supervision.

The Madeline Hunter model, an example of scientific supervision, identifies nine steps in presenting a lesson.[23]

● *Diagnosis*. Pretesting to determine a student's skill development relative to a learning objective.

● *Specific Objectives*. Identify appropriate objectives for a lesson based on pre-test information.

● *Anticipatory set*. Prepare students for learning by reviewing previous instruction and setting the stage for the new learning.

● *Perceived purpose*. Motivate students and clarify the purpose of the lesson.

● *Learning opportunities*. Match learning activities with students' learning styles to maximize results.

● *Modeling*. Provide students with examples of correct responses.

● *Check for understanding*. Make sure students understand the material.

● *Guided practice*. Provide opportunities for students to apply the new knowledge and receive corrective feedback.

● *Independent practice*. Provide opportunities for students to apply the new knowledge on their own.

Accountable supervision attempts to link student achievement to teacher performance. Given the multitude of variables that impact on student achievement, it seems impossible to identify specific teacher behaviors which could be held accountable for student achievement.[24] The foundation of some early merit pay plans attempt to do this.

Artistic supervision has been developed primarily by Elliot Eisner.[25] While it is difficult to quantify teacher effectiveness, the subjective nature of the artistic model makes it less attractive as a sole model for supervision. Perhaps a more effective approach would be to combine scientific, accountable, and artistic supervision.

Learning-centered supervision calls for an opening conference to establish rapport, a pre-observational conference to discuss the observations, an unfocused observation, a focused observation, observational analysis, a feedback conference, and a formative assessment conference.[18] Like pure clinical supervision, it requires a great deal of time and may best be reserved for beginning teachers or teachers having problems.

Bruce Joyce and Beverly Showers envision a need for "a major change in the ecology of professional life" based on the development of "a synergistic environment where collaborative enterprises are both normal and sustaining and where continuous training and study both of academic substance and the craft of teaching are woven into the fabric of the school, bring satisfaction by virtue of an increasing sense of growth and competence."[26] They propose a training program that includes these elements.

- Learning the meaning of horizontal transfer of learning.
- Developing high degrees of skill before attempting classroom implementation.
- Knowing when to use the new skill.
- Providing for practice in the workplace immediately following skill development.
- Providing for "coaching" by peers - the development of a peer support team.
- Generating a "learning how to learn" effect.

According to Joyce and Showers, the "coaching" component is critical and should include development of coaching teams. In highly developed coaching environments, colleagues view one another as sources of:

- Companionship.
- Technical feedback.
- Facilitators of application analysis.
- Helpers for adaption of a skill.[26]

Joyce and Showers emphasize the importance of transfer in a staff development process. There is a big difference between sitting in an audience and being told about a technique and working out the technique under coaching in the classroom environment. Transfer, the foundation for their staff development programs, assumes that given intensive training, which may include the purpose of a new strategy, guided practice and feedback, plus a need for application of the strategy, most teachers can learn to become proficient with new procedures.

Assessing Individual and Institutional Sources of Stress

Stress is real. Every person experiences stress at one time or another within a lifetime. Unaltered, stress can become the path to grief, disease, and premature death. This kind of stress is termed distress. Stress of a positive nature can lead to happiness, health, and longevity. Figure 4 compares positive stress, or eustress, with negative stress, or distress.[28] School administrators need to maximize the opportunities for staff, students, and peers to enjoy eustress and minimize the occasions when distress is produced by the work environment. Creating an environment characterized as a positive school climate is one where distress is negligible.

Figure 4.
Factors Leading to Positive and Negative Stress.

Eustress	Distress
Avoidance of stressful situations	Frequent encounter with stressful situations
Exercise	Being overly competitive
Physical activity	Overwork
Self-fulfilling work	Repetitive work
Diversions	Rationalization
Long range planning	Propensity to worry
Achievable goals	Living in the past
A positive outlook	Unrealistic goals
Belief in the "goodness of man"	Inappropriate amounts of sleep, relaxation, or inactivity
Periods of relaxation, inactivity	Improper diet
Proper sleep	Overweight, or underweight
Spiritual commitment	Dependence on drugs
Appropriate weight	Antisocial behavior
Positive family relationships	Solitude
Supportive friends	

Many factors relate to the personal lives of our employees and can not be controlled by the work environment. It is necessary for effective school administrators to be sensitive to the events taking place in the personal lives of their staff members and attempt to take this into consideration as stressful personal situations impact on the work performance of individuals.

To be privy to this kind of information, administrators must build trusting relationships and be accessible to their staff on a frequent basis in an informal way. The day to day troublesome factors that influence stress are not easily learned unless there is a firmly established, caring, relationship of mutual trust between the administrator and the staff. Staff development begins with the cultivation of this kind of relationship. Each administrator should have a staff development plan designed to build a trusting relationship with staff as well as a staff development plan to increase the formal skills of employees.

Conclusion

Staff development programs fail for a variety of reasons: poor planning and organization, a negative view of teachers by administrators, and inservice designs that focus on districtwide issues rather than the specific concerns of teachers. They are all too often occasions that could be termed "information assimilation," that is, sessions where participants act as passive observers with little opportunity for interaction.

Adult learners require a certain kind of learning environment. They are motivated to learn when their basic desires for a safe work climate, good salary with adequate fringe benefits, and fair treatment are met. But this is only partially responsible for generating motivation for adults. The most critical factor is the recognition, feelings of achievement, and increase in self-worth attached to new learning.[30]

Research has identified a number of attributes of effective adult learning models:

• The goals and objectives of the training are seen as immediately useful to teachers.

• The material presented is perceived as relevant to the personal and professional needs of the teachers.

• The teachers can see results within a short period of time, and feedback is available regarding the progress the teachers are making.

• The new learning makes the teachers feel good about themselves.

• The new learning is individualized.

• The teachers have input into the design and content of the inservice.

• The inservice is not seen as an attack on the competence of the teachers.

• The inservice is conducted in an atmosphere of trust, respect for the participants, and concern for their feelings.[30]

Even when all of the above characteristics are in place, inservice activities may result in short term benefits. In order for teachers to own the new technique, the innovation must move through a series of levels.

• Awareness: Little interest or involvement.

• Informational: A general desire to have more information but not a particular professional reason.

• Personal: The teachers begin to analyze the innovation relative to their own personal needs.

● Management: There is an expectation that the innovation will be implemented.

● Consequence: Impact of the innovation on learners is considered.

● Collaboration: Discussion with colleagues about implementing the innovation takes place.

● Refocusing: Teachers analyze the innovation for possible modification for more effective use.[31]

These have become known as the Stages of Concern of an innovation. For refocusing to take place and the innovation to become integrated, teachers have to feel that there has been administrative support all along the way. This type of change does not take place overnight. It takes time, lots of time. Development of a healthy climate of change and growth within a school takes from three to five years of well planned, persistent, meaningful activity.

Skill Accomplishment Checklist for Chapter Seven

Competence and Skills	Readings and Activities for Mastery
Competency: Design staff development and evaluation systems to enhance effectiveness of educational personnel.	See resources 1, 2, 3, 4, 5, 29, 30, 31 Activities: 1. Analyze the amount of staff development time available at each level of your school system, elementary, middle school, and senior high. Devise a plan to increase the amount of staff development time over the next five years. Be sure to review the teacher's contract and stay within the parameters established by that document. 2. Write to a variety of school districts of comparable size. Ask to receive a copy of their staff development plan. Summarize the documents received. 3. Design the "ideal" staff development plan for your school district. State the goals of the overall plan. Be specific in terms of time, objectives, followup, and plan evaluation procedures.
Skill A: System and staff needs assessment to identify areas for concentrated staff development and resource allocation for new personnel.	See resources 6, 7, 8 Activities: 1. Develop a needs assessment instrument to identify the gap between what is and what should be at the following levels: inputs, processes, products, outputs, and outcomes. 2. Develop a needs assessment instrument to assess the entry level skills of new personnel.

3. Administer the needs assessment instrument developed for item 2 and then design the plan to deliver the needed skill improvement program.

Skill B: Using clinical supervision as a staff improvement and evaluation strategy.	Readings: See resources 9-26 Activities: 1. Using the clinical supervision model, observe two new staff persons, two teachers generally considered to be master teachers, and two teachers identified as experiencing difficulty. Compare the effectiveness of the process for each group. 2. With the approval of the staff, conduct a two-week series of administrative monitoring activities. Be sure to observe each teacher in the building once each day. Prepare notecards to document what you observed. Meet with the teachers to discuss the process and what you learned at the end of the two weeks. 3. Design a contract to be used by staff for a year-long plan for either self-directed development or cooperative professional development. Be sure the design for cooperative professional development details the activities of each participant.
Skill C: Assessment of individual and institutional sources of stress and development of methods for reducing stress.	Readings: See resources 26, 28, 29 Activities: 1. Develop a plan to provide an administrator with an opportunity to interact with faculty on an informal basis. Be sure to specify how this activity fits into the amount of time available to the administrator. 2. Analyze your own activities, try to determine activities leading to distress and activities leading to eustress. Develop a plan to reduce the distress and maximize the eustress. 3. Study the current decision-making processes used in your district. Attempt to identify those practices that lead to the development of stress, both good and bad, within the system.

Resources

1. J. Getzels, "Administration as a Social Process," in A. Halpin, (ed.), *Administrative Theory in Education* (Chicago: Midwest Administration Center, University of Chicago, 1958).

2. B. Dillon-Peterson, "Staff Development/Organization Development - Perspective 1981," *Staff Development/Organization Development, ASCD 1981 Yearbook*, (Alexandria, Va.: Association for Supervision and Curriculum Development, 1981), p. 3.

3. B. Dillon-Peterson, "Staff Development/Organization Development - Perspective 1981" *Staff Development/Organizational Development, ASCD 1981 Yearbook* (Alexandria, Va.: Association of Supervision and Curriculum Development, 1981), pp. 11-36.

4. Theme issue, *Educational Leadership* 37, 5 (February 1980).

5. K. Wiles, *Supervision for Better Schools* (Englewood, N.J.: Prentice-Hall, 1967), pp. 3-5.

6. R. Kaufman and F. English, *Needs Assessment Concepts and Application* (Englewood Cliffs, N.J.: Educational Technology Publications, 1979)

7. R. Kaufman, "Needs Assessment," *Fundamental Curriculum Decisions, ASCD 1983 Yearbook*, (Alexandria, Va.: Association for Supervision and Curriculum Development, 1983) p. 57.

8. E. Eisner and E. Vallance, eds., *Conflicting Conceptions of Curriculum* (Berkeley, Calif.: McCutchan Publishing, 1974).

9. F. Wilhelms, *Supervision in a New Key* (Washington, D.C.: Association for Supervision and Curriculum Development, 1973), p. 1.

10. M.L. Cogan, *Clinical Supervision* (Boston: Houghton Mifflin, 1973).

11. S. McFaul and J. Cooper, "Peer Clinical Supervision: Theory vs. Reality," *Educational Leadership* 41, 7 (April 1984), pp. 4-9.

12. R. Goldhammer, *Clinical Supervision: Special Methods for the Supervision of Teachers* (New York: Holt, Rinehart, & Winston, 1969).

13. R. Krajewski, Editorial, *Contemporary Education* 49 (Fall 1977), p. 4.

14. R. Goldhammer, R. Anderston, and R. Krajewski, *Clinical Supervision: Special Methods for the Supervision of Teachers* (New York: Holt, Rinehart & Winston, 1980), pp. 208-211.

15. J. Brophy and T. Good, *Looking in Classrooms* (New York: Harper & Row, 1978).

16. A. Simon, "Peer Supervision: An Alternative," Association for Supervision and Curriculum Development, 1979 Annual Conference audiotape.

17. McFaul and Cooper, see 11.

18. A. Glatthorn, *Differentiated Supervision* (Alexandria, Va.: Association for Curriculum and Supervision, 1984), p. 2.

19. J. Lovell and M. Phelps, "Supervision in Tennessee: A Study of Perceptions of Teachers, Principals, and Supervisors," (Murfreesboro, Tenn.: Tennessee Association for Supervision and Curriculum Development, 1976).

20. C. Sullivan, "Supervisory Expectations and Work Realities: The Great Gulf," *Educational Leadership* 39 (March 1982), pp. 448-451.

21. W. Copeland, "Affective Disposition of Teachers in Training Toward Examples of Supervisory Behavior," Journal of Educational Research 74 (September-October 1980), pp. 37-42.

22. B. Joyce and M. McKibbin, "Teacher Growth States and School Environments," *Educational Leadership* 40 (November 1982), pp. 36-4.

23. M. Hunter, "Knowing, Teaching, and Supervising," *Using What We Know About Teaching* (Alexandria, Va.: Association for Supervision and Curriculum Development 1984), pp. 175-176.

24. D. Medley, "The Effectiveness of Teachers," in *Research on Teaching*, P. Peterson and H. Walberg (eds.) (Berkeley, Calif.: McCutchan Publishing, 1979), pp. 11-27.

25. E. Eisner, "An Artistic Approach to Supervision," *Supervision of Teaching* (Alexandria, Va.: Association for Supervision and Curriculum Development, 1982) pp. 53-66.

26. B. Joyce and B. Showers, *Power in Staff Development Through Research on Training* (Alexandria, Va.: Association for Supervision and Curriculum Development, 1983), p. 1

27. H. Selye, *Nature* (138:32) (1936).

28. D. Morse and M. Furst, *Stress for Success: A Holistic Approach to Stress and Its Management* (New York: Van Nostrand Reinhold Company, 1979), pp. 5-6.

29. R. Bents and K. Howey, "Staff Development-Change in the Individual," *Staff Development/Organizational Development, ASCD 1981 Yearbook*, (Alexandria, Va.: Association for Supervision and Curriculum Development, 1981), p. 12.

30. F. Wood and S. Thompson, "Guidelines for Better Staff Development," *Educational Leadership* 37:5 (February 1980), pp. 374-378.

31. G. Hall, R. Wallace, Jr., and W. Dossett, *A Developmental Conceptualization of the Adoption Process Within Educational Institutions* (Austin: Research and Development Center for Teacher Education, The University of Texas, 1973).

32. See 1989 Spring issue of *Educational Considerations Journal* for a comprehensive look at administrator staff development and the progress of the Leadership in Educational Administrator Development LEAD projects; also see K.J. Snyder and R.H. Anderson, *Managing Productive Schools: Toward an Ecology* (Orlando, Fla.: Harcourt, Brace, Jovanovich, Pub., 1986), chapter 11.

33. See Steffy, Betty, *Teacher Career Stages* (Lancaster, Pa.: Technomic Pub., 1989).

CHAPTER EIGHT
SKILLS IN ALLOCATING RESOURCES

School leaders must possess the skills to allocate human, material, and financial resources efficiently. Further, this must be done in an accountable manner to ensure successful student learning. Skills needed to accomplish this include:

- Budgeting, accounting, facilities planning, maintenance, and operation.
- Financial planning and cash flow management.
- Personnel administration.
- Pupil personnel services and categorical programs.
- Legal concepts, regulations, and codes for school operations.
- Analytical techniques of management, including financial management.

Behind any array of skills involved with the management of an enterprise are assumptions about the purposes of the enterprise itself and how it should be operated, both in the eyes of those in positions of authority and from those who receive the services of the enterprise. As has been noted elsewhere, these purposes should be clearly articulated and reflected in how resources are allocated.

In the late 1930s Chester Barnard, former president of the Rockefeller Foundation and president of the New Jersey Bell Telephone, developed an important distinction in resource allocation. He separated effectiveness from efficiency. Noted Barnard:

> "...we shall say that an action is effective if it accomplished its specific objective aim. We shall also say it is efficient if it satisfies the motives of that aim, whether it is effective or not."[1]

What Barnard established was that effectiveness had to do with results and efficiency had to do with intentions. It should also be obvious that what school administrators intend to achieve via resource allocation is not necessarily what they may actually achieve in terms of results.

Many economists and public policy experts, on the other hand, measure efficiency primarily in terms of cost and time savings. Effectiveness includes less quantifiable measures such as participation and ownership. Leonard Ayers, who wrote *Laggards in Our Schools* in 1909, collected data about overage children in their respective school grade levels.[2] By assuming that an "average child" would progress year for year and that children who did not were the result of "inefficiencies," Ayers developed his own index of efficiency for some 58 city school districts. Using his own yardstick he reasoned that an efficient school system was spending about 6.5 percent of its budget on repeaters.[3]

While Ayers' assumptions have since been shown to be fallacious, his ideas and the influx of "scientific management" studies ushered in what Raymond Callahan called the age of the "educational efficiency expert." About two decades of school superintendents and professors of educational administration combined forces to apply factory models to schools. The most well known of these was the platoon school invented by William Wirt who became superintendent of schools in Gary, Indiana, in 1908.[4,5]

Echoes of this past are heard in the modern day equivalent of the efficient use of resources within the accountability movement.[6] Ralph Tyler has cited three developments that propelled the accountability movement in education:

1. The increasing proportion of family income spent on taxes.

2. The failure of many children to meet basic literacy standards demanded for employment.

3. The development of new management procedures in industry and defense.[7]

School administrators still look toward business and industry for ideas to increase participation in decision making as well as increase efficiency. Among these ideas are quality circles that appear to have accounted for the worldwide dominance of Japanese products, from automobiles to computer chips, strategic management ideas used by international business and Peters and Waterman's analysis of successful American corporations contained in *In Search of Excellence*.[8,9,10]

There is a mounting body of literature in educational administration, however, that has begun to challenge the idea that schools can be correctly run on business models. If schools are merely one type of organization and business another, then the principles underlying one would or might apply to another. What works in the business world would work in the schools with minor adaptations. However, if schools are a peculiar type of organization, quite different from business, then what works in one would not necessarily work in the other.

Budgeting, Accounting, Facilities Planning, Maintenance, and Operations

Many school administrators appear to accept the notion that what accounts for success in business will work in the schools. Beginning with PPBS (Planning, Programming, Budgeting Systems), which Robert McNamara brought to the U.S. Defense Department from the Ford Motor Company, many educational administrators tried to implement these techniques but found the recordkeeping aspects unwieldy and the formulas and measures inappropriate for many aspects of learning, schooling, and school budgets. Similarly, when President Carter tried to use zero-based budgeting (ZBB)—justifying each program by starting from a budget of zero, many public sector administrators, including school administrators, tried to use it but found it unmanageable.

More recently, however, a number of school districts have successfully adapted budgeting techniques such as program and zero-based budgeting by simplifying reporting procedures and creating easy-to-understand budget documents (see Figure 1).[11] School districts from New England to California have also found that these techniques have helped them write more coherent budget reports and win community support for programs and budget increases. Even large systems report use of such approaches as school site budgeting to simplify procedures, decentralize, and control resources closer to those who are actually using them.[12]

While school administrators should feel free to experiment and adapt effective approaches, the importance of standard accounting procedures and reporting requirements cannot be overlooked.

Perhaps one of the best sources of information regarding financial management systems for school districts lies in the use of accounting principles developed by the Association of School Business Officials (ASBO). ASBO has created a series of recommended practices for school district accounting systems. These procedures are incorporated in the ASBO Certificate of Conformance Program. The accounting system should provide:

- An accurate record of all financial transactions.

- The basis for safeguarding the financial resources of a school system.

- Adequate information required for the realization of maximum revenue and use of the system's financial resources.

- The basis for determining if local, state, or federal financial requirements have been met.[13]

Figure 1. Westfield Program Budget.

Program Budget Crosswalk
Budget Fiscal Year 1982

The Westfield (Mass.) Public Schools includes in its budget document the following "Program Budget Crosswalk" to show the specific costs for each program and what percent of the total budget each program represents.

Program Description	Salaries 1,2,3	Services 4	Suppl-Matls 4	Other 6	Equipment 8	Total Expenses	Grand Total	Percent
Art	311,637	200	37,621			37,821	349,458	2.9
Attendance	14,581		100			100	14,681	0.1
Bilingual	47,699		2,705			2,705	50,404	0.4
Board of Education		15,800	889	1,500		18,189	18,189	0.2
Building Management	547,065	1,075	1,777			2,852	549,917	4.5
Business Education	187,308	2,100	7,750			9,850	197,158	1.6
Central Management	215,325	8,200	6,225			14,425	229,750	1.9
Computer Inst.	67,744	76,515	6,330		1,800	84,645	152,389	1.2
Data Processing	55,114	27,024	13,500			40,524	95,638	0.8
EPIC	33,359		3,115			3,115	36,474	0.3
Foreign Language	168,756	2,800	2,000			4,800	173,556	1.4
Guidance	239,598	1,000	15,388	200		16,588	256,186	2.1
Home Economics	147,411	600	6,614			7,214	154,625	1.3
Industrial Arts	183,391	1,575	24,480		2,973	29,028	212,419	1.8
Instr. Support	656,040	54,152	50,105	780		105,037	761,077	6.2
Insurance		81,291				81,291	81,291	0.7
Kindergarten	162,964						162,964	1.3
Language Arts	1,525,829		36,474			36,474	1,562,303	12.9
Maintenance Plant	216,639	91,160			74,395	165,555	382,194	3.2
Mathematics	702,883		9,185			9,185	712,068	5.9
Media Service - Lib.	137,187	725	36,145		409	37,279	174,466	1.4
Medical	56,472	9,038	2,150			11,188	67,660	0.6
Music	298,825	3,150	5,686			8,836	307,661	2.5
Plant Operation	587,699	260,645	682,792			943,437	1,531,136	12.6
Phys. Ed./Health	465,326		5,835		1,985	7,820	473,146	3.9
Reading - Remedial	117,994			6,322		6,322	124,316	1.0
Science	619,450	560	22,740		371	23,671	643,121	5.3
Social Studies	745,223		10,755			10,755	755,978	6.2
Special Education	664,166	289,721	17,150		11,000	317,871	982,037	8.1
Student Activities	84,458	25,716	19,555			45,271	129,729	1.0
Transportation		484,460				484,460	484,460	4.0
Tuition		166,658				166,658	166,658	1.3
Instr. Res. Ctr.	103,304	16,090	29,458	1,500		47,048	150,352	1.2
TOTAL	9,363,447	1,620,255	1,062,846	3,980	92,933	2,780,014	12,143,461	100.0

Source:
School Budgeting: Problems and Solutions (Arlington, Va.: American Association of School Administrators, 1982 ,p. 15.

Facilities Planning, Maintenance, and Operations

Facilities planning, maintenance, and operations have always occupied a very large place in the time and attention of school administrators. Very early in the century, school construction and school buildings became one of the most pressing activities of educational leaders. The first impetus for paying attention to school facilities was simply the health of school children in classrooms.

The health of the child is always of first account, whether in the home or in the school. Conditions have often been so unfavorable in the schools of the past that it is a question whether the value of the formal education received compensated for the injury done to the health.[14]

That statement was penned in 1903 in one of the first textbooks in school administration. Still another school administration text in 1917 took note of the dangers of poor sanitation:

The frequency and extent of epidemics among school children and the terrible toll they have taken are sufficient accusation against the school as a disease-distributing agency. Few conditions could be conceived of more favorable for the transmission of infection than an unsanitary school.[15]

Preoccupation with health and growing recognition of germs and how diseases were spread caused educators to develop ideas about where schools should be built. School lots should be "located on high ground, away from all objectional noises and all unsanitary conditions."[14] Four features were considered essential: (1) the ground upon which a school building would be erected; (2) such open space in and around the building that permitted landscaping and gardening to make entrances attractive; (3) the school garden; and (4) the school playground.

When it came to construction of the school building, the classroom was cited as the heart of the school. Accordingly, a school was to be constructed from the inside out. Because this appears to be accepted as common sense by educators today, it hardly seems worth mentioning. However, it was not common practice at the time:

When the schoolrooms have been planned and arranged with reference to lighting and convenience, the architect is likely to err in completing the rest of the scheme.[14]

Standards for classrooms and schools were uniform and precise (see Figure 2).

Figure 2.
Standards for Classrooms and Schools
from S.T. Dutton, School Management: Practical Suggestions Concerning the Conduct and Life of the School, 1903.

- A room was 28 x 38 feet, good for any grade.

- The long side of the room was exposed to light.

- The rows of desks should be placed so as to leave some vacant space in front on the side farthest from the windows for tables.

- The minimum height for a first story room was 13 feet.

- Natural slate blackboards should be placed on all wall space not occupied by doors.

- Chalk receivers should be beneath the blackboards.

- The floor of the schoolroom, as of all parts of the building, should be of maple or hard pine, selected stock, grooved, and closely fitted to prevent cracks for the accumulation of dust.

- School seats should be comfortable. The desk top has a slant of 15 degrees and should be capable of being raised if work requires it.

- All light should come from one side, preferably from the left.

- There should be a minimum of one-fourth to one-fifth floor space.

- Cloak rooms may be placed either along the corridor or in separate rooms adjacent to schoolrooms. If placed in the corridors, they should be connected and locked when not in use to prevent thieving.

- School corridors should be at least nine feet wide and be well lighted.

- Staircases should be placed at either end of the building; there should be no open wells.

- Every school building should have a small reception room, neatly furnished, where the principal or teachers may meet parents or other visitors.

- The heating of the schoolhouse should be such as to secure uniform temperature of 64 degrees to 70 degrees Fahrenheit.

- Thirty cubic feet of fresh air per minute for each person.

These standards came under swift attack in the new century. In 1929 Elwood P. Cubberley offered this critique:

> The time has come, everywhere, when the building of eight-room or twelve-room boxes, with windows regularly punctured in all of the outside walls, and with the only variation from typical classrooms being an office for the principal, usually on the second floor over the entrance hall, should stop. Such buildings may have satisfied the needs of the 1870 to 1890 period, but they do not meet the needs of the present in public education. Neither do the school buildings of the 1900 period, which added a teachers' room and an assembly hall, and they will meet the needs of the future even less.

Cubberley argued that such schools were obsolete because of these trends:

- Newer types of school curriculum in use.

- The need for differentiation in school work.

- The tendency of public education to undertake new educational and community services.

- The availability of new construction materials and the emergence of state school building codes.[16]

The second consideration concerning school facilities was cost. As buildings became larger, as construction standards more specific, as land became more valuable, particularly in the inner city, the value of school property escalated. A survey conducted by the U.S. Office of Education showed that in 1905 the total reported value of school property was more than $733 million, or approximately $47 per pupil enrolled. Thirty years later that value had increased nine times and stood at $255 per pupil.[17]

Following the baby boom of World War II, school construction began to increase and peaked in fiscal year 1966-67. Between fiscal years 1951-52 and the peak year of 1966-67, local school construction costs were estimated to be approximately $128 billion. Even after the enrollment decline began to set in nationally, school costs after 1968-69 through 1977-78 were estimated to be almost $52 billion.[18]

In 1965 Donald Leu in *Planning Educational Facilities* outlined these basic steps:

Determine Local Building Needs. Leu separated the overall future plan for all school building requirements from the planning of individual schools. Determining the adequacy of existing school facilities began with a review of existing educational programs compared to desired programs. This step produced a difference or gap that led to an examination of the adequacy of school facilities to house and deliver the desired educational program. This step ensured that the future was built into the concrete and bricks that followed.

Then the question of building location and land sites was pursued, along with costing the desired plants and considerations of building financing. The important part of this step guaranteed that program considerations were the driving force for school buildings.

The adequacy of school facilities also involved determining the school organizational pattern, such as K-6-3-3 or K-5-3-4, and others. Such patterns normally have been the result of expediency rather than program planning. Enrollment projections and a calculation of building capacity with each pattern must be estimated. Such calculations are the product of assumptions regarding desired/optimal class sizes for different grade levels and/or programs compared to the expected enrollment projected. Adjustments between the two result in a determination of the space requirements within an educational facility. Once again, the central notion is to move from program to plant and not to fit program into the plant.

Planning for an Individual School. Leu's second step was to put together a planning team: the board of education, superintendent and staff, a principal, teachers, students, representative non-instructional staff, curriculum specialists, a variety of educational consultants specializing in facilities, and the architect.

This team developed the building specifications that included a statement of goals and objectives and moved to program and room requirements. These considerations were then followed by specifications for ancillary activities and needs such as storage, toilets, playrooms/gymnasiums, custodial spaces, and general lighting guidelines.

Some of the criteria for determining the adequacy of a design are:

- Capability to support the desired program
- Safety
- Health

- Economy
- Flexibility
- Expansibility
- Aesthetics.

The architect's design will obviously be dominated by the priorities of the criteria. If economy is the most important factor, then obviously other criteria will suffer.

Selection of an actual building site should consider the size of the facility and the land topography such as elevation, drainage, soil, contour, and other natural features. Location is important, and officials and architects have to consider pupil safety, crime, zoning laws, sewer access, availability of public transportation, noise, odors and dust, and other natural hazards. Costs should include the initial land acquisition, site development — including the necessity of any prior building removal, installation of utilities, and street development. Some areas of the country actually require developers to provide land parcels for schools.

Financing the Capital Outlay Program for Facility Construction. Once an educational facility's costs are determined, school administrators must consider ways of financing construction. There is a variety of funding methods to consider:

- Bond issue (with or without state aid).

- One-time payment from operating fund revenue.

- Use of a capital reserve fund.

- Combination of the three.

Public resistance to school bond issues has steadily increased over the years. In fiscal year 1964-65, 74.7 percent of bond issues were approved compared to only 46.3 percent in fiscal year 1974-75. For this reason many school administrators are looking to other funding methods. [19]

In some areas of the country, school facilities are constructed on a pay-as-you-go basis using modular construction principles and the development of one basic school plan that is repeated to minimize architectural costs. [20]

Other Challenges

Enrollment decline has forced many school districts to close schools and attempt to sell them. Such campaigns are often accompanied by political battles to maintain neighborhood schools as well as the necessity to redraw school boundaries.

In closing a school building, some important steps to consider are:

Involve the Community. School buildings are more than structures. They symbolize important periods in people's lives.

Often a community's sense of identity is tied up in its public buildings, and since schools touch the largest part of the populace, it is no wonder that closing them evokes resistance. For this reason, communities must be involved in determining which schools to close. The facts and figures concerning the rising costs of education and the expense of maintaining schools with low enrollments must be calculated and made public.

Determine How the School Building Could Be Used. Under ideal conditions, disposed school buildings should help a community retain its sense of identity, add to the quality of life, and not detract from the tax base. For this reason school buildings, with little change in the actual facade, could be used for condominiums, office space, shopping malls, or other "smokeless" industrial/business purposes.

If none of these options are workable in a community, the buildings could be used as law colleges, business and training facilities, extensions of community colleges, or community/day care schools.[21] Staff development academies, early childhood education centers, and special education administrative centers are also possible uses.

Organize an Informational Campaign. Administrators can alleviate possible fears in the community through organizing a campaign that makes all of the facts public. Community forums and meetings, newspaper articles and flyers, block gatherings, and speeches to service and church groups are an essential element of school disposal efforts.

Plant Operation and Maintenance Costs

Next to instruction and fixed charges, plant operation and maintenance costs are the largest major school expenditures, estimated to be approximately 10 to 15 percent of all schools' operational budgets.[22,28]

School administrators must develop long term plans to maintain school facilities. In too many school districts, plant maintenance is curtailed to the point where only large scale expenditures can restore school buildings to a safe and adequate status. Ongoing maintenance costs to repair roofs, electrical wiring, external and internal walls, and other facilities and systems must be kept operational and safe. Making sure the members of the board of education regularly tour all school facilities prior to budget development is one way to keep a focus on the condition of schools and to ensure that the facilities remain safe, clean, and educationally functional.

Emerging Concerns

An emerging area of concern to school admnistrators is maintaining the safety of school facilities. For example, the widespread use of asbestos in school construction in a 20-year period between 1940 and 1960 as fireproofing, soundproofing, and to insulate pipes, walls, ceilings and boilers, has resulted in a potential health hazard of epidemic proportions. [23] As asbestos ages, it releases particles into hallways, classrooms, and other work spaces that can cause lung cancer or asbestosis, a severe scarring of the lungs.

The asbestos hazard is estimated to exist in approximately 121,000 schools now serving 80 million children.[24]

Other dangers in maintaining school facilities are the widespread use of pesticides, particularly a group of chemical compounds generally termed "chlorinated cyclodines" such as chlordane, heptachlor, and aldrin. These chemicals, which have been used extensively in treating houses and schools for termites and other insect pests, are known to have caused cancer in some laboratory animals. As a result, they are banned or subject to tight regulations in several states.

To assist in identifying potential hazards, a growing number of independent laboratories licensed by the American Industrial Hygiene Association now perform environmental audits of schools. School administrators are learning a new vocabulary about various toxic materials and substances and ways to detect them in services performed by such labs. Figure 3 lists common pollutants and the methods used to detect them.

Figure 3.
Some Common Pollutants and Their Detection Methods.

Pollutant/Toxic Substance	Detection Method
Asbestos, arsenic, lead, mercury, phenols	electron microscopy (blood, urine, and tissue)
Pesticides, PCB's, naphtha, kerosene, formaldehyde, benzene, chloroform, toluene, xylene	gas chromatography
Poisonous metals (aluminum, barium, cobalt, magnesium, manganese, zinc)	atomic absorption spectro-photometry
Common ions (ammonia, formic acid, nitrite, fluoride, sulfate)	ion chromatography

Figure 4.
Steps in the Removal of Pollutants.

1. Employ a Qualified Industrial Hygiene Laboratory
Health and environmental data should be gathered by a certified and qualified industrial environmental lab. Such labs are accredited by the American Industrial Hygiene Association (AIHA).

2. Notify County/State Health Departments
County/state health departments should be notified immediately of a suspected problem. In some cases these agencies perform free tests and analysis; most have the authority to close down a school or recommend actions if they believe a health hazard exists.

3. Take Emergency Steps — Location and Decontamination
Based on data gathered by either an accredited environmental lab and/or county/health department, emergency steps can be taken such as closing off suspected contaminated areas, supplying alternative sources of water, or suspending school for a specified time period to permit testing and location of the pollutant. Once a source of contamination is found, cleanup procedures should be undertaken immediately with the supervision of authorities or environmental lab consultants.

4. Re-Testing
Prior to any reopening of a contaminated area, testing must be done to determine if cleanup procedures have been effective. This is essential to maintain the public confidence and to protect against any possible legal liabilities.

5. Reopen School Environment
After retesting has confirmed a safe school environment, the school or area should be reopened quickly and used normally. This step quells rumors and puts the school back into "business as usual" without fanfare.

As more chemicals are used in everyday life, administrators will also have to worry about the safety of their drinking water, particularly if the water supply comes from ground or well sources. Such water may be contaminated with pesticides, inorganics such as arsenic, lead, and mercury, and fecal coliform. Air pollution and noise pollution are also more common than supposed and should be evaluated. Figure 4 outlines some recommended procedures if you suspect a pollutant in a school environment.

It is possible that school administrators will continue to encounter problems with such pollutants in increasing frequency as the dangers of indiscriminate chemical use and other substances become evident. To obtain information about possible dangerous pollutants, administrators and others may refer to:

● The National Library of Medicine of the National Institute of Health (NIH), which contains data on known and potential toxicants. Operational since 1978, its initial inventory consisted of 987 chemicals. Information is selected by the Oak Ridge National Laboratory.

● The Chemical Information System (CIS), maintained by the Fein-Marquart Associates of Baltimore, Maryland, under contract to NIH and the Environmental Protection Agency. Since 1972, this file has concentrated on mass spectrometry and includes 40 files on more than 116,000 chemical substances.[25]

Financial Planning
and Cash Flow Management

Expenditures for all forms of education, elementary and secondary (public and private) and higher education consumed about 3.4 percent of the Gross National Product in 1949. By 1967 the percentage of the GNP spent for education had doubled. In 1973 the percentage of the GNP spent for education exceeded all expenditures for defense.[26]

Since 1969, Americans have spent between 4.3 and 4.7 percent of their personal income for elementary/secondary education.[27] The figures belie the reality of the truly precarious state of education finances.

Historically, the first need was to establish a stable base of financial support for public education. Early American legislators realized that education for all was a building block for our democracy. However, their vision did not extend to taxation of all the people to pay for it.[28] Schools were financed with local taxation, tuition fees, and some state aid. Property tax was considered the fairest way to support education. As enrollments grew and costs increased, the inequities of this financial base appeared.

Property tax became a problem because of disparities in actual assessments taxes collected, exemptions types, and changing definitions of wealth. In modern society, land is only one form of wealth among many others.

As a result, many state legislators moved to create newer taxation standards to support public schools. Three types of standards are now used:

● *Fiscal Neutrality*. This standard shows the expenditures per pupil should be directly proportionate to the school district's wealth. Therefore, a state must develop a tax structure that forces equal funds to be collected from school districts not equal in wealth.

● *Equal Expenditures or Equal Inputs*. This approach to financing schools requires equal expenditures per pupil between districts or at least equality of educational offerings between districts.

● *Equal Outcomes*. Another look at the problem is to recognize that there must be inequality of inputs because students are different, but that this should lead to equality of output, the same results. Thus, poorer districts would have to spend more and richer districts spend less to realize equal outcomes.

These standards have evolved largely from litigation, initiated by the California Serrano Supreme Court decision. Over half of the states have experienced school finance litigation of one kind or another, and it is likely that such litigation will not cease as long as serious inequalities remain in the financing of public education.[27]

Cash Flow Management

Financial tightness forces school districts, like others, to improve their cash management practices. We recommend these steps to improve cash management practices:

• *Cash forecasting*. Develop a comprehensive plan based on short and long term receipts and disbursements.

• *Collections*. Improve billing practices for school districts that provide more cash for investment; for example, establishing late payment penalities or changing collection methods.

• *Improved bank relations*. Local school districts are often one of the biggest businesses in town. Shop around for the best bank interest rates possible and consider a more regional national market. This means developing competitive bidding procedures and engaging in negotiations on service charges.

• *Control of disbursements*. Manage the outflow of payments to take advantage of the district's funds for as long as possible. Unless there is a discount for them, making payments early is not a good idea, and the district may earn more money having the money in use elsewhere.

• *Concentration of cash deposits*. Collect promptly in one account and reduce time needed to mass resources for investment purposes.

• *Develop sound investment policies and procedures*. At the heart of good policies and procedures should be the notion that all available funds not essential to the district's operations should be invested. The policies should also require competitive bank bidding for treasury bills and certificates of deposits. Investments should be made early and be kept as long as possible.[29]

Personnel Administration

With 70 percent or more of most school budgets locked up in people, their salaries, and fringe benefits, it is no small wonder that personnel management has become increasingly important for school systems. Today, school administrators have to deal with tenure laws, grievance procedures, layoff rules, certification standards, teacher competency tests, salary schedules, and unchallenged evaluation techniques.

Two forces impacting on school district personnel offices and adding to increased paper work requirements are:

• Expanded federal and state requirements to demonstrate lack of discrimination in hiring, promotion, or dismissals on the basis of sex, race, or age.

• Union contractual stipulations that have brought about a requirement for improved evaluation procedures and techniques.

School district personnel offices also feel pressure over teacher burnout, layoffs, and employee problems with alcohol and substance abuse. As states alter certification requirements to include teacher competency testing adding more paper work, personnel administrators turn to automation as one solution to simplify recordkeeping and routine administration. Figure 5 outlines the personnel functions of school administrators.

Figure 5.
School System Personnel Activities.

Area

What School Administrators Do

1. Organization/Position Design and Description

- Analyze total work flow based on policy decisions

- Compare organizational structure to design requirements/desired outcomes

- Conduct position analysis to reveal discrepancies such as duplication of work or gaps in work assignment

- Construct alternative organizational/position designs for cost benefit analysis

- Select organization/position design that best fits overall requirements for effective work assignments

2. Staff Recruitment/ Selection

- Conduct staffing projections to identify organizational needs on short/long term basis

- Construct strategies for staff recruitment including markets/ locations most likely to have types of people required

- Engage in staff recruitment against specified targets to fill stated projections

- Define/refine selection procedures in harmony with state/ federal laws regarding discrimination practices and audit trails to prove no discrimination

3. Design/Administer Employee Compensation Systems

- Construct compensation system to reinforce organizational mission and basic work flow patterns

- Evaluate compensation system on equity, rationality competitiveness, retention, job performance, responsiveness, and promotion of career growth

4. Implement/Monitor Collective Bargaining

- Update compensation systems to promote effective organizational design and serve as the backup for collective bargaining required

- Provide backup data for collective negotiation

- Provide briefing sessions for administrative staff during negotiations

- Conduct staff development sessions for administrators after negotiations.

5. Process Grievance/ Arbitrations and Resolution of Work-Related Disputes

- Establish monitoring procedures to ensure responsible contract negotiations at all levels

- Establish procedures for processing work-related disputes contained in binding labor contracts

- Establish procedures for processing disputes regarding hiring, transfer, evaluation, and dismissal

- Maintain accurate records of all such disputes for future records/ references

- Monitor adherence to rulings on all work-related disputes

6. Monitor Work Climate/ Productivity

- Conduct climate surveys of schools and the total district

- Develop productivity and effective work load standards and measurements

- Monitor organizational productivity against established work standards

- Evaluate work flow patterns

7. Design/Implement Evaluating Procedures

- Design evaluation procedures and instruments that accurately reflect work achievement

- Conduct staff inservice training on proper use of measures

- Collect and record accurate and timely work-related achievement data

8. Retain Accurate Employment Record	• Establish procedures and recordkeeping systems concerning all aspects of employment such as certification, salary placement, promotion/tenure/transfer, dismissal, retirement, or termination data

One of the dilemmas school administrators face is educating the public about the complexities of managing a labor intensive organization such as a school district. Many people still envision schools as places where teachers instruct children and principals supervise teachers.

Part of the education of the public can take place when a personnel administrator briefs the school board (and hence the public) on personnel practices such as the steps in handling a grievance, arbitration, or transferring teachers according to contractual timelines and methods. Making union contracts public documents along with job descriptions of all administrative officers is another sound practice in dealing with public understanding of school district operations.

It can only have a positive effect if taxpayers realize that contract negotiations are an important part of deliberations. Multiyear contracts that call for across-the-board salary increases ensure automatic budget increases for future years. That leaves only supplies, equipment, and materials, normally a small percentage of any school budget, for budget cutting. Budget cutting comes too little, too late if contract negotiations have given away the financial store.

Pupil Personnel Services and Categorical Programs

Universal schooling through at least high school for all students has developed demands for other services also.

Counseling services once were thought to be part of a classroom teacher's responsibilities. An extension of a teacher's role as counselor was the homeroom. Homeroom was envisioned as a place where students learned and received instruction about a variety of problems not formally in the academic curriculum. [30]

Today the job of counseling has become a full-time one in most secondary schools. The titles of social workers, psychologists, psychiatrists, medical doctors, speech pathologists, learning disability specialists, and others now dot school district tables of organization. School personnel confront every conceivable type of social problem including alcohol and substance abuse, suicide, pregnancy, runaways, incest, and various forms of child abuse. Breakdowns in society have found their place in public schools with corresponding demands and counter-demands for services mixed in with opposition that such services represent an intrusion into the home and family.

Before adding pupil personnel services, school administrators should be aware of the practical and political problems of classifying students. The first recognition of differences in pupils was made in the 1890s for the blind, crippled, and mentally handicapped. [31] However, these traditional terms have not always served the pupils they were intended to help very well. Elliot L. Richardson, a former secretary of Health, Education, and Welfare, expressed concern regarding the use of "inappropriate labeling of children as delinquent, retarded, hyperkinetic, mentally ill, or emotionally disturbed." Richardson pushed for development of better classification practices and wider understanding in labeling students.[32]

Since then five criteria have been developed to assist schools in developing classification systems. They are:

1. *Reliability*—the capability of a classification system to be reproducible from one student to another with a different diagnostician.

2. *Coverage*—the classification system includes all of the characteristics of the individuals being classified.

3. *Logical consistency*—any set of criteria must be internally consistent and not mixtures of criteria. If a scheme is hierarchical, the assumptions underlying the relationships must be stated.

4. *Clinical utility*—since labeling of students can produce a self-fulfilling prophecy, the corresponding negative impact on the student should be offset by a positive gain in services based on a relationship to those services in a clinical setting.

5. *Acceptability to users*—any classification system must be good enough to be used by professional people on a day-to-day basis. If it is too complex, it will not be used. If it is too simplistic, it may do harm to both students and professionals by presenting only one dimensional perspectives.[33]

Educators and medical experts are in the process of changing the labels and definitions used in the public schools. There have been three classification systems for mental retardation in use in the U.S. alone, and a shift is occurring in examining systems for children who are blind, visually handicapped, or hearing-handicapped. The change reflects a move from structural to functional criteria. For example, functional labels include treatment needs and procedures to be employed, a feature often lacking in a purely structural definition of a handicap.[34]

With a blind student, a statement of a vision defect is replaced by categories such as total blindness, partial impairment of vision, social blindness, virtual blindness, and unspecified or undetermined blindness.[35] School administrators must be sensitive to labels and procedures that come to be accepted as role definitions in the school organization as they relate to pupil personnel services. Services should help and not hinder the growth of these students.

When considering the adequacy of the existing range of pupil personnel services in a district, school administrators may find it useful to employ these questions.

- What is the nature of the need, service, or condition that currently exists?

- In what ways is the need, service, or condition not being met now?

- In what ways is the need, service, or condition being addressed?

- What is the rationale for the school to be interested in meeting the need, providing the service, or addressing the condition being described?

- Is the school the appropriate agency or institution to meet the need, provide the service, or address the condition? If not, what agency or institution is better qualified, strategically positioned, or supported to do so?

- What will the impact be on the school if it employs the personnel to meet the need, provide the service, or address the condition?

- What are the costs and the benefits to the students, the school, and the community of accepting the responsibility, providing the service, or addressing the condition?

- What will happen if the school does not meet the need, provide the service, or address the condition?

- What problems will the school most likely face if it accepts the requirement to meet the need, provide the service, or address the condition (political, fiscal, contractual, legal, staffing/scheduling, curricular, organizational)?

- On what basis will the pupil personnel services be determined to be effective in the future? If they are judged not to be effective, how will or can they be changed or eliminated?

The area of pupil personnel services is one of the fastest growing sectors of many school systems. Careful attention should be given to answering thoroughly questions that document the needs and anticipate the consequences for expansion of this area.

Categorical Programs

The first person to advocate federal aid for education was Col. Timothy Pickering in 1783. Pickering proposed that surplus land in the Ohio Territory be used for public schools. The first federal legislation concerned with public education was the Land Ordinance of 1785. The Continental Congress determined that lands in the Northwest be divided into townships and that each township designate one section for public schools.[35]

Federal involvement in education as we know it today was slow to develop. In 1862, the Morrill Act donated federal lands for the establishment of colleges. MIT, Ohio State, and the University of California owe their origins to this historic piece of federal legislation.

President Andrew Johnson established a federal department of education in 1867, which was later reduced to a bureau in the department of interior. The Smith-Hughes Act, following World War I, promoted vocational education and home economics in secondary schools.

Following World War II, the Service Man's Readjustment Act, or the "G.I. Bill," helped veterans attend college. As a result, 8 million people went to school at a cost of more than $14 billion.

In 1950 Congress appropriated funds to local school districts to assist with hardships caused by increased enrollments due to large military installations. Public Laws 815 and 874 provided funds for facility construction and operating revenue. PL 874 marked the first time federal monies were used for general local school district operating costs.

Soviet success in the early space race to the moon resulted in the passage of the National Defense Education Act in 1958 with federal monies allocated to foster excellence in science, mathematics, and foreign language acquisition. To deal with problems of equity, the Elementary and Secondary Education acts of President Johnson's "Great Society" program ushered forth the massive and large scale federal funding of local public education experienced by most contemporary school administrators in 1965. Slightly more than one decade later, federal categorical funds had penetrated well over three-fourths of the nation's school systems. For the most part, federal programs brought with them rational planning models borrowed from economics, operations research, and industrial/business settings.

At the local levels, school administrators often struggled with new concepts and terminology that required hard data, feedback loops, action on data, and program adjustments and decisions. To obtain federal funds, local districts had to conform to federal guidelines. Even if the guidelines provided wide variations, they nonetheless mandated a type of thinking about programs that was not necessarily present before the Elementary and Secondary Education Act of 1965 was modified by the Education Consolidation and Improvement Act of 1981.

It becomes evident in reviewing various federal programs that administrators need a common set of skills to work with and implement categorical programs. Figure 6 lists some of the general administrative skills that will help administrators "handle" the programs.

Figure 6.
General Administrative Skills Required
to Develop Categorical Programs.

- Conduct a needs assessment (mostly to determine discrepancies)

- Construct appropriate programs with proper instruction modes (such as regular classroom instruction, learning labs, learning stations) to match a validated (agreed on) set of program objectives

- Accurately compute existing budgeting operations

- Develop a program budget that differentiates among various types of costs including per pupil expenditures, salaries, and fringe benefits

- Relate proper levels of professional staffing to program components

- Convert staffing assignments to mathematical descriptors (For example, FTE — full time equivalents)

- Clearly identify the client population and how it is to be served by the program

- Write an appropriate project narrative

- Select evaluation strategies and tools that match program objectives and report the results to various audiences

- Engage in team planning including teachers and parents at various stages of development and data feedback.

The federal presence in education was firmly established with ESEA (1965), and it is not likely that it will ever return to levels below pre-ESEA days. For this reason working effectively with federal programs is an important skill for a school administrator.

Legal Concepts, Regulations, and Codes for School Operations

The basis for legal standing of the schools rests largely upon "common law."[36] The genesis of common law lies in the customs, mores, and beliefs of a people and how they are acted on and interpreted in judicial proceedings to determine proper conduct. Common law is known as "case law," as contrasted with constitutional or legal power derived from statutes.

School administrators come to know school law from relevant legal suits or cases. The role of administrators, and in particular superintendents, is highly ambiguous because its power is also derived from case law and not statute. The actual power of the superintendency is more contractually defined by local school boards than state law.[37]

As a consequence school boards may not perceive a superintendent's actual authority correctly or clearly. The public is confused about the chief school officer's legal status, and the superintendent's ability to be a real innovator is sometimes hindered. This is evident particularly during collective bargaining because the superintendent is neither a member of the board nor an employee of the district, as are other employees. Does the superintendent represent teachers or principals to the board?

Administrators should also be aware of the general standards or expectations, peculiarly American, that dominate our educational systems. The precepts of equal opportunity, of personal freedom and the need for the individual to achieve his or her maximum potential have been the basis of extensive litigation procedures and will continue to be so. For this reason it is important to keep abreast of any rulings and understand the regulations developed to enforce them.[38]

In general, litigation and court rulings continue to revolve around these areas in public education:

- Religion and prayer.
- Finance and equity in school support.
- Collective bargaining.
- Student rights and problems.
- Employee rights.
- Desegregation.
- Handicapped students' rights.

Litigation Concerning Religion and Prayer

Determining the place of religion and which of its values to embrace in the school, its activities, and curriculum, continue to be sources of confrontation at all levels of American society. In *Abington v. Schempp* (1963) the U.S. Supreme Court held that Bible reading violated the establishment clause of the First Amendment. One year earlier the Supreme Court had banned school prayers, including a supposedly "neutral" statement adopted by the New York Board of Regents that said: "Almighty God, we acknowledge our dependence upon Thee, and we beg Thy blessings upon us, our parents, our teachers, and our country." In *Engel v. Vitale* case the court found that the state of New York could not sponsor a religious activity.

Bible reading and prayer continue to be sources of litigation in public schools. Controversies stemming from the "moment of silence" exercise at the beginning of a school day engender heated debate.[39] A 1983 survey of school administrators and superintendents in North Carolina indicated that prayer was conducted at various times in 31 percent of the public schools and that daily prayer was held in at least one of six schools.[40]

Right wing Christian fundamentalists have attacked public schools on various legal fronts. They object to:

- Teaching evolution or sex education.

- Not allowing prayer and Bible reading in the schools.

- Instilling a hidden set of values or moral principles sometimes referred to as "secular humanism."[41]

Secular humanism has become a "code word" among the New Right and is used to brand public school teachers, college instructors, liberals, feminists, atheists, civil libertarians, and internationalists.

The evolution controversy in science curriculum has led to a movement to teach "scientific creationism" as a curricular counterpoint to Darwin's ideas, but in *McLean v. Arkansas Board of Education* creationism was struck down as a violation of the Constitution because it promoted religion. The battle continues in other states.

Attempts to censor the schools and public libraries will continue, and for these reasons administrators need to be aware of the details and be prepared in the event their school system faces any litigation proceedings.

Litigation Regarding Finance and School Resources

Since 1968, 27 states have been involved in litigation regarding school financial support. Seventeen state high courts have ruled on these cases. In eight states, state approaches toward financial support were found acceptable within state constitutions. In nine states the opposite was determined. [27] The base of most of this litigation is the three standards we referred to earlier.

Perhaps the most famous case was the 1971 *Serrano v. Priest* decision by the California Supreme Court, which found that the quality of a child's education depended upon the resources of his school district and ultimately upon the pocketbook of his parents".[42] Thus, California's method of support for public schools was a function of wealth and it violated the concept of state "fiscal neutrality."

When many of the same arguments were raised at the federal level in the case of *San Antonio Independent School District v. Rodriguez* in 1973, in the only opinion of the U.S. Supreme Court on educational finance, the Court held that education was not a fundamental right under the U.S. Constitution, and, therefore, inequities in local/state financing could not be litigated at the federal level. This was particularly the case when there was no "suspect class" involved, and there was "an absence of any evidence that the financing system discriminates against any definable category of 'poor' people or that it results in the absolute deprivation of education — the disadvantaged class is not susceptible of identification in traditional terms."[42]

Apart from knowledge regarding taxation and finance, school administrators must know something about their personal liabilities and responsibilities for the fiscal operations of a school or system. Cases involving misuse of taxpayer funds are rather extensive in the bodies of almost every state. Administrators are also expected to take prudent steps to safeguard the property of the school district.

Another area in which school administrators are called on to establish policies and procedures relates to student fees. As various school systems experience fiscal difficulties in supporting a comprehensive educational program that includes cocurricular and extracurricular activities, they have resorted to charging students a variety of fees. The California State Supreme Court has ruled that school systems may not charge students fees even for extracurricular activities since these experiences are "educational in character."

The press to use every tax dollar by producing interest from short term investments has become rather widespread in school district financial management practices but obviously caution must be used in this area. In 1982, some 700 New York state school districts earned more than $100 million from such short term investments. However, when a major security firm went bankrupt, at least $45 million in investment capital of some 30 school districts in Alaska, Florida, New York, and California were left holding the bag. Noted one spokesperson for a state controller's office, "You can't regulate good sense on a local level … These districts are prey to anyone who can sell them on a high yield."[43]

To avoid costly litigation and financial loss, school administrators have been urged to move away from repurchase ("repos") agreements in favor of doing business with large commercial banks and investing in treasury bills.[44]

Investments can be protected by making sure that treasury notes pledged against district money have numbers and that the numbers are provided to the district as part of a written agreement. The notes backing the investment should be in a separate secured account in the district's name, preventing the backing paper from being used again. Banks rather than holding companies are a better choice for making such investments. While some insurance companies will provide a surety bond to protect against default, the costs may be prohibitive.

Collective Bargaining

Teacher unions and collective bargaining are here to stay in American education. While teacher unions/associations have been around since 1845, collective bargaining was not embraced as a "professional practice" at the local level until the 1940s as a matter of national policy. The American Federation of Teachers (AFT) even disavowed strikes until the 1950s.[45]

Intense rivalry between the NEA and AFT, as well as increased militancy among teachers in the 1960s, led to an all-time high of 114 teacher strikes or work stoppages capped by the 1968 statewide teacher strike in Florida backed by the NEA.

Legally, states have either adopted an outright collective bargaining law or enacted legislation that enables school boards and teachers to bargain together voluntarily. Only in a few states has the right of public employees to organize for bargaining been prohibited or limited by law.

A typical teacher union contract deals with salary and working conditions, including fringe benefits. While these may vary slightly from state to state and locality to locality, it is normal to find written contracts between teacher unions and associations with boards of education covering these clauses and concepts:

- Salaries, schedules, wage increases.
- Work hours.
- Work loads, scheduling.
- Assignment of personnel.
- Promotion, transfer, layoff provisions.
- Length of school day and year.
- Observations and evaluations of teachers.
- Preparation periods and extra duty assignments.
- Class size.
- Changes in curriculum, programs, innovations.
- Personnel files, charges against teachers, parental complaints.
- After school meetings, extra work assignments.
- Relief from clerical/non-teaching duties.

School administrators have come to understand through bitter experience that collective bargaining as it is practiced is frequently and unfortunately an adversarial process, pitting them against teachers and their unions. The same holds true for school boards.

> It requires that a board of education achieve a consensus among all interest groups but teachers and then defend that consensus against a consensus among teachers as developed and articulated

by a teacher organization. As a result, a board of education and school management engaged in bargaining must often abandon its neutral role of mediator and assume an active role as adversary to teachers.[45]

The evaluation of teachers within highly unionized settings is often difficult or takes so long that it can become virtually impossible to eliminate all but the most blatant forms of incompetency.[46]

Obviously, administrators working in highly unionized settings must be fully prepared for these circumstances. Whereas in most districts superintendents do not actually sit in on collective bargaining sessions or evaluate the classroom teacher, they should be well versed in what their subordinates are doing.

Student Rights and Problems

Modern school operations and student problems have come a long way since Gilbert Morrison stood before the 1904 annual meeting of the NEA and declared that one of the most serious problems facing high school was secret student groups.[48]

School administrators have come to understand complex new legal and social problems with each change in American society. Changing sexual mores, student pregnancy, one-parent families caused by escalating divorce rates, alcoholism and substance abuse, and the emerging student suicide phenomenon are just a few.

Before 1969 almost all matters involving a school's authority to discipline or control students in school settings were given to the state courts, who almost without exception provided wide latitude to school boards and their administrators to govern all facets of student life. All the courts required was that as long as school rules were rooted in a legitimate educational purpose, they could be defended and therefore upheld.

In 1969, though, the U.S. Supreme Court held in *Tinker v. Des Moines* that school authorities could not suspend students who had worn black armbands in a protest against the Vietnam War because such symbols were almost "pure speech" and protected by the First Amendment.

The Supreme Court noted that the wearing of the armbands was:

> ...unaccompanied by any disorder or disturbance on the part of the petitioners. There is no evidence whatever of petitioners' interference, actual or nascent, with the schools' work or of collision with the rights of other students to be secure and to be let alone.[42]

The judgment in *Tinker* that students had nearly the same rights as adults under the U.S. Constitution, while they attended school, radically altered traditional ideas of discipline. Student publications became impossible or difficult to censor; student activities and political activism expanded; student dress codes were more or less abolished, and the "due process" rights of representation were afforded to minors to be suspended or expelled.

It would be foolish to use the *Tinker* decision as the sole cause of the changes cited, but *Tinker* provided the legal umbrella for a wholly different look at the role of schools in disciplining students under the doctrine of in loco parentis. As parents have generally become more permissive with their children, this change has been reflected in the courts and the schools.

Employee Rights

The docile schoolmarm, long part of the American teaching work force, is long gone. Carefully prescribed rules and regulations regarding a teacher's personal life have disappeared.

As employees teachers have acquired the right to act like anybody else in our society, as noted by *The New York Times* columnist Gene Maeroff;

> Their personal conduct is no longer so circumscribed and now teachers are usually able to dress as they please, wear beards and long hair, be seen in public on dates, work in political campaigns, and even declare their homosexuality without losing their jobs. [49]

Teacher restrictions about criticizing the actions of their bosses in public have also been struck as unconstitutional. The classic 1968 case of *Pickering v. Board of Education* rendered by the U.S. Supreme Court concerned a letter written by a high school teacher to the editor of the local paper. The teacher's statement was highly critical of actions by his school board and superintendent concerning a proposed tax increase. The board felt that Pickering's letter was detrimental to the operations of the school district and was questioning the integrity of the board. Pickering was fired.

The U.S. Supreme Court rejected any claim that a teacher by virtue of his or her employment forfeits or abridges any rights enjoyed by all citizens under the Constitution.

The implications of *Pickering* for school administrators are that teachers or anybody else don't need advance approval to speak critically of school board or superintendent actions. Teachers and principals may draft letters to the newspapers critical of their superiors' actions like any other citizen. While their actions may be questionable professional ethics, they cannot be legally presented.

Other areas of caution for administrators and school boards were opened up with the Supreme Court ruling in the *Board of Education of Paris Union School District No. 95 v. Vail* (1984). The Court let stand a Circuit Court ruling on the question of whether a teacher who was given verbal assurances by officials of two years' employment but was hired under a one-year contract (due to a local policy) had a constitutionally protected right to be employed for two years. The Circuit Court ruled in favor of the employee. Clearly, school officials must be careful in making promises to an employee that differ from the terms of the contract, even though an oral contract may be prohibited under state law. [67]

Sexual Discrimination

Compensation systems that differentiate between males and females have been voided as well. In 1937 the Indiana Supreme Court held that there was no rational basis for a personnel classification that treated married women differently.

Title IX of the Education Amendments of 1972 (PL 92-318), which prohibits certain forms of sex discrimination, has brought about expanded athletic programs for girls in elementary/secondary education and higher education. It has also sought to end discrimination in course selections and offerings and provided legal mechanisms for women to file grievances if they believe they had been discriminated against.

Complaints against school systems have also moved into job discrimination in school administration. Women have organized groups to take action against school districts that have appeared to practice discrimination against them.

Complaints can be filed with the Office of Civil Rights (OCR), which has the legal clout to investigate. Such investigations can be exhaustive and time consuming for local school administrators who must respond to such charges. OCR looks for patterns of appointments or trends in recruitment that result in discrimination. An examination of data sources indicates that approximately 16 percent of the 43,000 principals in the U.S. are female and only between two and four percent of the nation's superintendents are female.[50]

Women's organizations charge that female candidates are often asked illegal questions about home, family, and personal lives in interviews. Most consultants who conduct superintendency searches are male, and school boards, even when the majority of members may be women, are not aggressive enough in seeking qualified female candidates for administrative positions.[51] These conditions perpetuate a male-dominated administrative hierarchy that will not be changed overnight and that will be a source of continuing litigation for many local school districts and their administrative staffs.

School Desegregation

Few areas of education have been subject to greater litigation than desegregation of the public schools. Again and again the federal courts have been called to clarify and rule the adequacy of efforts by boards of education and school administrators to adhere to the law.

Brown vs. Board of Education (1954) marked the beginning of the end of the "separate but equal" concept of education. The impact of *Brown* must be judged in the long view. By bringing into focus almost 100 years of legal segregation, the court set new standards of both operational and legal expectations for public education. By setting such a new standard, public opinion could be swayed and re-crystallized around a new set of principles by which the schools would function in the future.

However, the U.S. Supreme Court had to rule again in *Cooper v. Aaron* (1958) that even when state authorities were hostile to school desegregation efforts, as in Little Rock, the school board could not renege on its obligation to provide education with the argument of maintaining law and order. Twenty-five years later, a federal district judge in Little Rock, Arkansas, ruled that two largely white suburban school districts had contributed to racial isolation and segregation and ordered the consolidation of the school districts.

A controversial aspect of the U.S. Supreme Court's rulings on school desegregation has been the busing issue. Because of the nature of many school systems — cities are part of larger county governmental units — desegregation could not occur without the aid of the school bus.

The issue came to a head in *Swann v. Charlotte-Mecklenburg Board of Education* (1971). The U.S. Supreme Court found that Charlotte-Mecklenburg was a state-enforced dual segregated school system in violation of *Brown*. It also overturned objections about using busing for integration purposes. The Court's message was clear. The school district had to use busing as a method to achieve a unitary school system that was in fact desegregated.

School busing for purposes of achieving racial integration has been contested in both state legislatures and Congress ever since *Swann*. Efforts to use busing to integrate the Los Angeles Public Schools were halted, however, when voters approved an initiative halting mandatory transportation for integrating that public school system.

Litigation continues in the issue in many school systems. The matter is far from settled politically, socially, economically, and educationally. Some feel it will not be resolved until housing patterns are also changed. Public schools cannot escape from either being blamed for perpetuating remnants of racial segregation nor from being used as a tool to eliminate such remnants in the larger society.

Rights of Handicapped Pupils

Nowhere have judicial concepts such as due process and equal protection been more important than in education of the handicapped. Two landmark cases have firmly established these principles.

In *Mills v. Board of Education of the District of Columbia* in 1971, and *Pennsylvania Association for Retarded Children v. Commonwealth of Pennsylvania* in 1972, retarded students could not be denied entrance to the public schools without due process. The policies in dispute in both cases violated the Fourteenth and Fifth amendments.

When due process was embodied in historic PL 94-142, it defined procedural due process for the handicapped as follows:

- The right to notice.

- The right to hearing.

- The right to personal presence.

- The right to counsel.

- The right to raise issues.

- The right to protection against arbitrary rulings and the right to fairness and impartiality.

- The right to a hearing time.
- The right to proof of damages.
- The right to introduce evidence.
- The right to a hearing before a tribunal of jurisdiction.[52]

Furthermore, the notion of the LRE (Least Restrictive Environment) or *mainstreaming*, is at heart a legal concept, not an educational one. It has been expressed legally in such terms as, "the less drastic means," "the reasonable alternative," or the "less intrusive alternative."[52]

Another ruling dealt with whether or not states can require handicapped students to pass competency tests to receive high school diplomas. The U.S. Supreme Court refused to hear a case in which a local district had awarded high school diplomas to handicapped students who had passed their IEP's (Individualized Educational Plans) but had not passed the New York competency tests required of other students.

While a trial judge ruled initially in favor of the students, both the state's intermediate and highest courts reversed the decision saying that handicapped students had no property right to a diploma nor any right to be free from the stigma of being denied one.

A similar ruling concerning student competency testing for all students was reached in the case of *Debra P. v. Turlington* (1981). Further legal battles should clarify the role of the courts in protecting student rights and ensuring that competency tests are valid indicators of true learning and later success in life.[53]

Another important ruling on the rights of handicapped students is *Irving Independent School District v. Tatro* (1984) in which the Supreme Court upheld Congress's goal in enacting the Education for All Handicapped Children Act. They held that "related services" were part of a free appropriate education to be provided by public schools and then circumscribed circumstances of related services as: (1) only handicapped children are eligible; (2) the service must be necessary to enable a student to benefit from special education; and (3) the service must not require a physician for its administration. The Court did not address the issue of whether schools would be required to obtain equipment for services.[67]

Analytical Techniques of Management

Today school administrators are expected to know and use advanced management techniques from colleges and universities, corporate leaders, and from their own professional readings and conference attendance.[54]

No matter the source, the analytical techniques of management are:

- Decision theories.
- Organizational theories.
- Financial concepts/applications.
- Planning and evaluation techniques.

- Program management techniques (curriculum and instruction).

- Political theories, politics, and policy development.

Contrary to what some may think about the place of theory in the day-to-day operations of a school, almost all actions have some theoretical base, even if it isn't known to the practitioner. This is particularly true of organizations like schools, which have evolved over many years. Schools are contrived social organizations. They are not "natural" in this sense.

To explain, understand, describe, and predict actions in the schools, administrators must deal with theory, and believe it or not, there is nothing as practical as good theory because it does just that: it helps, it describes, it explains, and it predicts.

Decision Theories

Decision theory deals with the types of decisions made in social organizations, of which schools are one type. There are two categories of social decision processes: (1) citizen or individual decisions and (2) proxy decisions.[56]

When two professionals make individual choices that can be counted as in voting, this is a process of collective choice, *citiprocesses*. The second type of decision is made by a "proxy" or representative. This occurs when a person makes decisions for others, as when a union leader represents teachers at the bargaining table. Sometimes as it occurs in organizational life, the decision-making process is a hybrid of the two types of basic process.

For example, the operation of a school district is largely hybrid decision making. It typically begins with an election of a school board (a citiprocess), delegation of authority to a superintendent and administrative staff (proxiprocess), participation by lay and professional committees (citiprocesses), and arbitration of labor-management disputes (a proxiprocess).

Knowing which organizational component contains which dominant process is useful in examining and analyzing improvements in decision making. In school systems, administrators and union leaders make decisions as proxiprocesses. As such, a proxy leaders face three problems:

(1) Understanding the differences between their preferences and those of the people they represent.

(2) How to acquire data and information about how these people feel about issues upon which decisions must be made.

(3) Weighing opinions, information, and data and trying to judge the merit of the input by collation of the data and collation problems (sampling, etc.).

When a school superintendent as a proxy decision maker does not receive clear instructions from the school board by a majority vote and does not know how the community or staff feels about a particular issue, then a personal or individual decision must be made.

And the consequences of such an action? Proxy decision makers can have their choices reversed or eliminated if they fail to read the board, community, or staff correctly on an issue. Decision theorists can identify the choices to specific mathematical forms. These enable decisions to be reduced to those actually available in any given set of circumstances.

Citiprocesses are influenced and hinge on adversarial relationships (collective bargaining) or the formation of coalitions or political parties. Internally, the proxiprocess involves committees, delegated roles, and formal/informal social groups where pure adversarial relationships are rarely found. Proxy decision makers often rely on consultants to provide expert advice on technical problems.

School administrators as proxy decision makers must never forget that groups do not have preferences, only individuals do. Any data that supposedly represent a group, political or otherwise, should be viewed with a good deal of caution if not downright skepticism.[57]

Organizational Theories

Schools and school systems are organizations, and efficiency and effectivenesss are matters of great concern to those within such organizations and to those served by them. What standards or models can be applied to schools by which they can be assessed?

Educators and non-educators alike have used an industrial model of effectiveness for many years in examining the processes and organization of schools.[58] Schools superficially can be likened to industrial/commerical models, in that they have a core function (teaching/instruction). This function is managed by a principal of a school building (plant) that is part of a school system. The system in turn is managed by a superintendent. The superintendent is accountable to a board of trustees (the school board).

This model assumes that the core functions are responsive up and down the line, first to the principal and then to the superintendent. Presumably, the superintendent, by being responsive to the school board, is being responsive to environmental demands. According to the model, when the board changes policy, administrative actions bring about the changes.

From this perspective school administration can be defined as "a social process concerned with identifying, maintaining, controlling, and unifying formally and informally organized human and material energies within an integrated system designed to accomplish predetermined objectives."[59] Such definitions have led to an emphasis on MBO (Management By Objectives) and to an attempt to develop budgeting systems that are tied to objectives within the core functions to permit greater control of costs.[60]

Yet, there is a good deal of research and observation that contradicts this organizational model borrowed from industrial settings. Schools are not that simple. They just don't work in such a way as to permit the application of industrial/commercial models. Charles Bidwell observed that in practice schools were loosely knit structures requiring internal coordination that was quite different from the typical bureaucratic structure of industry. He noticed that school administrators did not focus on control by results and were in some instances more responsive to "the interests of their faculties than to systemwide requirements."[61]

Sociologist Dan Lortie also examined school structure and administrative controls. He took account of these factors:

- School boards frequently find it difficult to enunciate clear objectives and deal with substantive matters.

- The power of a school superintendent is very limited compared to other types of organizations, and the superintendent is normally isolated from the day-to-day operations of the schools.

- Managerial controls often found in business organizations are lacking in school systems.

- Control over teachers is confined largely to initial selection and later to bureaucratic rules.[62]

Robert Dreeben confirmed both Bidwell's and Lortie's views of schools as places largely immune from administrative policy directions. Dreeben simply stated that "the school system hierarchy does not serve as a direct transmission line for the communication of policy decisions designed to influence teachers' classroom activities."[63] Teachers do not follow orders in the same sense that a military organization would conceive directions from top to bottom in an organization.

One of the most influential of organizational theories of schools has been advanced by Karl Weick. Weick called schools "loosely coupled systems." By this he meant that "coupled events are responsive, but that each event also preserves its own identity and some evidence of its physical or logical separateness."[64] The line from the classroom to the principal's office is not the kind of authoritative line of command one would find in military or industrial organizatons. Rather, the classroom and the principal's office are more or less "attached" but each is still separate.

The advantages of organizations like schools that are "loosely coupled" are:

- Some parts of the organization can be effective, while ineffective parts can be sealed off.

- The organization is not expected to be responsive to small changes in the immediate environment.

- The organization can innovate quickly by confining the innovation to one unit and need not require the approval of the others.

- Local adaption is encouraged as well as a greater variety of potential responses to one situational (all at once) without a need to iron out all of the contradictions.

- Independent units not completely dominated by others possess greater autonomy and hence personal rewards for those within such units.

- Coordination costs among units are minimized.

The disadvantages of schools viewed as "loosely coupled systems" are:

● Moving a total organization is extremely difficult, requiring a monumental effort in obtaining a working consensus among units.

● The organization can be "adrift" or exist in a state of inertia for a long time if no one feels like changing it.

● Contradictions in operations can be expensive; mistakes are often repeated and can become built into the structure itself.

● Autonomy is or can be a major barrier to the requirement for better communication and change.

● While coordination costs may be low, duplication of labor and materials may offset the low coordination costs.

Innovations that are superimposed on schools and that require them to behave in any other way than "loosely coupled systems" may be doomed to failure. Clearly, management theories applied to schools must be modified by the reality of a school district's organization.

Financial Concepts and Applications

Financial management continues to be a major challenge for school administrators. One Big Eight accounting firm has developed questions to assess the quality of a district's management and control (see Figure 7). Prospective school leaders may wish to consider each, as they pertain to their situation.

Figure 7.
Assessing Fiscal Management and Control.

The Adequacy of Accounting Controls

1. Does the chief financial officer report to the chief executive officer?

2. Does the system issue regular, timely, and responsive financial management reports?

3. Does the school district conduct regular reviews and actual performance of revenues and expenditures and of the initiation of action, if appropriate?

4. Does the school district have an established set of accounting policies and a procedures manual?

5. Does the district review the extent of expenditure-control systems, e.g., encumbrances, position control, contract monitoring?

6. Does the school district conduct periodic reviews of revenue sources?

7. Does the district review the extent of its internal audit function?

The Adequacy of the Procurement System

1. Does the district maintain a system of centralized procurement?

2. Does the district consult a purchasing manual?

3. Does the district encourage competitive bidding?

4. Does the district maintain a receiving, inspection, and quality control function?

Reviews of the Financial Stock of the District

1. Does the district maintain a financial review program?

2. Does the district check the comprehensiveness of its own reviews?

3. Are such reviews conducted on a regular basis?[159]

Public Disclosure

1. Does the school district maintain a policy statement regarding disclosure requirements?

2. Does the school district and its officers adhere to that statement?

In 1979-80 the Association of School Business Officials (ASBO) conducted a national survey on financial management practices, emphasizing school district investing, borrowing, and school-banking relationships.[66]

They found that:

- 86 percent of the states regulated school financial practices with state laws.

- 60 percent of the states possessed two or more sources of regulations pertaining to school financial management practices.

- 86 percent of the states permitted use of general school funds for investment purposes.

- 65 percent of the states limited the length and amount of investments.

- 18 percent of the states imposed a statutory limitations on arbitrage.

- 45 percent of the states allowed school districts to use out-of-state banks.

Figure 8 outlines specialized concepts and terms relating to school district financial management practices.

Figure 8.
Terms Related to School Finance.

Arbitrage: The practice of borrowing money by a school district at one lending rate and investing it at a higher rate, thus earning income as a result.

Cash Investment Pooling: The consolidation of all cash accounts from separate funds into one or a few accounts for investment purposes.

Direct Deposit Payrolls: Placing the entire payroll into a bank to improve employee access to their salaries.

Cash Budgeting: Determining the timing of receipts and disbursements of a school district to project fund availability for investment purposes at specific time periods.

Cash Flow Schedule: An annual determination normally by month of the expected net receipts and disbursements based on historical financial data trends. Such a schedule forms the basis for cash budgeting.

Repurchase Agreements or "Repos": A type of security, normally U.S. treasury bills, purchased and sold at a later date. The "Repo" is owned by the investor until payment at maturity. Other types of investment securities are certificates of deposit (CD), U.S. government treasury bills or bonds, federal agency securities, or state and municipal obligations.

Float: The amount of cash that remains in a checking account after all checks have been written and cleared the account. The sum can be a source of short term investments.

Many school districts have not used banking services as fully as they could because they:

- Use only one bank (usually a local institution selected haphazardly).
- Do not bid for banking services.
- Do not use savings accounts.
- Are not aware of the fees charged for use of various banking services.

Many school administrators have been slow to earn more for the school district via short and long term investment practices and cash budgeting methods. Clearly, administrators will have to become more sophisticated and aggressive using solid financial management procedures when possible.

Conclusion

Any organization is moved by the ideas that are in the minds of those in charge. There are two types of ideas: those that deal with operations and processes and those that deal with what an organization's ideals are and how they come into being. Ideas about how to organize schools and how to measure what they do have been powerfully influenced by the Industrial Revolution.

Unlocking the potential of schools to become more effective may involve a painful retracing of the way school leaders think about them. Understanding how we perceive schools and what we want them to do is more difficult than simply accepting schools as they are and looking for ways to make them better.

Allocating resources is therefore a twofold process: first, examine the fundamental nature of the enterprise, and second, discover and implement the most effective processes that will realize those purposes.[68], [69], [70], [71]

Skill Accomplishment Checklist for Chapter Eight

Competency and Skills	Reading and Activities for Mastery
Competency: Allocate human, material, and financial resources efficiently, in an accountable manner to ensure successful student learning	Readings: See resources 1, 2, 3, 4, 58, 62, 63, 64 Activities: 1. Learner could develop a list of changes implemented in the district and determmine how many used the simple input-output model used in economics. Then list any problems encountered with each change. How many faltered due to schools being considered as "loosely coupled systems?" 2. Using Mintzberg's *Structure in Fives* (ref. 51), list each of the components of accountability and how they relate to one another and what precedents each had prior to the modern day terminology for older practices. 3. PPBS and later ZBB (refs. 16, 17) were attempts to tie allocation strategies, budgeting, and learner outcomes together. They were largely failures. What do they assume about school operations in order to work? Read thoroughly Walcott's *Teachers vs. Technocrats* for a case study of the failure of PPBS (ref. 164). At the heart of the matter is the definition of organizational "rationality." How are schools different?
Skill A: Facilities planning, maintenance, and operation	Readings: See resources 20, 21, 23, 25 Activities: 1. Develop a site by site description of each school building listing specifics such as an accurate room use record (regular classrooms, special programs, storage, resource rooms, etc.) and a detailed site description indicating any type of problem encountered such as drainage, retain walls, erosion, pollution. Also list all major building and site work completed on the building since construction.

2. Develop a schedule of when potential pollutants and toxic chemicals/pesticides have been used in the building for routine maintenance and operation. Discuss findings with local/county department of health.

3. Do you have an asbestos problem? Consult A. Natale and H. Levin, *Asbestos Removal and Control*, Asbestos Control Technology, P.O. Box 183, Maple Shade, N.J. 08052. This book deals with a step by step description of asbestos removal, explores legal liability, special insurance required, and methods to ascertain the dangers of airborne asbestos.

Skill B: Financial planning and cash flow management

Readings: See resources 14, 15, 16, 27, 29, 65

Activities:

1. Does your district use cash investment pooling? Investigate with your bank the consolidation of all cash account of separate funds into one for investment purposes. Investigate what state laws pertain to use of funds on short term investments. Check with your accountant as to how accounting records must be maintained.

2. Establish a cash flow pattern in your school district by setting up a simple chart that lists by month total expected receipts, disbursements, and net balances. This will indicate the "netflow" of cash available for investment purposes. This is the key to cash budgeting. Two decisions must be made: time horizon used and level of detail/specification called the "level of aggregation." The time horizon refers to the period used for cash flow schedules (monthly, quarterly, annually). Do you have cash available for investment purposes? When and how much? Consult historical data regarding when the district has a cash surplus or a cash deficit.

3. Conduct a payroll disbursement pattern to determine the amount of cash that may be available for short term investments. This is accomplished by determining the amount and percent of payroll checks cashed by day beginning with "payday," until 100 percent has been cashed. Do you have funds available for investments? When and how much?

Skill C: Personnel administration

Readings: See resources 8, 30, 31

Activities:

1. Do job descriptions exist for each position in the school district? A job description should contain statements

pertaining to overall objectives and functions for each specific job title, organizational relationships, expected contact with others, type of supervision the job holder will receive, and the necessary education and experience required. Each specific job duty should have a parallel job standard that is quantitative in nature. For example, if a job duty is to "involve teachers in decision making," one standard would be "hold teaching staff meetings once per week." The duty is made quantitative in nature so that it can be evaluated. Assess the quantity and quality of the job descriptions in your school district.

2. Conduct staffing projections for your school or district. First compile a list of positions and note the turnover by grade level, subject area, and certification area. Look at possible expected retirements? Develop a one- to five-year expected staff turnover. Consult with state data regarding availability of replacements who are fully qualified. Develop specific recruitment strategies to ensure able replacements.

3. Analyze your current administrative compensation system. What are its strengths and weaknesses? How can these be improved?

4. How well do current personnel records and practices comply with Title IX, EEOC requirements? Are accurate records kept of all candidates, rating sheets used, lists of interviewers and summary comments in case of a Title IX, EEOC review? If not, what steps must be taken to be in compliance?

5. Evaluate the strengths and weaknesses of the district's teacher collective bargaining agreement. Is there an unbroken line of authority from the board to the classroom teacher uncompromised by any union veto power? What is the history of grievances in the district? How have they been resolved? What contract language has given the administration the most problems? How should it be changed?

6. What are the existing problems with the teacher evaluation instrument? Using the publication *Evaluating Teacher Performance* by Educational Research Service of Arlington, Virginia, 1978, assess the strengths and weaknesses of your current teacher evaluation program and instrument. List the major problems you expect to encounter trying to change your current instrument.

Skill D: Pupil personnel services and categorical programs.

Readings: See resources 32, 36, 52, 53

Activities:

1. Trace the problems in using the existing set of categories in describing and diagnosing varying types of students with handicapping conditions. What problems have been encountered? What classifications are required to be used? How could the classifications be altered?

2. What educational problems exist with creating the least restrictive environment (LRE) for pupils in your school/district? How could mainstreaming be improved?

3. Has your district/school experienced shifting problems in the area of serving some students, such as an increase in the numbers of students called "learning disabled" from "mentally retarded"? What are the causes of the shift? How can the problem be addressed better educationally?

4. Graph the amount, kind, and breadth of federal/state categorical programs in your school or district. What are the trends? What criteria would you use to determine if the funds received were put to good use? What problems has your school/district encountered with such categorical funds?

5. How has your district developed the required skills to develop categorical programs described in this chapter? Is there a training program to develop such skills? Conduct a skill based needs assessment to determine who possesses such skills.

Skill E: Legal concepts, regulations and codes for school operations

Readings: See resources 38, 42, 67

Activities:

1. Categorize the types of legal questions most prevalent in your school/district. In what areas do you find the most problems? Why? What applicable state law is helpful? How could or should such laws be changed to provide greater clarity in school operations?

2. Trace the expansion of social problems in the schools into the problems your school/district is currently encountering in the area of pupil rights and school discipline. How should or can school regulations/policies/codes be altered to assist school administrators in doing a better job?

3. Interview veteran school administrators and ask them how their personal liability has increased over the years as far as lawsuits and legal vulnerability are concerned. Compile a list of all of the lawsuits currently being litigated against your school/district and all administrative personnel. What areas have the greatest frequency? How long does it take them to be resolved? What are the insurance risks involved in being a school adminstrator?

Skill F: Analytical techniques of management

Readings: See resources 1, 2, 3, 13, 36, 47, 56
Activities:

1. Keep a weekly log of all problems that had to be resolved in your school/district in which you were involved. What types were they? What data was necessary to resolve them? How was the data used? Which problems were the most difficult? Why?

2. Develop a skill inventory for a major administrative position in your district. What skills must the person possess prior to coming onto the job? What skills must the person use on the job? What evaluation tools or methods can be used to assess skill levels? What are the most common skills missing in prior applicants for the position?

3. Obtain copies of five major reports prepared by the administration for the school board in the last 1-2 years. What were the dominant types of analytical techniques used? How were problems identified? How was information related to resolving identified problems? How were the problems actually resolved?

4. Analyze the quality of any long range plan that has been developed in your school district. What was the data base? What decisions were reached with the data base? What assumptions were used in constructing the plan (programs, facilities, curriculum, testing, etc.)? How does the district know if the plan was followed? How is the plan monitored? What happens if the plan is ignored? What is the value of such plans?

Resources

1. C.I. Barnard, *The Functions of the Executive* (Cambridge, Mass.: Harvard University Press, 1966), p. 20.

2. L. Ayers, *Laggards in Our Schools* (New York, 1909).

3. L. Ayers, as cited in R.E. Callahan. *Education and the Cult of Efficiency* (Chicago: University of Chicago Press, 1962).

4. R.E. Callahan, *Education and the Cult of Efficiency* (Chicago: University of Chicago Press, 1962).

5. H.J. Otto, *Elementary-School Organization and Administration* (New York: Appleton-Century-Crofts, Inc. 1954), pp. 137-141.

6. See F.J. Sciara and R.K. Jantz (eds.), *Accountability in American Education* (Boston: Allyn and Bacon, Inc. 1972).

7. L.M. Lessinger and R.W. Tyler (eds.), *Accountability in Education* (Worthington, Ohio: Charles A. Jones, 1971), pp. 1-6.

8. P.C. Thompson, *Quality Circles* (New York: American Management Association, 1982).

9. H.I. Ansoff, *Strategic Management* (New York: John Wiley and Sons, 1979).

10. T.J. Peters and R.H. Waterman Jr., *In Search of Excellence* (New York: Harper and Row, 1982).

11. Donald L. Hymes, "Schools Begin Budget Recovery," *The School Administrator*, (October 1984) pp. 11-12.

12. Donald L. Hymes, *School Budgeting: Problems and Solutions* (Arlington, Va.: American Association of School Administrators, 1982), pp. 12-15.

13. "Guidelines to Establish a Certificate of Conformance Program for Financial Reporting by School Systems," Association of School Business Officials, Information Bulletin No. 14, February 1971, p. 7.

14. S.T. Dutton, *School Management: Practical Suggestions Concerning the Conduct and Life of the School* (New York: Charles Scribner's Sons: 1903), p. 48.

15. H.E. Bennet, *School Efficiency: A Manual of Modern School Management* (Boston: Ginn and Company, 1917), p. 86.

16. E.P. Cubberley, *Public School Administration* (Boston: Houghton Mifflin Company, 1929), p. 561.

17. U.S. Office of Education, "Biennial Survey of Education, 1934-1936," Statistics of State School Systems, 1935-1936. *Bulletin* 1937, No. 2. Volume II, Chapter Two, p. 55; also *Bulletin* 1931, No. 20, Volume II, pp. 40-41. Washington, D.C. Government Printing Office, 1932, as cited in P.R. Mort and W.C. Reusser. *Public School Finance* (New York: McGraw-Hill Book Company, Inc. 1941), p. 329.

18. Costs are expressed in constant 1977-78 dollars. U.S. Department of Commerce. Bureau of the Census, *1972 Census of Governments*, Volume 6, Topical Studies No. 4: Historical Statistics on Governmental Finances and Employment, 1974: Government Finances, various years, as cited in *The Condition of Education 1980* Edition, National Center for Education Statistics, U.S. Government Printing Office, Washington, D.C., p. 42.

19. National Center for Education Statistics, annual reports on *Bond Sales for Public School Purposes* as cited in Digest of Education Statistics 1979. National Center for Education Statistics, U.S. Government Printing Office, Washington, D.C., p. 72.

20. D.J. Leu, *Planning Educational Facilities* (New York: The Center for Applied Research in Education, Inc. 1965).

21. See also E. Bussard and A.C. Green. *Planning for Declining Enrollment in Single High School Districts.* National Institute of Education, U.S. Office of Education, U.S. Government Printing Office, Washington, D.C. 1981).

22. *The Condition of Education 1979 Edition.* National Center for Education Statistics U.S. Government Printing Office, Washington, D.C. p. 157.

23. K. McCormick, "Asbestos: The Clock is Ticking in Your Schools, and Inaction Could Prove to be Devastating," *The American School Board Journal*, 171:4 (April 1984) pp. 33-36.

24. P. Shabecoff, "Study Cites Lack of E.P.A. Action on Asbestos Peril in U.S. Schools," *New York Times*, February 1, 1984, pp. 1 and A. 17.

25. The data in this section on pollutants was extrapolated from M. Corey, "Specialized Environmental Databases Provide Vauable Information," *Newsletter* of Clayton Environmental Consultants, 14 (September 1983) pp. 1 and 6. See also P.H. Howard, G.W. Sage and A. LaMacchia, "The Development of an Environmental Fate Data Base, *"Journal of Chemical Information and Computer Science*," 22 (1982) pp. 38-44.

26. U.S. Department of Commerce, Bureau of Economic Analysis, *Survey of Current Business: U.S. Department of Health, Education, and Welfare*, National Center for Education Statistics, *Statistics of State School Systems: Financial Statistics of Institutions of Higher Education*: Social Security Administration, *Compendium of National Health Expenditures Data*: Council of Economic Advisors Economic Report of the President, as cited in *The Condition of Education 1980 Edition*, National Center for Education Statistics, U.S. Government Printing Office, Washington, D.C. p. 38.

27. A Odden, C.K. McGuire and G.B. Simmons, "School Finance Reform in the States: 1983," Report No. F83-1 (Denver, Colorado: Education Finance Center, Policy Analysis and Research, Education Commission of the States, 1983) p. 18.

28. F.W. Cyr, A.J. Burke, and P.R. Mort, *Paying for Our Public Schools* (Scranton, Pennsylvania: International Textbook Company, 1938), p. 13.

29. S. Schoenfeld, A.H. Bierce, and R.O. Scott, "Cash Management: An Exercise in Utility," *Management Focus* 31,2 (March-April 1984), pp. 14-19.

30. R. Strang, *The Role of the Teacher in Personnel Work*, (New York: Bureau of Publications, Teachers College, Columbia University, 1953), p. 105.

31. A.A. Hitchcock and others, "Milestones in the Development of Personnel Services in Education," in *Personnel Services in Education*, N.B. Henry (ed.) The Fifty-Eighth Yearbook of the Study of Education (Chicago, Ill.: University of Chicago Press, 1959), p. 287.

32. As cited in N. Hobbs (ed.), *Issues in the Classification of Children* (San Francisco: Jossey-Bass Publisher, 1975), p. vii.

33. R.L. Cromwell, R.K. Blashfield, and J.S. Strauss, "Criteria for Classification Systems," in Volume I, *Issues in the Classification of Children* (San Francisco: Jossey-Bass Publisher, 1975), pp. 4-25.

34. J.W. Filler, C.C. Robinson, R.A. Smith, L.J. Vincent-Smith D.D. Bricker, and W.A. Bricker, "Mental Retardation," *Issues in the Classification of Children* (San Francisco: Jossey-Bass Publisher, 1975).

35. S.W. Tiedt, *The Role of the Federal Government in Education* (New York: Oxford University Press, 1966), p. 15.

36. See M.W. McLaughlin, *Evaluation and Reform: The Elementary and Secondary Education Act of 1965/Title I* (Cambridge, Mass.: Ballinger Publishing Company, 1975).

37. J.B. Stedman, "Education in America: Reports on Its Condition and Recommendations for Change," Issue Brief Number Ib83106, the Library of Congress, Congressional Research Service, Major Issues System, June 16, 1983.

38. H.H. Punke, *The Teacher and the Courts* (Danville, Ill.: The Interstate and Printers and Publishers, Inc., 1971), p. 7.

39. P.A. Zirkel and I.B. Gluckman, "Silent Meditation: It's the Law," *Principal* 63,5 (May 1984), pp. 50-51.

40. As cited in F.W. English, "Emerging Issues for School Administrators," in *NCRPE Bulletin* 10,4 (Fall 1983); data obtained "N.C. Schools Promote Religion, Study Contends," *Education Week*, September 21, 1983, pp. 3-4.

41. M.H. Mitchell, "Whether Secular Humanism Is Religion: Analyzing the Legal Argument That Public Schools Violate the Establishment Clause When They Teach Secular Humanism," *NCRPE Bulletin* 10,4 (Fall 1983), pp. 50-63.

42. D.L. Kirk and M.G. Yudof, *Educational Policy and the Law: Cases and Materials* (Berkeley, Calif.: McCutchan Publishing, 1974), p. 582.

43. S. Ranbom, "Schools' Investments Hit by Bankruptcy of Securities Firm," *Education Week* 3,35 (May 23, 1984), pp. 1, 4; A. Wilentz, "Firm's Bankruptcy Affects 3 Districts," *Newsday*, May 22, 1984, p. 23.

44. See also A. Mitchell, "Broker Testifies on School Investment Flap," *Newsday*, June 6, 1984, p. 21.

45. C.R. Perry and W.A. Wildman, *The Impact of Negotiations in Public Education: The Evidence from the Schools* (Worthington, Ohio: Charles A. Jones Publishing Company, 1970), p. 3.

46. R. Brody, "Why It's So Hard to Fire Bad Teachers," *Newsday*, May 8, 1983, pp. 7-8, 24-27.

47. See W.C. Carey, *Documenting Teacher Dismissal: A Guide for the Site Administrator* (Salem, Ore.: Options Press, 1981).

48. G. Morrison, "Secret Fraternities in High Schools," *Journal of Proceedings and Addresses of the Forty-Third Annual Meeting of the National Education Association* (June 1904), pp. 484-490, an as cited in A. Flowers and E.C. Bolmeier, *Law and Pupil Control* (Cincinnati: The W.H. Anderson Company, 1964), p. 13.

49. G.I. Maeroff, "Teachers Now May Act Just Like People," *The New York Times*, July 4, 1976, p. 12.

50. See E.H. Jones and X.P. Montenegro, *Climbing the Career Ladder: A Research Study of Women in School Administration: A Report to the National*

Institute of Education Minorities and Women's Program, U.S. Education Department, (Arlington, Va.: Office of Minority Affairs, American Association of School Administrators, 1982).

51. C. Shapiro, "We'll Sue Your School Board to Win Equity for Women Administrators," *American School Board Journal* (May 1984), pp. 43-45.

52. As cited in D.R. Barbacovi and R.W. Clelland, "Public Law 94-142: Special Education in Transition," (Arlington, Va.: American Association of School Administrators, p. 4).

53. M.M. McCarthy, "The Application of Competency Testing Mandates to Handicapped Children," *Harvard Education Review* 53,2 (May 1983), pp. 146-164.

54. W.G. Spady and G. Marx, *Excellence in Our Schools: Making It Happen* (Arlington, Va.: American Association of School Administrators, 1984).

55. J.V. Baldridge and T. Deal, *The Dynamics of Organizational Change in Education* (Berkeley, Calif.: McCutchan Publishing, 1983).

56. D.J. Clough, *Decisions in Public and Private Sectors: Theories, Practices, and Processes* (Englewood Cliffs, N.J.: Prentice-Hall, 1984).

57. G.M. Kaufman and H. Thomas (eds.), *Modern Decision Analysis* (New York: Penguin Books, 1977).

58. M.B. Katz, *The Irony of Early School Reform* (Boston: Beacon Press, 1968).

59. S.J. Knezevich, "Management Strategies," in H.J. Walberg (ed.), *Improving Educational Standards and Productivity*, (Berkeley, Calif.: McCutchan Publishing, 1982).

60. G.S. Odiorne, *Management by Objectives* (New York: Pitman Publishing Corporation, 1965).

61. C.E. Bidwell, "The School as a Formal Organization," J.G. March (ed.), in *Handbook of Organizations* (Chicago: Rand McNally and Company, 1965).

62. D.C. Lortie, "The Balance of Control and Autonomy in Elementary School Teaching," in A. Etzioni (ed.), *The Semi-Professions and Their Organization* (New York: The Free Press, 1969).

63. R. Dreeben, "The School as a Workplace," in R.M.W. Tavers (ed.), *Second Handbook of Research on Teaching* (Chicago: Rand McNally, 1973).

64. K. Weick, "Educational Organizations as Loosely Coupled Systems," *Administrative Science Quarterly* 23 (December 1978).

65. S. Schoenfeld and L.S. Maisel, "How to Rate Your City's Management," *World* 4 (1981), pp. 16-17.

66. F.L. Dembowski, *A Handbook for School District Financial Management* (Park Ridge, Ill.: Association of School Business Officials, 1982).

67. R. Dean Jollay Jr. and Ann M. Holmes, "Supreme Court Decisions Affecting Education: The 1984 Term and a Look Ahead into 1985," paper prepared for The Information Exchange, the Office of Governmental Relations, the American Association of School Administrators, 1984.

68. Bratlien, Maynard J., "Techfinance: A Computer Oriented Simulation in Planning and Budgeting." National Conference of Professors of Educational Administration, Western Michigan University, Kalamazoo, Michigan, August 15, 1988.

69. Childs, Stephen T. and Shakeshaft, Charol. "A Meta-analysis of Research on the Relationship Between Educational Expenditures and Student Achievement," *Journal of Education Finance*. 12, No. 2 (Fall, 1986), 249-263.

70. Odden, Allen. "A School Finance Research Agenda for an Era of Education Reform," *Journal of Education Finance*. 12, No. 1 (Summer, 1986), 49-70.

71. Pipho, C. "Making Hard Choices," *Phi Delta Kappan*. 69, No. 3 (November, 1987), 182-183.

CHAPTER NINE

SKILLS IN EDUCATIONAL RESEARCH, EVALUATION, AND PLANNING

School leaders need skills in conducting research and using research findings to improve program evaluation, long range planning, school operations, and student learning. The following four skills top the list:

- Research design and methods including gathering, analyzing, and interpreting data.

- Descriptive and inferential statistics.

- Evaluation and planning/futures models and methods.

- Selection, administration, and interpretation of evaluation instruments.

Respect for educational research, evaluation, and planning among school leaders has increased considerably since the 1960s and 1970s. In a 1982 study of school superintendents, Ohio State University researchers found a surprisingly high regard for educational research. Over half of the 1,321 respondents to the AASA-sponsored study said educational research is "usually useful" or "highly useful." Only 3 percent said research is not useful.[1]

The press for accountability and quality control has prompted this higher regard for educational research. School leaders have become aware that conducting and interpreting research are critical to program evaluation and long range planning. Also, there has been a marked change in the levels of preparation that today's administrators have in contrast to a decade ago. Greater emphasis on research, planning, and evaluation is evident in most preparation and inservice programs. School leaders realize that the public is no longer satisfied with being told that the schools are "doing a good job." The people want to know how good. To respond, administrators need to master basic skills in educational research, evaluation, and planning.

Research: Definition, Problems, and Value

Research is a systematic effort to investigate and solve problems. Educational researchers try to find answers to such complex issues as the effect of administrative behavior on student performance; relationships between teacher behavior and student performance; and the impact of various levels of administrator and teacher job satisfaction on their performance. State and national political leaders seek research findings to help them develop policy or push legislation for higher teacher salaries and more support for school programs. Policy makers want research evidence that "proves" the effectiveness of one type of school organization over another or determines the most effective teacher-supervisor ratios to improve student achievement.

No Quick Answers. Unfortunately quick answers are missing. Educational research is an inexact process often conducted by biased people. No research method can ensure that an educational problem will be solved. There are always uncertainties. Some conclusions are abstract and general as in basic research, which deals with theory and the nature of things, or others are concrete and specific, as in applied research. Most educational research attempts to link theory with practice. Educational researchers differ on their opinions about how useful educational research and theory development are to educational practice.[2] In spite of the many obstacles in educational research and theory development, researchers and practitioners must combine efforts to study what is useful to schools. Because of the pressures intensified by numerous national education reports and the growing criticism of schools and colleges of education, educational leaders are pushed to provide immediate solutions to school and classroom problems. The time pressure has increased activity in *applied research* and downplayed the usefulness of *basic research*. While applied research is usually directed at quick answers to solve immediate problems, basic research requires longer time periods, tests for relationships and causality, and draws conclusions about data under investigation. For example, applied research would be comparing two methods of teaching reading to third grade students. Basic research would be developing ways to measure the degree of openness in a school climate.

The true value of research is not merely to provide quick answers to practical problems. Rather, its value lies in developing theory and advancing knowledge so that its answers are sound and lead to problem solving. Impatient to solve problems, many educators have adopted new programs that later research proved valueless or even detrimental to the education process.

Research and Effective Schools. A classic example of the use of quick answers to solve practical problems is nationwide school improvement programs based on effective schools research. School practitioners, including state education department officials, need answers to instructional problems and often run through research stop signs to win the race with time. They may parrot the widely touted "five correlates" from the effective schools research as the answer to creating highly successful classrooms in all school settings.[3] Research evidence supports the notion that tightly coupled, streamlined schools can improve test scores. The development of uniform curriculum and "essential elements" in each subject, single textbooks, workbooks, and standardized tests, however, is a return to schools of yesteryear characterized by frontal teaching, uniform instruction, and tighter discipline contracts.

Several researchers have presented compelling caveats about the problems inherent in blindly accepting research on effective schools.[4] These researchers and many public school leaders support further conceptual and theoretical development as well as further empirical research. They point out that no one can accurately define an effective school and that the focus on instructional outcomes is too limited. Critics also claim that schools are labeled as effective on the basis of assessments of instructional outcomes at only one or two grade levels in one or two curriculum areas in selected elementary schools.

Research on effective schools has produced several positive results, however, such as:

● Optimism that schools can be organized to enhance instruction and student achievement.

● Clues to a number of factors that school leaders can stress to produce more efficient school operations.

● Common vocabulary to improve communication between public school and university personnel.

Because many methodological and conceptual problems remain before valid and reliable models can be applied to all schools, school leaders need adequate research skills to avoid the temptation to apply quick fixes and give simple answers.

Research Designs and Methods Include Gathering, Analyzing, and Interpreting Data

Research design and methods of data gathering are too complex for indepth treatment here. Readers should consult a good basic research textbook to gain a stronger foundation in research.[5,6,7] However, there are several important skills that should be and are included.

Research Designs and Methods. Four research designs commonly distinguished are the descriptive method, the causal-comparative method, the correlational method, and the experimental method. These designs differ in significant ways. If the interest is in the relationship between a principal's use of supervision and teaching performance, for example, different approaches can be taken to analyze this problem.

Descriptive Method. Gathering teacher perceptions through interviews or self-report questionnaires to determine the effectiveness of the clinical supervision approach is an example of the descriptive method (see Figure 1). The treatment may or may not have caused any change in teaching performance.

Figure 1.
Design for Descriptive Method.

$$T \rightarrow O$$

T = Treatment, ie., clinical supervision

O = Data gathered to determine teaching performance

Causal-Comparative Method. An example of the causal-comparative method would be research that applied clinical supervision techniques to a select group of teachers and applied no supervision to another select group of teachers. The researcher would compare the teaching performances of the two groups to determine whether teacher behaviors or styles differed. While this design may show relationships and is similar to the *correlation method*, it is not really adequate for determining causality. Some factors other than clinical supervision may cause differences in teaching performance (see Figure 2).

Figure 2.
Design for Causal-Comparative Method.

$$G_1 \rightarrow T \rightarrow O$$
$$G_2 \xrightarrow{\hspace{1cm}} O$$

G_1 = Group 1, T = treatment ie., clinical supervision, O = Measurement of impact,

G_2 = Group 2, $\longrightarrow$ = no treatment, O = measurement for impact

---

If the *treatment group* has higher teaching performance scores than the *control group*, it could mean that the treatment caused the difference, that some other factor caused the difference, or the groups were different to start with since no random selection was used to determine either group.

Experimental Method. The experimental method is necessary to infer causality. This design involves random selection of subjects, precise measures of teacher behaviors, consistent applications and control of the treatment, and accurate measures of research outcomes. For example, researchers could ask trained clinical supervisors to provide precise and extensive supervision for one randomly selected group of teachers and no supervision to another randomly selected group of teachers. Since clinical supervision is an independent variable, then any difference in teaching performance of supervised teachers can be attributed to supervision. The true experimental design is considered the most powerful research method because it provides adequate controls for all sources of internal invalidity. That is, it isolates the variable/s that caused the change in the dependent variable, i.e., teaching performance (see Figure 3). If the treatment group has higher teaching performance scores on the posttest, it is very probable that the treatment caused the difference.

Figure 3.
Design for Experimental Method

$$R_1 \ O_1 \rightarrow \ T \ \rightarrow \ O_2$$
$$R_2 \ O_3 \xrightarrow{\hspace{2cm}} \ O_4$$

R_1 = Random selection of experimental group, O_1 = pretest of teaching performance, T = treatment (for example, clinical supervision), O_2 = posttest of teaching performance
R_2 = Random selection of control group, O_3 = pretest of teaching performance, $\longrightarrow$ = no treatment, O_4 = posttest of teaching performance.

Factors Affecting Internal Validity. For research to have internal validity, the goal must be to establish experimental controls that will allow for a conclusion that differences occur as a result of experimental treatment. The eight classes of extraneous variables that if not controlled, can weaken research designs are:

1. *History*. When instructional treatments extend over a period of time, it is possible that other events occur that may account for results.

2. *Maturation*. While an instructional treatment is in progress there may be natural growth occurring in the learners (biological, psychological, or sociological), which is more instrumental than the instructional treatment in producing desired results.

3. *Testing*. Students who take the same test twice, as in a pretest/posttest design, sometimes perform differently in the posttest as a result of their having taken the pretest.

4. *Instrumentation*. If the measuring instruments are changed during an evaluation study, any apparent changes in pupil performance might be more directly associated with the shift in measuring devices than with the educational phenomenon being evaluated.

5. *Instability*. Most measures used in evaluation investigations are less than perfectly reliable.

6. *Selection*. In evaluation studies where the performance of two or more groups is being analyzed, the effect of an educational intervention can be confounded if the students constituting the groups are selected differently.

7. *Mortality*. If two or more groups are involved in the evaluation study and pupils drop out of one or more of the groups, the results of the study may be confounded.

8. *Statistical Regression*. When learners are selected for an evaluation study because of their extremely high or (more often) extremely low scores on a test, their performance on subsequent tests will tend to "regress" toward the mean of the distribution because of statistical unreliability of the measuring device used.[8]

The term *external validity* refers to the representativeness of the findings of a study.[8] The hope in conducting research is that findings can be applied at a later date to groups of subjects in other locations. Obviously, internal validity must be present before external validity can be considered. To control for internal and external validity, one quasi-experimental and two truly experimental designs are introduced. (Refer to two other sources for information on more complex factorial and ex-post facto designs such as Tuckman.[7])

True Experimental Designs. Two true experimental designs include:

- posttest-only control group design.
- pretest/posttest control group design.

The **posttest-only control group** design is potentially the most useful true design.[7] It can be diagrammed as shown below. A "T" designates a treatment and a blank space designates a control (no treatment). An "0" designates an observation or measurement and each 0 is numbered (i.e. 0_1, 0_2, 0_3, and so on). The letter R designates that selection of subjects was made through use of a table of random numbers. A diagram of the design would be:

$$R - T \rightarrow 0_1;$$
$$R \longrightarrow 0_2$$

This design uses two groups (samples) randomly (R) selected from the population. One group receives treatment (T) and the other group receives none. Random selection of the groups controls for selection and mortality weaknesses, and treating only one group controls for history and maturation. In addition, no pretest is given to either group to control interactions between testing and treatment and for sample testing effects. The appropriate method of analysis for posttest only control group design is a comparison between the mean for observation number one, 0_1 and the mean for observation number two 0_2.

> Example: Dr. Bill Johnson of Accountability City Schools decides to test the impact of his new principal inservice program. He randomly selects 20 of his elementary principals and requires ten of them to undergo extensive training on four of the eight AASA administrator skills. The other ten principals receive no training. The posttest scores significantly favor the treatment group. Thus, he concludes that training has caused a difference.

Pretest-Posttest-Control Group Design. Another extremely useful true experimental design is the pretest-posttest control group design. A diagram of the design is:

$$R - 0_1 - T \rightarrow 0_2;$$
$$R - 0_3 \longrightarrow 0_4.$$

One of the two randomly selected groups receives the treatment (T) while the second group, the control group, does not. This design includes a pretest for both groups. Although this design controls the same weaknesses as the posttest only design, it introduces an additional small problem. There is no control for a testing effect (in other words, gain on posttest due to experience on pretest) which may reduce the internal validity; nor is there control for possible sensitization to the treatment that subjects might gain by having a pretest, thus affecting external validity. Under most situations, the posttest only control group design should be used since random assignment of subjects to groups is considered adequate for control of selection bias.[7] However, if school leaders are interested in measuring the degree of change produced by a treatment, then pretest data are necessary. That is, they can compare the mean scores of $0_2 - 0_1$ with the mean scores of $0_4 - 0_3$ to determine whether treatment produced a change or differential effect on the groups.

> EXAMPLE: Dr. Bill Johnson wants to validate the results he found using the posttest only control group design. Therefore, he randomly selects 20 more elementary principals—ten in the experimental group and ten in the control group. He then adds a pre-test covering the same four administrator skill areas. One group is trained and the other is not trained. Bill then compares the posttest scores to determine the impact of the training.

Quasi-Experimental Designs. These designs are not completely true experimental designs because they control some but not all of the sources of internal invalidity. However, in the real world of education, especially public schools, these designs are often the most applicable.[8] Administrators and teachers are leary of "researchers" looking for "good" or "bad" effects caused by a treatment or lack of it on students. The welfare of research subjects frequently overrides any benefits that may come from true experimental designs.

Quasi-experimental designs carry experimental controls and work with minimum class time disruption. No control group is required. They are also superior to one-shot case studies or the one group pretest, posttest designs that are the most frequently used designs for public school research and evaluation. The basic quasi-experimental design diagrams in a time-series design such as:

$$0_1 \ \ 0_2 \ \ 0_3 \ \ 0_4 \ \ T \ \ 0_5 \ \ 0_6 \ \ 0_7 \ \ 0_8.$$

> EXAMPLE: Dr. Johnson wants to determine if the administrative performance of his 15 central office administrators will improve as a result of an intensive week long inservice retreat in which five of the AASA skill areas are stressed. Dr. Johnson gathers relevant performance data on all 15 administrators in each of the four months before and after the retreat. He finds that 12 administrators' performances gradually improved each month after the retreat. Thus, the training is probably causing the change.

In this approach, a series of observations are collected over equal time periods.[6] Tests that are administered over a period of time (0_1, 0_2, and so on) measure the effects of treatment (T) (for example, new curriculum or teaching strategies), and provide control for maturation and to some extent for history. Although the time-series design does not control for history as well as a true experimental design, it does help researchers determine the influence of the history factor and, therefore, is more adequate than alternative single-group designs.

Time-Series and Alternative High School Program. In actual studies the time-series design has proven to be a valuable tool in measuring the impact of new alternative high school programs on attendance; teacher, student, and parent attitudes; and grade point averages. Data were collected at equal time intervals on each student in the program beginning one year prior to the program and for one year after the program was underway. The researcher concluded that the program caused a positive change in most factors and was able to control major concerns about history, maturation, and instrumentation.[9] The time-series design has also proven useful in evaluating the effects of Chapter I programs on student achievement in math and reading.[10]

Traditional pretest, posttest designs for experimental research are of limited use in most school research because student enrollment fluctuations, testing effects, and several other intervening variables create invalidity problems. Therefore, the time series design is more practical for school leaders attempting to measure the impact of programs.

Gathering, Analyzing, and Interpreting Data

Data gathering strategies and processes will vary according to the questions most pertinent to a researcher. Some problems lend themselves better to surveys, some to case studies, and some to documentary research. Investigators must select a method or combination of methods that they believe will produce a solution.

The Survey. Surveys are more widely used and often the most successful method to determine present educational trends or attitudes, to compare present conditions with those of the past, and to forecast events of the future. Other labels for the survey are the descriptive survey, the normative study, and the status study. In collecting data for a survey, educational leaders consult sources that give them the most complete, current, and accurate information on the subject. Researchers either make direct observations, administer questionnaires and other paper pencil instruments, or conduct interviews.

Questionnaires. Carefully constructed questionnaires or those that have been validated through frequent use can help gather information in a relatively short time period. The three-round delphi method takes considerably longer (see the planning section of this chapter). Questionnaires, unfortunately, are weak because they are impersonal. In addition, construction of good questionnaires is complicated[6,7,11].

The Interview. Interview methods use national and local opinion surveys with considerable success. Using this method helps investigators obtain exact information from many individuals through face-to-face contact. Confidential information can usually be gathered if interviewers present requests honestly and intelligibly. Two important rules in the interview method are:

● The preparation of the interview guide and the conduct of the interview must be carefully planned.

● After a sample has been selected investigators should obtain some commitment of cooperation from these individuals before an interviewer arrives.

The principal advantages of the interview method over the questionnaire method are its adaptability, which allows for immediate feedback, and the opportunities for obtaining greater depth from the meaning of the responses.

Skillful interviewers can lead subjects to reveal key information that they would not reveal on a questionnaire.[6]

John Goodlad of UCLA and his associates used observations, questionnaires, and interviews to produce *A Place Called School*. They formulated questions about schools and transformed the questions into more specific ones for questionnaires and interviews. The staff modified existing techniques for systematically observing classroom practices and adopted them to use in the study. After fieldtesting the tools and processes, the survey methods were used to compile a large body of data about 38 schools. These 38 schools produced data from 8,624 parents, 1,350 teachers, and 17,163 students. Goodlad states that, "We cannot generalize to all schools from the sample. But certainly the 'thick descriptions' compiled from several different perspectives raise many questions about schooling and about other schools...."[12] From these "thick descriptions" many common elements emerged with implications for all schools.

Case Studies. Data gathered for case studies are in many ways similar to the "thick descriptions" used by Goodlad. Case study methods entail intensive study of a single individual, several individuals, school, or several schools at one particular point in time or over a period of time. Like those achieved in typical surveys, case study results or conclusions are more descriptive than prescriptive. The method helps identify causative factors and may suggest procedural changes. Case studies usually involve accumulation of considerable data, and with careful analysis, investigators isolate cause and effect relationships that explain the observed behaviors of subjects or institutions. The results can produce guidelines or suggestions that can be generalized to similar situations.

The naturalist, who conducts research in natural settings, cautions researchers about drawing conclusions from "thick descriptions" conducted either from rationalistic or naturalistic paradigms. Naturalists do not attempt to form generalizations that will hold at all times in all places, but to form working hypotheses that can be transferred from one context to another depending on the degree of "fit" between the contexts.[13]

Documentary Research. When investigators are interested in events and conditions of the past, they turn to documentary research, which includes collection and analysis of historical documents. The most important steps in this method of research include location of the records, their external and internal evaluation, and interpretation.[14] Records as sources of data can be numerous—eyewitness accounts of events, letters, diaries, legal records, affirmed files, newspapers, board minutes, and artifacts of many kinds. Primary sources are preferred over secondary sources because of the chance of error.

It is important that school leaders possess skills in selecting the best research designs to fit the problem to be investigated. The credibility of research findings relies on the research design and methods used. If the experimental survey, case study, documentary investigation, or a combination of methods is selected for a given research project, then careful planning is required. Choice of the wrong method can lead to invalid results and costly decisions.

Descriptive and Inferential Statistics

School leaders in most cases are not statisticians, but they must possess the basic skills to interpret and in some cases conduct research. Their task is not to conduct precise research and produce perfect reports that appear in experimental psychology journals. Their aim is to make policy and program decisions based on what is best for the schools and the students. Therefore, a distinction should be drawn between *statistical significance* and *practical significance* of data.[15] To determine statistical significance, calculate the probability that a given event could have occurred by chance. Practical significance is a judgment call based on the level of statistical significance, number of subjects in the study, and the importance and political impact of the results. Administrators must know the rules to determine the levels of significance and importance to school programs.

Statistics is one of the most basic tools school leaders need to understand and use as they interpret scores from the many educational tests administered in our schools. Even reading a test manual to evaluate the adequacy of a test for a particular purpose requires statistical knowledge. More important, if school leaders are to benefit from research literature, an understanding of statistical concepts and methods is essential. Within practical restraints, this section of chapter nine identifies and briefly describes data analysis procedures that are of basic importance to school leaders. For the computational mechanics of plugging numbers into formulas, refer to a standard statistics text or completion of a graduate statistics course. Several excellent standard and programmed statistic texts are available.[16,17,18]

Statistics. Statistics deals with the collection, organization, and analysis of data. Statistics is also the science of reaching sound conclusions from incomplete data. How is this possible? School leaders must first understand that they can and should use the basic concepts of descriptive and/or inferential statistics in their decision making about school programs. The following outline identifies statistical concepts that should be learned by all administrators. Without these basics they cannot make informed decisions about school programs.

Descriptive Statistics

I. **DEFINITION** —statistics used to describe and summarize data.

II. **FOUR MAJOR TYPES**

    A. **MEASURES OF CENTRAL TENDENCY**

        1. **MODE**—the score occurring most frequently
        2. **MEDIAN**—the midpoint of a distribution
        3. **MEAN**—the average of the scores
           a. The statistical formula for mean

$$\overline{X} = \frac{\leq x}{N}$$

$\overline{X} =$ the mean of the distribution
$X =$ the raw score
$N =$ the number of raw scores
$\leq =$ "the sum of "

Example: Comparing mode, median, and mean

Raw Scores	Mode is the value occurring most frequently in a distribution.
X	4
4	8
8	8 The Mode is 8.
8	10
10	16
16	20
20	

Median is the midpoint of distribution. (In median — half of frequencies are below, half are above. In this example the median is halfway between the two center values of 8 and 10.) (The median is an appropriate average to use when there are usually high or low numbers.)

```
4
8       10
8     +  8   The Median is 9.
10    2 18
16      9
20
```

Mean is the average of the score.

```
     4
     8
     8    The
    10    Mean (X̄) is 11
    16
    20
 6  66
    11
```

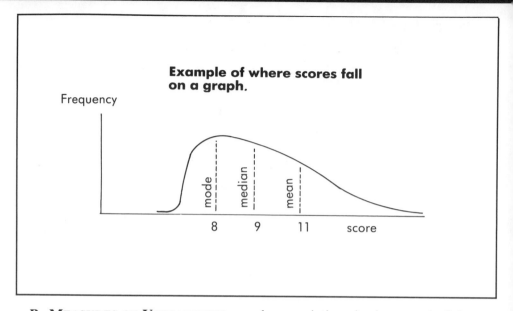

Example of where scores fall on a graph.

B. MEASURES OF VARIABILITY — show variations in the spread of the scores

1. **RANGE**—the difference between the highest and lowest score +1. Using the raw scores above: 20 - 4 = 16 + 1 = 17

2. **VARIANCE**—refers to the distribution of scores around the mean. Mean scores become less representative of group scores as the variance increases.
   a. The statistical formula for variance

$$S^2 = \frac{\Sigma\, x^2}{N}$$

S^2 = the variance of the sample

$x = X - \overline{X}$ = the difference between the raw score and the mean

N = the number of raw scores

Σ = "the sum of"

3. **STANDARD DEVIATION**—The standard deviation is the square root of the variance. It tells you whether most of the scores cluster closely around the mean or are spread out along the scale. The larger the standard deviation, the more spread out the scores. Standard deviation is also useful for comparing groups and provides the basis for standardizing test scores by computing IQ's, stanines, and scale scores. It is used more often than other measures of variability.

Frequency Distributions and Standard Deviation

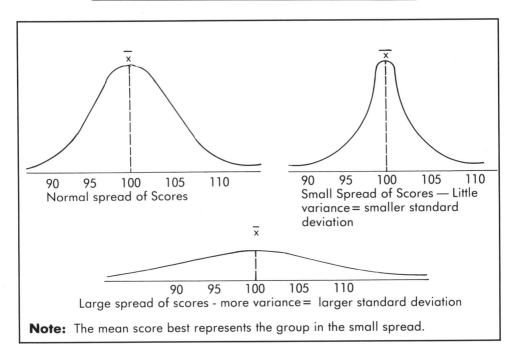

Note: The mean score best represents the group in the small spread.

a. The statistical formula for standard deviation

$$S = \sqrt{\frac{\lessgtr x^2}{N}}$$

S = the standard deviation of the sample
x = the difference between the raw score and the mean
N = the number of scores

Remember—standard deviation is the square root of variance.

The Measure of Variability

Techniques in the measure of variability are the most important statistical skills needed by school leaders. Mean scores, for example are frequently used to measure the achievement level of all students in a given school district, school, or grade level. Policy is made and programs are initiated or changed based on a statistic (i.e. mean scores) that may not tell the true picture since they hide the range and distribution of individual scores.

C. **Measures of relationships** — are expressed as correlational coefficients.

1. **Correlation coefficients** indicate the degree and direction of relationship of variables
    a. Correlation coefficient of + 1.00 (or -1.00) indicates the variables are highly related.

    b. Correlation coefficient of .00 indicates no relationship

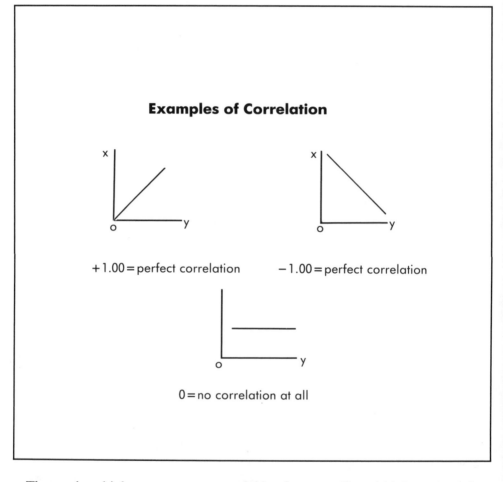

Examples of Correlation

+1.00 = perfect correlation   − 1.00 = perfect correlation

0 = no correlation at all

Thus, when high scores on one variable, for example, administrator performance, are associated with high scores on a second variable, for example, hours of inservice, the variables are said to be positively correlated. The same is true if both scores are low.

When high scores on one variable, i.e., high administrator performance scores, are associated with low scores on a second variable, i.e., very few hours of inservice and vice versa, the variables are said to be negatively correlated.

However, some variables show no tendency to vary or change together. In this case, it is reported that there is no correlation between the variables, for example, administrator performance and amount of inservice.

The amount of relationship or correlation is not causation. That is, improved administrator performance may not be caused by the amount of inservice. But an accumulation of correlational evidence can, in some cases, help build a credible case for causality between two variables.

D. **MEASURES OF DISPERSION** (or measures of relative position) express how well an individual has performed compared to all other individuals in the sample.

● **PERCENTILE RANK** indicates the percentage of scores that fall below a given score.

a. If a score of 70 corresponds to a percentile rank of 82, the 82nd percentile, this means 82 percent of the scores in the distribution are lower than 70.
For example, school administrators must understand percentile ranking to compare the distributions of achievement test scores in their districts with state and national scores.

b. The median of a set of scores corresponds to the 50th percentile. Of course the "national norm" is always at the 50 percent percentile.

The illustration indicates that students who have a rank of 82, did better than 82 percent of the students and not as well as 18 percent.

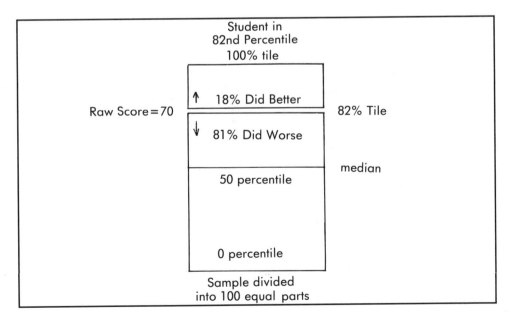

Student in
82nd Percentile
100% tile

Raw Score = 70

↑ 18% Did Better

82% Tile

↓ 81% Did Worse

median

50 percentile

0 percentile

Sample divided
into 100 equal parts

III. CHARACTERISTICS OF THE NORMAL CURVE

A. Fifty of the scores are above the mean and 50 percent are below the mean.

B. The mean, median, and mode are the same.

C. Most scores are near the mean.

D. A score occurs fewer times the farther it is from the mean.

E. A normal distribution is symmetrical and unimodal.

F. Ninety-nine percent of the scores tend to be plus and minus 3 standard deviations from the mean.

G. Over ninety-five percent of the scores lie within 2 standard deviations (plus and minus) from the mean.

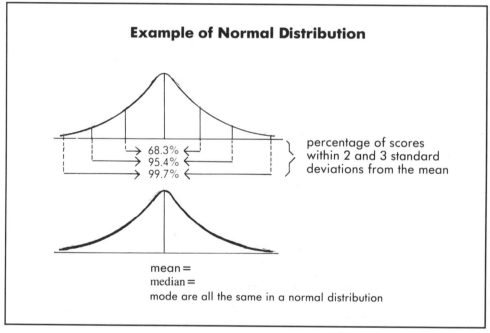

Example of Normal Distribution

68.3%
95.4%
99.7%

percentage of scores within 2 and 3 standard deviations from the mean

mean =
median =
mode are all the same in a normal distribution

For a normal distribution, the shape of the curve depends on the size of the variance or standard deviation. A small variance S^2 results in a "higher hump," a large variance gives a flatter curve.

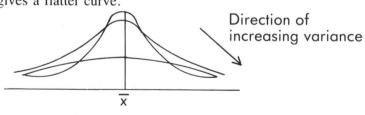

Direction of increasing variance

$\overline{x}$

H. **SKEWED DISTRIBUTIONS**— occur when a distribution is not normal

   1. Negatively skewed if the extreme scores are at the upper end of the distribution.

   2. Positively skewed if the extreme scores are at the lower end of the distribution.

   Skewed distributions can, of course, indicate that a test is too easy, too difficult or inappropriate for a particular group.

Example of Skewed Distributions

If the distribution of scores is skewed (where all the scores are at one or the other), the curve will not be symmetrical and the three measures, mean, median, and mode will not be equal.

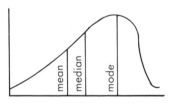

Left "negative" skew scores
tend to be in higher end.

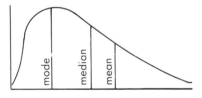

Right "positive" skew score
tend to be in lower end.

Inferential Statistics

I. **DEFINITION**— statistics used to determine how likely it is that the results of a sample, or samples, are the same results that would have been found for the entire population.

II. **TYPES OF INFERENTIAL STATISTICS**

A. T TEST - Statistical procedure used to determine if statistically significant differences between the means of two samples; that is, differences not likely to be due to chance.

EXAMPLE : Suppose we randomly assign students to two groups to compare the effectiveness of two methods of teaching reading. The groups are placed in different instructional situations for a semester. They are then tested in reading and their mean scores are determined. The two groups are different in their mean achievement scores. We need a way to determine if the differences that appear between the two groups are merely a result of chance factors, or if it can be attributed to the different teaching styles. The test is an appropriate statistical tool to test the difference.

First, one must reject what is called the "null hypothesis." The null hypothesis states that the two samples to be tested for mean differences are nothing more than one of many pairs of random samples from the same population where the mean of the differences in means is 0; that is, *the difference between the means is a function of chance alone*. If the difference between the means is unlikely to be a function of chance alone, the null hypothesis is rejected.

Next, establish confidence intervals or probable limits within which the population mean falls. In other words, a 95 percent confidence interval corresponds to .05 probability level that differences are due to chance.

a. Statistical formula

$$\bar{X} \pm 1.96 \ SE_{\bar{X}}$$

$$SE_{\bar{X}} = \text{Standard error of mean} = \frac{S}{\sqrt{\bar{X}}}$$

Note: with sample size of 500 or more, see Table of T in a statistics book.

Ninety-nine percent confidence interval—corresponds to .10 probability level of chance occurrence.

a. Statistical formula

$\bar{X} + 2.58\ SE_{\bar{X}}$ Note: with sample size of 500 or more.

Now, run the t test:

$$t* = \frac{\bar{X}_1 - \bar{X}_2}{\sqrt{\left(S_1^2 / n_1\right) + \left(S_2^2 / n_2\right)}}$$

*Where t = the value by which the statistical significance will be judged.

$\bar{X}_1$ = mean of group 1 n_1 = number of subjects in group 1
$\bar{X}_2$ = mean of group 2 n_2 = number of subjects in group 2
S_1^2 = variance of group 1
S_2^2 = variance of group 2

---

1. If the obtained value is less than the tabled value, then the null hypothesis is held true, and any differences in data can be attributed to chance alone.
2. If the obtained value of t equals or exceeds the tabled value, the null hypothesis is rejected, and we must attribute the differences to something other than chance, i.e., teaching styles.

Example Using T Test

Two classes of 25 students each obtained the following results on the final examination in statistics:

$$\text{Class 1: } \bar{X}_1 = 85 \qquad S_1^2 = 400.15$$

$$\text{Class 2: } \bar{X}_2 = 79 \qquad S_2^2 = 989.85$$

Test the hypothesis that the two classes do not differ in average performance on the exam, that is $C_1 = C_2$.

Solution:

$$t = \frac{\bar{X}_1 - \bar{X}_2}{\sqrt{\left(S_1^2/n_1\right) + \left(S_2^2/n_2\right)}} \quad \begin{matrix} = 6 \\[6pt] = 1.52 \end{matrix}$$

$$t = \frac{6}{1.52} = 3.95$$

Thus:
3.95 = obtained value
2.01 = book value at .05 with 49
degrees of freedom.

- Reject the null hypothesis and conclude that the two classes do differ significantly in their performance.

B. ANOVA—Analysis of variance. A statistical procedure designed to analyze the differences between the means of two or more samples. It analyzes the variations in groups and yields an F value that is interpreted like the T value. In this procedure, a different form of the treatment is applied to each of the groups, then the values of the treatment group means are compared.

ANOVA is a very important test that lends itself to a wide variety of research problems and is also the basic unit of many more complex experimental designs. It is one of the most widely used statistical procedures. Detailed explanations of ANOVA can be found in statistics textbooks.

Computer Program Statistical Package for the Social Sciences (SPSS)

Computer programs on these and other statistical tests are available in most larger school district research divisions, universities, and regional research laboratories.

One of the most widely used computer programs to run statistical analyses is the Statistical Package for the Social Sciences (SPSS). SPSS provides a variety of tests and analyses. Figure 4 includes a sample of SPSS procedures that are accomplished by computer.

Figure 4. SPSS Procedures for Statistical Analyses.

Procedure	SPSS Procedure Name
mean	CONDESCRIPTIVE OR FREQUENCIES OR BREAKDOWN
Standard Deviation	FREQUENCIES OR BREAKDOWN
t - test for unmatched groups	T - TEST (GROUPS)
Chi - square	CROSSTABS
Analysis of variance	ANOVA
Factor analysis	FACTOR

School administrators need a working knowledge of these basic statistical concepts and tools to interpret and conduct research to provide better schools.

Program Evaluation, Planning Models, and Methods

In recent years, school leaders have been provided a fairly large number of evaluation models from which to choose. We do not wish to compare the merits of various evaluation models here but present a few of the more helpful ones.

Evaluation of educational programs is an inexact science. To evaluate means to "value" something. Thus values are involved; indeed, they must be. The choice of evaluation as a useful process, the definition of its role, what is studied, how it is studied, how resources are allocated, all involve value judgments. Judgments are made regarding the relative value of various evaluation means versus evaluation ends.[19] The intellectual, emotional, and physical well being of numerous students can be helped or harmed as a result of program evaluations. Two excellent sources that describe the importance of constant attention to rigorous evaluation standards are *Standards for Evaluation of Educational Programs, Projects and Materials*, developed by the Joint Committee on Standards for Educational Evaluation, and an AASA publication *Evaluating Educational Programs* by Mitchell Lazarus. These sources present practical ideas and strategies on evaluation, ranging from evaluation standards, planning, choosing a test, and interpreting test scores to new evaluation methods and reporting results.[20,21]

Two evaluation models that have been most helpful to school leaders are the Goal-Attainment Model and the CIPP Model.

Goal-Attainment Model. The origin of this model is usually associated with the work of Ralph W. Tyler of the University of Chicago.[22] Tyler believes that the degree to which a school can reach its goals determines its direction and success. Careful formulation of educational goals transformed into measurable (i.e. behavioral) objectives gave impetus to an evangelic fervor that spawned the belief that "Anything worth teaching can be written in behavioral form" or "If you can't write it down, you can't teach it." Tyler advocated measuring student achievement to determine the degree to which the previously established goals were achieved. The goal-attainment model includes helpful steps for school leaders and state and national accrediting agencies.[23] The model consists of eight steps.

1. Involve members of the total community.

2. Construct broad goals and specific objectives.

3. Translate specific objectives into forms that are communicable and that facilitate learning.

4. Develop measurement instrumentation.

5. Carry out periodic measurement.

6. Analyze measurement data.

7. Interpret analyzed data.

8. Formulate recommendations for program change or modify the goals and objectives.

The CIPP Model. This program evaluation model, used for decision orientation, was developed by evaluation specialists Daniel Stufflebeam of Western Michigan University and Egan Guba of Indiana University. Stufflebeam has been more active in refining the CIPP Model during recent years. The term CIPP, an acronym, represents four types or stages of evaluation: context, input, process, and product. These four states of evaluation lend themselves to making four types of evaluation decisions. Planning decisions to determine objectives are made in *context* evaluation. Structuring decisions to design evaluation procedures are made in *input* evaluation. Implementing decisions to use, monitor, and improve these procedures are made in *process* evaluation, and recycling decisions to judge and react to the outcomes produced by these procedures are made in *product* evaluation.[24]

The CIPP model has been widely used to evaluate programs in and out of education.[25, 26] A wide variety of evaluation instruments are used to gather important data to include in the evaluation. (See skill accomplishment checklist for Skill "D" at the end of this chapter.)

The Texas Education Agency (TEA) initiated an accreditation and renewal process to guide 1,100 local school districts.[27] The TEA model has been influenced by the Goal-Attainment and the CIPP models. Figure 5 displays these influences and similarities. One recent school evaluation simulation produced by the National Study of School Evaluation provides a useful teaching resource that requires participants to apply many of the concepts included in the evaluation models in Figure 5.[28]

School leaders must continue to upgrade their program evaluation skills to give more concrete evidence to the public of the success of our school systems. This concrete evidence can be produced by combining testing information, other research and evaluation methods, and good judgment. According to Paul Salmon, executive director of AASA, "School improvement councils, self-studies, visits by external evaluation teams, examinations of whether existing programs are meeting real needs, all contribute to the evolving science, or art, of effective evaluation."[21]

Evaluation, Planning, and Futures Methods

Educational planning is a process to "get there from here" in the most efficient and effective manner possible. The process is vital to meet the megachallenges described in Appendix A and to meet the minichallenges faced daily in a school building or classroom. The purpose of this section is to introduce the most useful planning and futures methods for school operations.

A key function of the school district, and therefore the responsibility of school leaders, is to manange change through careful planning. Every educational problem, program, and decision is the result of some change that has happened or one that school leaders wish to initiate. The following steps are necessary to manage change effectively.

1. Specify the objectives of the change and anticipate the problems that will be created by change.

2. Create programs to accomplish the objectives and manage the problems.

3. Gain the acceptance of the entire administrative team and other key people who are involved or affected.

4. Establish an effective communications network to manage disagreement and agreement in the change process.

Figure 5.
Comparing Evaluation Models.

Goal-Attainment (Metfessel and Michael)	CIPP (Stufflebeam)	TEA (Division of Accreditation)
1. Involve members of the total community. 2. Construct broad goals and specific objectives. 3. Translate specific objectives into forms that are communicable and facilitate learning.	1. **Context Evaluation** Attempts to isolate the problems or unmet needs in educational setting. This leads to identification of general goals and specific objectives that should be the focus of an educational program.	1. **Goal and Goal Indicators** Broad statements of desired student characteristics, related to knowledge, attitude, or physical peformance. Should cover reasonable range of student learning areas that school district and community makes commitment to pursue.
4. Develop measurement instrumentation.	2. **Input Evaluation** To provide information needed for decisions regarding which instructional resources to use and in what manner they should be used to promote achievement of objectives identified.	2. **Self-Study** Student needs assessment by comparing student achievement to goal attainment, establish the priority of student learning needs in specific areas of concern. Program Analysis -- use student learning needs to analyze program. What program deficiencies might have caused student learning needs?
5. Carry out periodic measurement.	3. **Process** Monitor actual instructional objectives to help instruction and decision makers anticipate and overcome procedural difficulties.	3. **Five Year Plan** Priorities plan to reach targeted student learning objectives in five years or less. Also a plan of targeted improvements in student goal achievement. Strategies to achieve these objectives may be new, modified, or intensified efforts chosen by district.
6. Analyze measurement data. 7. Interpret analyzed data. 8. Formulate recommendations for program change or modified goals and objectives.	4. **Product** Analyze outcomes produced by the program. Outcomes are related to objectives. Comparison is made between expectations and actual results. This helps decide whether to continue, terminate, modify, or refocus instructional programs.	4. **Annual Evaluation** Product-Student Achievement; Process-Implementation Strategies. Were the annual student learning objectives achieved? Were the implementation strategies carried out as planned? Were the implementation strategies the right ones? What changes in the plan's objectives or strategies should be based on annual evaluation?

5. Provide a budget and resource system that will help key people receive the necessary money and other resources at the right time and place.

In the 1980s, planning has changed in nature, scope, and purpose. School leaders have grown to appreciate the old saying; "Plans are sometimes useless, but the planning process is indispensable." Planning will not predict the future with complete accuracy nor solve all problems. A proper planning process, however, will reduce the number of surprises or "gotchas" and help revise the original objectives and the methods of assessment. Thus, optimizing staff and student performance rather than accurately hitting the original target is the mark of a good planning process.

People Plan the Plan

The most important point to remember about the planning process is that "people plan the plan." School managers can apply the most sophisticated planning techniques and be miserable planners unless key colleagues are involved, trusted, and recognized for their expertise and contributions.[29] Old truths in this concept keep coming back in the forms of "quality circles" and *In Search for Excellence.* People in education do not want and in most cases do not need a "boss." They need a leader with the skills to bring out the very best talent and desire in each staff member. Planning is through people not through plans. An AASA critical issues report, *Planning for Tomorrow's Schools*, emphasizes the point that educational planning "may reside less in its technical adequacy or vision than in the processes it conditions and the political environment within which it functions. By bringing together all of the groups who have an interest in a district's educational plan (and by letting them shape the plan through their discussion and debate), the district gains support for the resulting plan.[30] AASA and Bill Cook have initiated strategic planning certification programs for school leaders. The program provides a step-by-step results oriented discipline for strategic planning. Videos and books on the process are available from AASA.

Planning: How To Do It

1. Establish a planning team that includes:
   a. Professional and support staff members
   b. Parents and students
   c. Superintendent and one member of the Board
   d. Ten community leaders including the media

2. Develop a plan for planning
   a. Determine the type of planning — facilities, curriculum, personnel development, bond issue, and so on
   b. Identify goals and goal indicators and put them in priority
   c. Conduct a needs assessment within the schools and the community
   d. Determine greatest needs and put them in priority
   e. Establish a time line (for example, one year, two years)
   f. Establish milestones for continuous assessment of goal accomplishment
   g. Determine the person(s) responsible for each component of the plan
   h. Allocate resources by placing a price tag on each step
   i. Establish a reporting system through internal and external information systems.

Nominal Group Technique (NGT). NGT is a good planning method to encourage group members to view themselves as critical to the planning or problem-solving process.[31] This technique provides a structured group meeting following a prescribed sequence in the problem-solving steps and using low variability among planning groups containing six to ten people. A large number of independent ideas are generated using the techniques. Participants in the NGT process feel less threatened and gain a strong sense of accomplishment.

NGT consists of five steps:

● *Step 1:* Silent generation of ideas that are put in writing by each participant. The question under consideration is shared with each group member. The group is then charged to write ideas in brief phrases or statements that will answer the question.

● *Step 2:* Round robin recording of ideas—participants are asked to give one of their ideas that will be recorded on a flip chart or a black board. No discussion takes place at this point. Each participant gives an idea or passes until all of the ideas generated by the group have been recorded.

● *Step 3:* Each idea is clarified and discussed in the order in which they were presented. This step is designed to eliminate misunderstandings that might have arisen concerning the ideas presented.

● *Step 4:* Vote on item importance—each participant is asked to rank order a specific number of items, usually five, plus or minus two. Each participant places the item number and its rank on separate cards. The votes are counted and discussion is encouraged to clear up misunderstandings about item information.

● *Step 5:* Final vote—From the process a priority list of answers is obtained.

KIVA. Excellent for involving many people, the KIVA method also offers a clearer perspective of the past, present, and future events in the planning process. KIVA consists of seven steps (see figure 6).

Figure 6. KIVA Method.

Step 1. Divide the people into three equal-sized groups and label group 1 as "past experts," group 2 as "present experts," and group 3, "future experts."

Step 2. Seat group 1, "past experts," in chairs arranged in a circle and ask them to present a history of the problem or plan and record each idea on a flip chart. After 20 minutes, tape the "past" information on the wall so that it is visible to all group members. Note only "past experts" are allowed to talk in Step 2; the present and future experts observe from behind the circle of chairs.

Step 3. Ask group 2, "present experts," to present the current events affecting the plan or idea and repeat the process in step 2. Only "present experts" are allowed to talk.

Step 4. Next group 3, "future experts," present possible, probable, and likely events that will impact or be initiated by the plan and repeat the process in steps 2 and 3. Only "future experts" are allowed to talk.

Step 5. The combined groups move into one big circle and discussss the past, present, and future events, and their implications, problems, and strong points.

Step 6. The KIVA leader should attempt to reach consensus on the most important needs that the school or district should address.

Step 7. The most important needs become the priorities upon which the planning process begins.

Luvern Cunningham, in "From Visions to Development: A Learning Resources Center - Based Community Education Systems Model," USAID/Washington, Grant Agreement No. AID/1A-G1169, prepared by San Jose State University, 1978.

Gantt Chart. The Gantt Chart provides an orderly method for graphically displaying the steps in a planning project. The task to be completed and the person responsible are listed down the left side of the chart. The time requirement to accomplish each task is located at the top of the chart. Figure seven provides an example of a Gantt chart to initiate and evaluate a new curriculum program.

Each activity and required resource is included along with the time duration and sequence. The last step in the construction of a Gantt chart is progress posting. Progress is normally posted at regular intervals so that activities that are off schedule can be identified and corrective action taken.[29]

**Figure 7.
Gantt Chart.**

Activity and Person/s responsible	Jan.	Feb.	March	April	May
1. Conduct needs assessment	1——28				
2. Identify and prioritize needs		1——15			
3. Select evaluation teams		2/16 — 3/4			
4. Develop news releases	1/1 ——————————————————— 5/29				
5. Design program strategies			3/5——7		
6. Inservice for staff			3/7—— 4/3		
7. Initiate program				4/3—— 5/7	
8. Monitor program impact				4/5—5/15	
9. Conduct final evaluation					5/15-18
10. Final report					5/19-25

Program Evaluation Review Technique/Critical Path Network (PERT/ CPM). PERT is a more complicated version of the Gantt Chart that includes the duration of the project, the interrelationships among the activities, and the time factors called "slack time" and "critical path." Scheduling of the project and promised completion dates are based on the network time calculation for the critical path.[32] This technique can prove to be very helpful in the preparation of the operating budget or in planning school facilities.

A PERT network is a "flow diagram" consisting of the activities and events that must be accomplished to reach the program objective, showing their logical and planned sequences of accomplishment, interdependencies, and interrelationships. The PERT network begins with the final event. An event is a point in time when something either ends or begins. It is represented by a circle and assigned a number. The sequence is in chronological order. Activities, which are indicated by straight lines connecting two events, involve the expenditure of resources and lead to the accomplishment of an event. Beginning with the final event, the administrator works backward to other events that must precede it; for example, what events must come before, after, or at the same time as the particular event. In figure eight for example, the steps involved in producing videotapes of simulated problems for principals are diagrammed. We start with the original idea to final distribution for principals to use for self - improvement. In the PERT chart we show six steps. (We have simplified the steps for the purposes of this discussion.) If there is a delay in one of the steps—for example, it takes longer than two weeks to film the simulations—then the inservice coordinator checks the PERT chart to see how this delay will change the overall schedule.

Notice that in the PERT diagram the time required for each step is given. Writing the script for the simulation takes three weeks; filming the simulations takes three weeks. Thus, the films will be ready for duplication in six weeks. The total six-week sequence is what is known as the *critical path*: the specific sequence of activities and events whose completion is critical to the entire project. What the inservice coordinator has done is to estimate the least possible amount of time needed for completion of the critical path. The method of estimating project completion time is known as the CPM (Critical Path Method).

Futures Methods

Preparing school leaders to anticipate and manage the future has become a major thrust of the University Council of Educational Administrators, AASA, and other organizations. This emphasis on educational futures has revitalized interest in educational planning among public school and university practitioners and professors. This interest in planning for the future has created a whole new species of intellectual: the professional futurists or futurologist. This creative futurist analyzes economic, educational, social, and technical trends and their impact on institutions and society. Based on this analysis the futurist designs two or three forecasts. These forecasts are valuable tools for managers. The education division of the World Future Society (WFS) has made a definite impact on educational leaders. The WFS, Hudson Institute, and other futures groups have added respect to the field that has led to at least 400 colleges offering futurist courses.

Figure 8. Sample Project Using PERT.

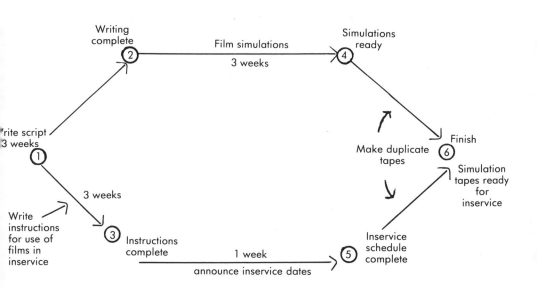

Public schools have been adding futures components to social studies, science, and English curriculum, and the use of futures methods are widespread in gifted and talented programs.

Vision and School Leaders. There is no question that America's parents and others are searching for managers who have vision to lead the public schools. Administrators who lack vision probably will survive in today's educational environment. But the schools and systems under their direction will not cope successfully over the long haul without those special people who know where they are going and what it will take to produce successful students.

San Diego Superintendent Thomas Payzant put it this way: "As shapers of the future of education, we must have a vision of what it should and can be. School leaders must be able to transform ideas into action that help schools become places of learning that can make a difference in the lives of children."[37]

Few universities or corporations, although there are exceptions, have worked to develop visionaries among their students or staff. As such, it must be assumed that those who possess such creative and intuitive thinking processes are either self-taught or have an innate perception as to the role vision plays in organizational success. Daniel Duke, University of Virginia Professor of Educational Administration, writes that the difference between more effective and less effective school leaders boils down to two factors: Effective leaders (1) possess and are able to articulate a vision of effective schooling, and (2) they allocate their time in ways that increase the likelihood of realizing that vision.[38] School leaders, however, can use various techniques to help develop a vision of the future and effective schools, and enable others to share in that process. One of the best exercises follows:

Step 1   Select a group of 25 community and school leaders for a one-day workshop.

Step 2   Select a keynote speaker to present ideas on the future of the nation, state, and local community.

Step 3   Ask participants to close their eyes, relax, and project themselves to the environment of the year 2015.

Step 4   Tell participants that you have received the word that the school district has been selected as one of the top three districts in the United States in 2015.

Step 5   Ask each person to write down three or four reasons for the national recognition.

Step 6   Conduct a mock television interview and ask each person to state the three reasons why the district won the recognition.

Step 7   Record all responses.

Step 8   Organize task forces around the major reasons to begin working toward making them a reality.

Intuition in School Management. In these times of change, school leaders must make decisions about people and programs in a hurry. Intuition as a method or resource to make decisions is receiving heightened attention in publications such as *The Wall Street Journal, The Futurist, Fortune, Administrative Management* and *The School Administrator*. Intuitive management, much more than gut level decision making, is based on the ways a person uses both hemispheres of the brain to make decisions. Much research on the human brain reveals that the American education system is basically "left brained." We are taught to be logical, to use language, to stress mathematical and analytical reasoning, and to be deductive in drawing conclusions. We are taught systematically how to learn, and not to be out of step. It's like the Japanese motto: If the nail sticks out, hammer it in."

Now we are discovering that leaders in business, government, and education have far higher scores on intuition in making decisions. Walt Disney, for instance, had both the ability to use right-brain, inductive, holistic artistic hunches and was also an analytical "left brained" thinker. After Disney's death, the Walt Disney Corporation hit troubled financial times because too many left brained, systematic people were making decisions. Once the corporation was directed to the use of the integrative right/left brain approach to intuitive management, the corporation gained new momentum.[37]

Trust Your Hunches. School leaders must trust their hunches more and not always rely on the facts. Conventional wisdom may not be superior wisdom. We must realize that genuine intuitive insights are not under conscious control or will. Predicting when they will come is nearly impossible.

This intuitive hunch came to Ray Kroc of McDonalds fame in 1960. His laywer advised against spending $2.7 million for the McDonalds name. Ray Kroc closed his office door, yelled and screamed, threw things out of windows, called his lawyer back and yelled, "Take it!" He said he "felt in his funny bone, it was a sure thing."

School leaders are caught between the thunder and the lightning of education. They must logically and intuitively reach out and "take it" if education is to keep pace with the world around them.

Scenarios. One of the better methods to plan probable, possible, or preferable futures is by developing scenarios of the future. A scenario is a description of a series of future events that produce an outcome. In writing a scenario, persons describe these future events and the eventual outcome by placing themselves in the future, describing the changes in their surroundings, and reflecting on how and when the changes occurred. Scenarios have been used as helpful tools in educational planning.[33]

Delphi Technique. The Delphi technique was initiated in the early 1950s as an Air Force-sponsored Rand Corporation study.[35] The technique involves a series of questionnaires that ask a panel of experts to provide an opinion or prediction concerning the topic. The first round asks for general information. The second round consist of items developed from the first round and requests panelists to respond to forced choice, Likert-type items. The third round provides panelists with group averages from the second round usually in the form of a mean, mode, medium, or interquartile range. Panelists are asked to reconsider their second round responses based on the collective data. Individual panelists are asked to consider changing their response to move closer to the group norm or to state a reason they feel that a minority position is in order. A fourth questionnaire provides each participant with new consensus data and a summary of minority opinions and requests a final revision of responses.[29]

Skills in educational planning and related futures methods are vital for school leaders in coping with the complexities of the future and in planning and making decisions for developing effective school programs. People make the plans and school leaders need staff support to be effective planners. The techniques of planning are the second consideration. School administrators who can create the right planning attitudes and can apply the right techniques will take a major stride toward earning the label "school leader."

Selection, Administration, and Interpretation of Evaluation Instruments

A variety of evaluation instruments are available to school leaders. The most useful material for this purpose is the *Program Evaluation Kit* developed at the Center for the Study of Evaluation at UCLA.[36] These six small books include instruments and methods to assist evaluators in measuring program implementation and impact.

Standardized testing by far dominates the practice of program evaluation nationwide. According to Mitchell Lazarus, "There is a growing body of professional opinion to the effect that standardized testing, while usually the fastest, cheapest way to evaluate, is sometimes not the best way.[21] The AASA book, *Evaluating Educational Programs*, written by Lazarus, presents helpful information to school leaders about the pitfalls in testing and how to avoid them and suggests practical alternatives and methods that have been proven to work.

It is important to select or design an instrument that fits the local school situation. Evaluation teams of teachers and administrators who help institute the program priorities should write appropriate objectives and select and/or design evaluation instruments, and well written criterion-referenced tests. No one instrument should be the only tool to gather data to make judgments about programs, teachers, administrators, and students. Staff, student, parent, and expert opinion should be balanced with norm and criterion-referenced tests.

Reporting Test Results. It is important to remember that school performance results may be negative. Rather than take a defensive posture, outline the steps your district plans to take toward improvement. Also, before informing the news media, inform all school employees about assessment procedures and scores. All staff should be informed about the nature of the testing program, what the tests are supposed to show and not show, and how the results are going to be used to improve student performance. Following staff meeting or other communication, individual efforts should be made to inform parent groups and others. Newsletters can help. Releases, individual visits, and press conferences can be used to inform the news media. Skills in selecting, analyzing, interpreting, and reporting the results from evaluation instruments are a critical part of a school administrator's arsenal.

Conclusion

School leaders must be skilled at interpreting and conducting research, evaluating programs, and planning for the future. Each skill is dependent on the other and must be mastered. Preparation programs have stressed these skills in recent years, but for many reasons, busy school administrators have not always used the available knowledge. Inservice programs are too often focused on immediate problems or "quick fix" information. School leaders realize that the public is no longer satisfied with information describing the process of education. They are asking for a product and a payoff for the programs. Therefore, the basic skills included in this chapter are critical if America's school administrators are to win greater support for our schools.

Skill Accomplishment Checklist for Chapter Nine

Competency and Skills	Reading and Activities for Mastery
Competency: Conducting research and using research findings in decision making to improve long range planning, school operations, and student learning.	Readings: See resources 2 - 8. Activities: 1. Learner could design a sequential list of topics usually included in a research plan. 2. Learner could identify a local educational problem and identify the important variables, develop the hypotheses, gather the data, test and draw conclusions.
Skill A: Research designs and methods including gathering, analyzing, and interpreting data.	Readings: See resources 3, 4, 5, 6, 7, 8, 12, 13, 14 Activities: 1. Student could be presented with three educational problems and required to select and defend the proper research design. 2. Student could be assigned to develop and pilot test a questionnaire. 3. Learner could be assigned to develop an interview schedule and interview five superintendents, principals, or professors. 4. Learner could be presented with data gathered by questionnaires or interviews and ask to analyze and interpret the findings.
Skill B: Descriptive and inferential statistics.	Readings: See resources 5 and 16. Activities: 1. Learner could be given a set of test scores and required to calculate the mean, median, mode, and standard deviation. 2. Learner could be given test scores from two groups given different treatments and required to select the appropriate statistical tool and calculate for statistical significance at the .05 level.

Skill C: Evaluation and planning/futures models and methods.

Readings: See resources 15, 19, 20, 23, 24, 25 - 31, 32, 33, 35.
See also R. Kaufman and F. English, *Needs Assessment: A Guide To Improve School District Management*, (Arlington, Va.: AASA, 1976).
Activities:
1. Learner could conduct a local needs assessment about educational concerns.
2. Leaner could apply the CIPP Model to the evaluation of a simulated or actual program.
3. Learners could use the School Evaluation Simulation developed by NSSE, resource #28.
4. Learner could conduct a delphi study and write a scenario based on the results.
5. Learner could conduct a literature search on intuitive management and determine its benefits and problems for school managers.
6. Learner could develop a plan to improve a building maintenance or curriculum program using both a Gantt chart and PERT diagram.

Skill D: Selection administration, and interpretation of evaluation instruments

Readings: See resources 5, 11, 20, 23, 36. Also see B. Tuckman, *Evaluating Instructional Programs* (Boston: Allyn & Bacon, Inc., 1979). This test includes excellent examples of instruments.
Activities:
1. Present the learners with an evaluation problem and require them to select and defend their choice of instruments to gather data.
2. Require learner to distinguish the strengths and weaknessess of norm and criterion-referenced tests.
3. Require learner to interpret a set of test scores using percentiles, stanines and grade equivalents.
4. Require learner to develop a plan for releasing district or schoolwide test scores to the media.

1. L.L. Cunningham and J.T. Hentges, *The American School Superintendency 1982*, (Arlington, Va.: American Association of School Administrators, 1983).

2. E. W. Eisner, "Can Educational Research Inform Educational Practice?"; and E.L. Baker, "Can Educational Research Inform Educational Practice? Yes!", *Phi Delta Kappan* 65 (March 1984).

3. J.I. Goodlad, "A Study of Schooling," presented to the Stanford Teacher Education Project, Stanford, Calif., Jan. 23, 1982; B. Rowan, S.T. Bossert, and D.C. Dwyer, "Research on Effective Schools: A Cautionary Note" *Educational Researcher* 12, 4 (April 1983), p. 24.

4. L. Cuban, "Effective Schools: A Friendly But Cautionary Note," *Phi Delta Kappan* 64, 10 (1983), p. 695-696; D. MacKenzie Research for School Improvement: An Appraisal of Some Recent Trends" *Educational Researcher* 12, 4 (April 1983), p. 5-14.

5. F.N. Kerlinger, *Foundations of Behavioral Research: Educational, Psychological and Sociological Inquiry (2nd Edition)* (New York: Holt Rinehart & Winston, 1973).

6. W. Borg and M. Gall, *Educational Research: An Introduction (Fourth Edition)* (New York: Longman, 1983).

7. B. Tuckman, *Conducting Educational Research (2nd Edition)* (New York: Harcourt Brace, Javonovich Inc., 1979).

8. D.T. Stanley and D. Campbell, "Experimental and Quasi-Experimental Designs for Research on Teaching," N.L. Gage (Ed.), *Handbook for Research on Teaching* (Chicago: Rand-McNally, 1963), p. 171-296; J. Hoyle, "Has Your Research Design Been Weak Lately?" *CEDR Quarterly* 2, 3 (Fall 1978), 18-19.

9. J. Hoyle, "Evaluating an Alternative High School Program," *NASSP Spotlight*, published by the National Association of Secondary School Principals, Reston, Va., September 1975.

10. J. Hoyle and R. J. Stalcup, "A Report of the Evaluation of Dougherty County's Chapter I Program in Mathematics and Reading - Grades 1-6 For the Period of September, 1981 - June, 1982," Dec. 1982, p. 4.

11. L.W. Anderson, *Assessing Affective Characteristics in the Schools* (Boston: Allyn & Bacon, Inc., 1981), pp. 239-260.

12. J.I. Goodlad, *A Place Called School* (New York: McGraw-Hill, 1984).

13. E. Guba and Y. Lincoln, *Effective Evaluation* (San Francisco: Jossey-Bass, 1981).

14. T. Hillway, *Handbook of Educational Research* (New York: Houghton Mifflin Co., 1969), pp. 43-45.

15. W.J. Popham, *Educational Evaluation (Englewood Cliffs, N.J.: Prentice-Hall, 1975), pp. 239 and 249.*

16. *B.L. Turney and G.P. Robb, Statistical Methods for Behaviorial Science: With Feedback Exercises* (New York: Intext Pub. Inc., 1973).

17. C.T. Fitz-Gibbons and L.L. Morris, *How to Calculate Statistics* (Beverly Hills: Sage Publications, 1978).

18. J. Bruning and B. Kintz, *Computational Handbook of Statistics (2nd Edition)* (Glenview, Ill.: Scott Foresman, 1977).

19. D.R. Krathwohl, "The Myth of Value Free Evaluation," *Educational Evaluation and Policy Analysis* 2, 1 (January–February 1980), p. 44.

20. *Standards for Evaluation of Educational Programs, Projects and Materials*, developed by the Joint Committee on Standards for Educational Evaluation (New York: McGraw-Hill, 1981).

21. M. Lazarus, *Evaluating Educational Programs* (Arlington, Va.: American Association of School Administrators, 1982).

22. R. Tyler, "General Statement of Evaluation," *Journal of Educational Research* 35 (1942), pp. 492-501.

23. N.S. Metfessel and W.B. Michael, "A Paradigm Involving Multiple Criterion Measures for the Evaluation of the Effectiveness of School Programs," *Educational and Psychological Measurement* 27 (1967), pp. 931-943.

24. D. Stufflebeam, J. Walter, W. Gephart, R. Hammond, H. Merriman, and M. Provus, *Educational Evaluation and Decision Making* (Itasca, Ill.: F.E. Peacock, 1971).

25. J. Gilberg and E. Scholwinski, "Improving the Utility of Schools Psychological Reports Through Evaluation Using Stufflebeam's CIPP Model," *School Psychological Review* 12, 3 (March 1983).

26. J. Hoyle, "Evaluation and Corrective Therapy: Help?", *Journal of Corrective Therapy* (October 1978).

27. TEA, "Accreditation Planning Process" (Austin, Texas: Texas Education Agency, 1984).

28. *School Evaluation Simulation*, developed by the National Study of School Evaluation, (Falls Church, Va.: NSSE Pub., 1984).

29. W.G. Cunningham, *Systematic Planning for Educational Change* (Palo Alto, Calif.: Mayfield Pub. Co., 1982).

30. American Association of School Administrators, *Planning for Tomorrow's Schools* (Arlington, Va.: American Association of School Administrators, 1984), p. 9.

31. A.L. Delbecq and A. Vande Ven, *Group Techniques for Program Planning*, (Glenview, Ill.: Scott Foresman and Company, 1975) for an example of the NGT for solving school problems, see J. Hoyle, "Teacher Versus Administrator: A Growing Crisis," *Planning and Changing* 9, 4 (Winter 1978) and *Educational Digest* (May 1979).

32. R.L. Granger, *Educational Leadership* (Scranton, Pa.: Intext Pub. Co., 1971), pp. 128-138.

33. C. Dede and D. Allen, "Education in the 21st Century: Scenarios as a Tool for Strategies Planning", *Phi Delta Kappan* (January 1981).

34. H. Kahn, and others, *The Next 200 Years* (New York: Morrow and Co., 1976).

35. T.J. Gorden and O. Helmer, *Report of Long-Range Forecasting Study*, Rand Corporation, 1964.

36. L.L. Morris (ed.), *Program Evaluation Kit* (Beverly Hills: Sage Publications, 1978).

37. T.W. Payzant. "Making a Difference in the Lives of Children: Educational Leadership in the Year 2000," Paul B. Salmon Memorial Lecture, delivered at the annual convention of the American Assocation of School Administrators, New Orleans, February, 1987.

38. D.L. Duke, *School Leadership and Instructional Improvement* (New York, Random House, 1987), p.33.

PREPARING THE BEST SCHOOL LEADERS

The scope and complexity of the skills in this book designed to foster successful school leaders may be viewed flatly as "overwhelming." On the other hand, the reader may conclude falsely that, "If I master all the skills, I can be a guaranteed success!" Neither belief is realistic for these reasons:

• It is possible to acquire a good level of proficiency in almost all of the skills described, though few administrative jobs require the same level of expertise in all of them.

• Educational administration is not static, but interactive and dynamic. Simply mastering these skills ignores the reality of the whole job.

• The knowledge base of educational administration constantly is being expanded and refined.

Mastery of all eight skill areas at the highest level may not be possible. School leaders, however, can aspire to mastery of the structural components of each area and strive to remain current throughout their careers.

Additionally, there is no clear research evidence that the study of each skill, and the employment of each recommended management system component, will result in outstanding success by administrators. It is striking, however, that major attributes of the eight skill areas, and the recommended delivery systems, (i.e., management, content, clinical, field, professional and renewal components) are found in the programs of most universities, academies, Leadership in Educational Administration Development projects, and institutes.

Delivery Systems and the Book

Delivering, applying, and evaluating the eight major skill areas is easier said than done. University faculty and practicing administrators, however, have adapted these recommendations with success. This section suggests programs and procedures to deliver and/or apply the eight major skill areas at the following levels:

• University preparation programs in educational administration.
• School district management training academies.
• State agency school-management training programs.
• State LEAD projects.
• National professional organizations, academies, seminars, and workshops.
• Self-help programs.

Listed below are major program delivery components for these training levels. Some delivery components may apply to more than one level.

University Preparation Programs

University preparation programs should reflect contemporary management concepts and technologies. Students and professors engaged in this enterprise should be well-grounded in the foundations, theories, and research findings that support serious study of educational administration as an academic discipline. Educational administration has gained status as a university field of study as a result of the scholarly contributions by a number of distinguished professors. They have placed the study of educational administration on an equal plane with business administration, public administration, and other related applied disciplines.

Continued efforts by the National Council of Professors of Educational Administration (NCPEA) and University Council for Educational Administration (UCEA) are producing new ideas that strengthen preparation of school leaders. Also, Division A of the American Educational Research Association is a leading force in examining the concepts of educational administration through research and critical analysis.

Management System Components. Based on these developments and this book, university preparation programs should include the following management system components.

1. *Diagnosis Capability.* Assessment procedures should be developed not only for program entry, but also to diagnose competencies of graduate students in each of the eight skill areas and in speaking and writing skills. The faculty and an advisory committee of practicing administrators should construct the performance indicators, and determine minimum mastery levels for admission, counseling, placement, and completion. Diagnosis capability should be divided into two separate activities as follows:

• *Paper/Pencil Tests.* Multiple choice, short answer, and essay tests can be designed for each of the eight skill areas. Beginning students should achieve a minimum score of 70 percent, and a score of 80 percent should be required for students who have a master's degree or state administrative certification. A central file for test score data management should be kept to monitor student progress. The exam can be administered by a faculty member assigned to coordinate the diagnostic system, and it can be scored by a faculty member assigned to develop test items for each of the eight skills. Results should be shared with a program assessment committee as information and should be given to the student's adviser for counseling purposes.

• *Assessment Centers.* Students are tested and interviewed at assessment centers to evaluate their abilities, potentials, strengths, weaknesses, and motivation.(1) The test, which can take from one day to one week, should include simulated administrator games, "in-basket" exercises, and personality and persuasive speaking tests. Typical administrative dimensions evaluated include leadership, decision making, speaking, writing, and scholastic aptitude. Industry has found that the assessment center technique is an effective method of managerial selection. Education also is finding this to be true.

— The NASSP Assessment Center. One of the most comprehensive assessment center models grew out of the National Association of Secondary School Principals (NASSP) Assessment Center Project. Each center is conducted by a group of six highly trained assessors who observe and evaluate 12 to 20 candidates in various exercises and simulations. Participants are evaluated on these 12 skill dimensions: problem analysis, judgment, organizational ability, decisiveness, leadership, sensitivity, range of tolerance, and oral and written communication skills.

These 12 skill dimensions are critical to the success of building principals, but are only one part of the program to develop school leaders. Because each of the skill dimensions is a subset of the eight AASA skill areas, a more comprehensive center program has been developed to assess the AASA skill areas common to all levels of administration.

— The National Executive Development Center (NEDC). AASA's comprehensive assessment center, the National Executive Development Center (NEDC), provided participants with an Educational Administrator Effectiveness Profile (EAEP) which diagnosed and mapped out strengths and weaknesses, and included an assessment by five colleagues. (To improve the EAEP, AASA and the Meadows Foundations have initiated the Diagnostic Executive Competency Assessment System (DECAS) under the direction of Nolen Estes and Ben Harris at the University of Texas, Austin.)

• *Impact of Centers.* After several years of evaluation by a team from Michigan State University, the performance measures for the NASSP Center are positive. High correlations exist between assessment ratings and job performance of candidates selected as principals and assistant principals.

Research indicates that exercises in the assessment center program reflect the tasks that principals are required to perform on the job and that mastery of these tasks is essential to successful performance. The evaluation team concluded that the NASSP assessment center is valuable for the selection of school administrators. Data are being collected to measure the impact of AASA's NEDC.

Centers are operated in conjunction with AASA, NASSP, school districts, regional service centers, and universities. Several university departments of educational administration have played roles in supporting the assessment center concept that, in part, has been included in UCEA-sponsored training activities for many years. Simulations and other assessment techniques that tap a wide variety of administrative behaviors and skills have been integrated into instructional programs by many departments of educational administration.

It seems clear that the diagnostic capability of a preparation program is the first step. Professors must develop a wide array of methods to determine the mastery level of graduate students or practicing administrators in each of the eight skill areas.

Continuing study is needed to update the cognitive instructional objectives in each of the eight skill areas. The responsibility rests with departments of educational administration and leading practicing school administrators.

2. *Design Capability.* University graduate programs should be designed to challenge students to master all eight skill areas. Realistic group activities, simulation, management games, assessment centers, and related field exercises and materials are vital.

Based on the diagnostic information about each student, individualized degree or certification requirements can be met. For this reason it is recommended that the initial exam be completed as part of the program application process. Based on this information, a student program could consist of regular courses, workshops, readings, internships, assessment centers, action projects, and research activities.

3. *Instructional Capability.* The faculty member teaching each of the skill areas should have had some practical experience and/or a record of scholarship in that area and be a full-time professor. Use of qualified adjunct or clinical professors, especially selected practicing administrators, for regular and short courses, and class presentations, also is important. In addition, a professor, superintendent, or principal could teamteach a course. The use of simulation games, guest speakers, videotapes, computer simulations, scenario presentations about the future, role-playing, panel presentations, and case studies are some of the instructional activities that can help students master the eight skill areas. Part-time or "one-shot" teaching will not accomplish in-depth mastery learning. Time for ideas and concepts to "percolate" in the minds of students and the professors is vital to the university experience.

4. *Resource Capability.* The university's total resources should be applied to ensure graduate program quality. Vital ingredients are carefully selected lectures, seminars, and courses, and relationships with professors in educational administration and other disciplines. Professors and students should have access to a library that includes electronic retrieval and search capabilities.

5. *Program Evaluation Capability.* Continuous scrutiny of program design, delivery, and effectiveness is essential to monitoring program quality. Programs should employ assessment mechanisms that systematically use performance information on both students and graduates as a basis for modifying program content and method. Among the better ways is to conduct a self-study and then invite two or three leaders in educational administration to conduct an external evaluation, including a written report containing specific recommendations. The National Council of Professors of Educational Administration continues to update criteria and information related to program quality assessment. Also, the UCEA has a program preparation center at Arizona State University that compiles data on the quality issues surrounding the selection, training, and evaluation components of preparation programs. The new National Policy Board on Educational Administration will become the standard bearer for quality and evaluation in the next decade.

• *NCATE.* The National Council for the Accreditation of Teacher Education (NCATE) has a major role to play in evaluating educational administration programs. NCATE is an important figure in the program evaluation picture and will be seeking standards of quality in administrator preparation in the future.

Professors. There is little doubt that the most important ingredient in program quality is the professor. Professors hold the key to quality, and most are responding to meet the needs of school leaders.

Content Components. Contemporary graduate programs should contain several content concentrations from which individual student programs can be constructed. The content of the program should be based on data produced through diagnosis of individual students. A common core of requirements should be included:

1. Administrative, organizational, political, and learning theory (covers climate, instructional management, and politics skills).
2. Technical areas of administrative practice (covers time management, legal codes, staff evaluation and development, and resources skills).
3. Behavioral and social sciences (covers climate, politics, curriculum, and research skills).
4. Philosophical, sociological, and historical foundations of education and educational administration (touches all skill areas).
5. Research, planning, futurism, and evaluation (impacts all skill areas).
6. Instructional management, curriculum, and new instructional technologies (covers climate, instructional management, and curriculum skills).

It is important to stress that none of the skill areas can be considered completely mastered because of the constant change in education and schools. However, outstanding school leaders need a grasp of the minimum essentials to provide a secure foundation for learning new skills that will aid them in adjusting to rapid change and new knowledge as they build new programs and renovate old ones. Men and women must be prepared to see the interrelationships between and among specializations and to weigh them against broader social and educational goals.

Administrator preparation programs also should continue to incorporate common content drawn from scholarly inquiry of professors of educational administration, business, sociology, psychology, political science, economics, literature, and other related disciplines. Supported by continued research, this solid knowledge base is being developed as the common ground to launch a successful career in any area of specialization in educational administration, including the professorship.

Clinical Components: Field Experiences. Campus-based and field-based clinical experiences are essential elements in preparing school leaders. Clinical arrangements should provide opportunities for students to compare experiences with the content component. This comparison allows students to diagnose sources of difficulties and identify problems, to develop plans and strategies, and to assess outcomes. Opportunities should be provided for systematic observations and participation in several field settings under the joint supervision of faculty and practitioners.

A field experience should be integrated into each of the eight skill areas, and each department or program should provide this vital component by attempting to:

• Establish a program advisory committee of school administrators who meet with the department faculty several times per year.

• Urge members of the department's program advisory council to identify potential "administrative stars" who should enter the graduate program.

• Devise a plan for release time and possible paid internships in selected school districts.

• Develop seminars at school sites that are team-taught by professors and members of the program advisory council.

• Recapture many of the old "lab school" clinical concepts to create observation opportunities similar to the clinical model used in medical training.

Professional and Renewal Components. Faculty and students in the department or program should hold memberships and participate actively in professional organizations. Memberships in local, state, and national groups provide excellent opportunities for renewal through conferences, workshops, academies, and individual contacts to exchange ideas about specific problems or programs. The National Council of Professors of Educational Administration (NCPEA) and UCEA offers the best opportunity for professors to exchange ideas about preparation programs and teaching strategies.

Another professor-oriented organization that makes major contributions to the improvement of administrator preparation is Division A of the American Educational Research Association (AERA). AERA provides research findings and ideas on teaching methods, and materials to improve the scholarship and practice of educational administration.

Among the leading professional organizations for practitioners are the American Association of School Administrators, the National Association of Secondary School Principals, the National Association of Elementary School Principals, the National School Boards Association, the Association of School Business Officials, the National Organization for Legal Problems in Education, and the Association for Supervision and Curriculum Development. Most of these associations have state affiliates that provide a multitude of professional renewal opportunities for practitioners and professors.

School District Management Training Academies

Many school district have organized their own management training academies for school administrators to:

• Establish an assessment center for skill diagnosis.
• Update and upgrade specific skill areas of the existing leadership team.
• Organize a more "tailor-made" training program for advancement of administrators, not simply letting potential administrators acquire training anywhere.
• Emphasize specific goals and objectives of the district in the content form identified by the district.

The contents of this book can be used to develop surveys of skills that must be learned by the on-board administrative team, as well as the base for drafting proposals and programs to establish the specific skills that must be learned to improve leadership and enhance instructional effectiveness.

State Departments of Education

Many state agencies also have developed administrative academies for superintendents and principals.

Because this book was developed on the basis of a consensus of practitioners and professors, it can be used collaboratively by state education agencies, universities, and professional associations in defining and executing jointly operated training programs.

In addition, several states have, or are in the process of upgrading and expanding requirements for, administrative certification. The contents of this book can be used to validate such new requirements and assure legislative bodies and the public that new certification laws are professionally comprehensive and realistic.

Self-Study and Group Study Programs

Because this book encompasses a broad scope of educational leadership skills, individual school administrators may use it to update and improve their skills. The citations could serve as skills checklists, and the recommended reading as directed further study. Administrative colleagues could use this book as a guide for group study and discussion, setting out a schedule of meetings that cover the eight skill areas in as much detail as they feel necessary.

After using the book, individual or groups of administrators could take the areas where they feel they need additional training; enroll in selected university/college courses, workshops, or seminars; or develop proposals for state funding for a training program in their own district.

Research on the Skills

Although research has not been conducted to determine the extent to which the delivery system components have been integrated into current preparation programs, extensive research has been conducted to determine the validity and relevance of the eight skills areas and their subskills. Michael McClellan, in his dissertation research, gathered perceptions from a national sample of superintendents about the relevance of the competencies and related skills in the *AASA Guideline for the Preparation of School Administrators*.[2] The analysis of the data revealed strong agreement among the superintendents about the critical importance of each of the 50 competencies and skills included in the *Guidelines*. Don Piper, University of North Dakota professor, and Wallace Edgell, in his dissertation research, found the same strong support among professors of educational administration.[3] These national studies established a valid common skill base that not only has influenced new certification plans in several states, but also has influenced university-based preparation programs to focus more on outcomes.

In fact, Edgell reported that 141 professors of educational administration, and 31 department heads in UCEA institutions, indicated that their departments presently were meeting 75 percent of the recommendations in the *Guidelines,* and that they could meet 100 percent within three years. The *Guidelines* also have proven to be useful for program developers in state and national administrator academies and in numerous school district leadership development efforts.

"In Search of Excellence in the Superintendency," a study supported by the Meadows Foundation and conducted by doctoral students at the University of Texas, identified performance areas and skills (based on the AASA *Guidelines*) required for effective job performance in the superintendency; priorities placed on performance areas and skills by effective superintendents in the nation; and determined current staff development needs of Texas superintendents.[4] The results indicated that the role of the superintendent and his or her effectiveness cannot be viewed as single issues or separate from the context of the district. This national study questioned 157 superintendents who were identified as "effective" by professional organizations, universities, and state departments of education in each of the states. These effective superintendents tended to rank the performance areas of school climate and curriculum among the top three of the eight major performance areas. Finance ranged from first to seventh place, depending upon the demographics of the superintendent's district. (The ranking increased as the district became less metropolitan. Finance was the most important to rural superintendents.)

Mitchell Hall, in his dissertation research, found striking similarities in his national study comparing "effective" secondary principals with a random sample. Effective principals tended to rank the performance areas of instructional management and curriculum among the top three of the eight major performance areas. Other skills ranged from first to seventh place, again depending upon the demographics of the school.[5]

The findings of these studies make it clear that the present practice of preparing all students in the same way for administrative roles is inadequate. Beyond the generic knowledge core, preparation and inservice programs should differentiate the program for students who wish to lead districts and schools in certain locations with unique characteristics and with particular enrollment sizes. The university degree programs, and professional development activities, also should be differentiated for a student on the basis of the experience and skills that the individual brings to the program.

Skills Impact on University Preparation

Since the skills were first presented in the *Guidelines* document and later in the first edition of this book, most university preparation programs have given attention to the recommendations for program improvement. Although some programs adopted more of the recommended guidelines than others, brochure descriptions and personal conversations with a significant number of professors reveal that almost all programs have included selected components in their curriculum or delivery system. The terminology may be different, and there may be six, ten, or

20 performance areas to meet the current mission statements and program goals of the department; but the AASA impact is there. This may seem to the uninformed observer to be building conformity to standards, but the research findings alone indicate the acceptance and relevance of the skills. What has happened is that university faculty scan and monitor the knowledge base of the discipline and select the components that best fit their instructional needs.

Skills Impact on Professional Development

A good example of the impact is the Texas LEAD Center. The center, part of the LEAD national network, was partially funded through a two-year grant by the Institute for Educational Leadership in Washington, D.C. According to Director Joan Burnham of the Texas LEAD Center, it is a collaborative endeavor, pooling the resources and expertise from key entities in the state concerned with the professional development of school administrators. Consortium cosponsors are the Texas Association of School Administrators, the Texas Elementary Principals and Supervisors Association, and the Texas Association of Secondary School Principals. In addition to the presidents of the three cosponsoring organizations, a seven-member governing board includes leaders representing business and industry, the state education agency, colleges of education, and regional education service centers. A 33-member advisory committee offers further statewide access to expertise, guidance, and resources.[6]

The Texas LEAD Center focuses primarily on research and development. To accomplish its mission of strengthening educational leadership development, the Center concentrates on five major functions:

- Collecting information on leadership skills, training, and practices
- Developing and delivering leadership training services
- Providing technical assistance and consultation
- Disseminating and supporting utilization of information
- Fostering interorganizational collaboration

The LEAD Center's primary strategies are:

- Training of trainers.
- Use of work teams (task groups) made up of administrators, other educators, and private sector leaders.
- Development of state and national networks to provide input in training and planning and to disseminate LEAD information.

The overall domains or job performance statements that were developed and validated by the Texas LEAD Center were adapted from the eight AASA Leadership Outcome Goals found in Chapter 1.

The adapted domains include the following:

- Promote positive school climate
- Directing school improvement
- Instructional management
- Personnel management

- Administration and fiscal/facilities management
- Student management
- Professional growth and development
- Strengthening support for schools.

Under the leadership of LEAD Center Director Joan Burnham and Edward Manigold, associate executive director for programs and professional development for the Texas Association of School Administrators, efforts are under way to validate the job performance domains for Texas school administrators serving in each of five positions: business manager, curriculum director/instructional supervisor, director of personnel, elementary and secondary principal, and superintendent.

The Center has published a helpful document titled, *Management and Leadership Development for School Administrators: A Guide for Developing Management and Leadership Skills.* The booklet offers suggestions for strengthening the capabilities of all administrators through a systematic approach for developing both sound district professional development plans and individual self-improvement plans. (For more information on the LEAD Center and its activities, contact Dr. Joan Burnham, Texas LEAD Center, 1101 Trinity St., Austin, TX 78701-1994; (512) 477-9014.)

For information on the 90 or more Principal Centers and administration academies, see the *National Directory of Principals' Centers* published by The Principals' Center, Graduate School of Education, 336 Gutman Library, 6 Appian Way, Cambridge, MA 92138; (617) 495-1825.

The National Policy Board

The National Policy Board on Educational Administration was established as a result of a recommendation in the report of the National Commission on Excellence in Educational Administration released in 1987. The Board includes representatives from national organizations with interests in educational administration, including AASA, NCPEA, and UCEA. A recent report by the Board titled, *Improving the Preparation of School Administrators: An Agenda for Reform* includes a nine-item agenda that has far reaching and controversial suggestions for improving administrator preparation. Two of the more controversial items call for (1) an Ed. D. to become a principal or a superintendent and (2) a national professional standards board to develop and administer a national certification examination. The Board has several key functions, including:

- Monitoring the implementations of the Commission's recommendations.
- Conducting periodic reviews of preparation programs for administrators and professors.
- Encouraging the development of high quality programs for preparation of administrators.
- Producing position papers on critical natural policy issues in education.
- Holding forums for discussion of issues in educational administration.
- Generally ensuring good communication across interest groups about policy.[7]

Programs Utilizing Guidelines

A number of exemplary preparation programs have adapted all or part of the guidelines into their curriculum and program goals, including:

• The University of Texas, Austin
Contact person: Dr. Nolen Estes
Telephone: (512) 471-7551

• The University of Nebraska, Lincoln
Contact person: Dr. Robert Stalcup
Telephone: (402) 472-3726

• West Virginia University
Contact person: Dr. Edward Lilley
Telephone: (304) 293-3707

• Montana State University
Contact person: Dr. John Kohl
Telephone (406) 994-0211

The Professional Studies Model

The National Commission on Excellence in Educational Administration has recommended the following to departments of educational administration: "Administrator preparation programs should be like those in professional schools which emphasize theoretical and clinical knowledge, applied research, and supervised practice."[8]

Many significant efforts have been launched in the past 20 years to develop a successful professional studies graduate degree program in educational administration. Several universities have tried and tested various field-based, extended weekend, summer, or mid-week-day graduation programs for full-time administrators, including the University of Illinois-Champaign, Boston College, Boston University, Kansas State University, the University of Cincinnati, the University of Utah, and the University of Oregon.

The established need to educate new and superior school leaders has made the professional studies model the "hottest ticket" in the discipline of educational administration. This heightened emphasis has leaders and professional associations recommending that building-level and central office administrators should hold a professional studies doctorate.

The Professional Studies Doctorate

As mentioned earlier, the idea of a professional studies doctorate is not new.

Doctor of Engineering, Doctor of Business Administration, and Doctor of Education degrees have been granted for many years. The rationale for the degree is to improve applied knowledge and skills of practitioners in professional fields rather than prepare them as researchers. With the onset of reforms in education, national commissions, state advisory committees, and universities are recommending a professional studies doctorate with the following characteristics:

• Grant the more professional Ed.D., rather than the traditional research-based Ph.D.

• Select a cohort of 10-12 students who have the talent for and interest in a career in public school administration.

• Develop a working balance between on-campus courses and varied field-based experiences that will allow the cohort of students to keep their jobs while pursuing the degree. Extended weekend sessions in school districts and intensive seminars on campus are examples.

• Emphasize field-based research that focuses on evaluating school effectiveness and other outcomes important to guiding effective schools. The results would benefit the collaborating school districts, offer students useful research skills, and contribute to higher quality dissertations.

• Have university "cohort" faculty and public school superintendents and principals, i.e. clinical faculty, team teach the intensive summer seminars and extended weekends.

• Conduct a comprehensive performance assessment for each student during the first semester to encourage professional growth and individualized learning.

• Stress the use of intuition and higher order thinking skills to help produce leaders with vision who can plan schools for the future.

• Assure student attendance and active involvement in state and national professional conferences and in state legislative activity.

• Develop a curriculum that will balance the classic literature in theory and educational history with the latest research on school effectiveness and the realities of school and school leadership.

Opportunities must also be provided for students to conduct systematic observations and to participate in several field settings under the joint supervision of university faculty members and field-based practitioners. The eight skills areas should guide these activities. In addition, professors and students should have access to a complete library that includes electronic retrieval and search capabilities. Lack of access to such a library is a major reason why non-traditional, off-campus programs are uneven in quality.

Planning and Implementing the Professional Studies Model

Changing an 80-year-old, tradition-bound, respected, liberal arts graduate studies program to a university/school district collaborative "practical" model can be a complicated task. It is not easy for professors to add on a new degree program or phase in new components. Moreover, upper-level administrators, with traditional leanings for the prestige activities of presenting papers to learned societies and publishing in scholarly journals, may not be inclined toward "field activities" and "professional degrees. These attitudes of university faculty and adminstrators alike can literally kill efforts to design professional studies degree programs.

However, university leaders are beginning to reach out to public schools. The issues of illiteracy, growing school dropout rates, and the high percentage of entering college freshmen requiring expensive remediation have caught the attention of both administrators and professors. Some of the more dramatic views call for combining a state's higher education and public schools into one comprehensive system offering schools for students beginning at age three and continuing into adult life-long learning programs.[9]

Initiation of a professional studies model is the key, and the following steps may assist university planners in the process:

1. Secure support from faculty colleagues. Present a general rationale and the model in this text to colleagues for discussion purposes. If support to pursue the model is present, take the next step.

2. Approach the (department/school/college) dean and academic vice president to tap their interests in the model and leave the proposal for them to read and consider.

3. If the central administration supports the spirit of the model, take the next step.

4. Create three task forces and ask for faculty and graduate students to volunteer based on interest. Provide each person with the following material, which provides alternative professional studies programs and practical suggestions on implementing programs.

• Chapter 10 of this text book.
• Access to *Excellence: The Oregon Wednesday Program*, (Eugene, Ore.: Division of Education Policy and Management, University of Oregon, March 1988).
• J.R. Hoyle, *Educational Administration: Knowledge and Faith.* The President's Lecture presented at the National Council of Professors of Educational Administration, (Tuscaloosa, Alabama, August, 1989).
• D.E. Griffiths, R.T. Stout, and P.B. Forsyth, "The Preparation of Educational Administrators," in D.E. Griffith, R.T. Stout and P.B. Forsyth, eds., *Leaders for America's Schools: The Report and Papers of the National Commission on Excellence in Educational Administration*, (Berkeley, Calif.: McCutchan Pub. Co., 1988), pp. 384-405.
• D.C. Thompson, "A Working Partnership: Training Administrators in a Cooperative Field-Based Model, *Educational Considerations,* 15, 3, (Fall 1988) pp. 17-20.
• *The Education of North Carolina's Teachers: A Doctoral Program for Senior School Administrators*, A Report to the President of the University of North Carolina, Chapel Hill, North Carolina.
• *Preparing Tomorrow's School Administrators in Texas*, a Report by the Educational Administration Advisory Committee to the Texas Higher Education Coordinating Board, Austin, Tx. March 1988.

• *Professional School Administrator Program*, a brochure published by the Department of Education, Office of Admission, 104 B, Campion Hall, Boston College, Chestnut Hill, Mass. 02167.

• *Weekend Ed.D. Program in Educational Administration*, a brochure published by Boston University, School of Education, 605 Commonwealth Ave., Boston, Mass. 02215.

5. Ask each task force to meet and respond to the following questions:

• Task Force on Students

-How are students selected?
-Should students be practicing administrators?
-Should students be classroom teachers with administrator certification?
-Should students be classroom teachers with no course work in educational administration?
-Should students be selected from fields outside of education?
-Should those selected be only those recommended by school administrators?
-What are the admissions criteria?

• Task Force on Course work and Clinical Experience

-How is a balance maintained between a required course sequence and individual student needs?
-Should weekends, summers, two days each month be used for inclass work?
-Should the same class time configuration for the clinical experiences in the school district be used?
-Are research techniques taught on campus, in the field, or both?
-How can classes be scheduled in disciplines outside of educational administration?

• Task Force on Staffing and Advising

-How can professors team teach and maintain current student and class loads?
-Should clinical professors (i.e., superintendents, principals, etc.) be hired on a part-time or permanent basis?
-Do two professors serve as advisors for each group of students?

6. Ask each task force to select two leading school administrators to get their reactions to the questions and possible solutions.

7. Plan a two-day retreat for professors, selected school administrators, and representatives from state administrator groups to discuss the task force reports and develop a strategic plan for the model.

8. Secure funding to pay administrators to teach and organize extended field experiences in school districts.

9. Begin the first class and evaluate the progress each semester. Invite LEAD and state education department staff to assist in this effort.

Beginning the professional studies degree program is a challenge. The major obstacle is change itself. A second problem is the overload and stress placed on the key actors during the first year of implementation. The struggle will pay dividends, though, preparing professionals who can lead America's schools of the future.

Conclusion

What knowledge and skills must be taught in preparation programs and staff development activities to produce the leaders we need? What skills are most vital to school leaders for continued success? These questions have few simple answers.

As stated already, there were mixed opinions in the literature about what a total preparation or training program should include. There was little more agreement about common elements taught in the programs, and who should do the teaching. The answers to the exact relationship between the type of preparation and the quality of on-the-job performance is still elusive. However, the professional studies model holds great promise to find that relationship.

The theory base that derives from interpreting research findings, and from observing best practice at all levels of educational administration, led to the *Guidelines for the Preparation of School Administrators*, and subsequently, to this textbook. We have attempted to stress the importance and application of management skills to bring more systematic order to the study or educational administration. Our attempt should help practicing and future administrators develop a more comprehensive and practical knowledge base.

We do, however, offer these conclusions about the study and practice of educational administration:

• *The ultimate purpose of preparation and inservice training is to improve practice.* Training is a means to an end. That end is improved practice that translates to improved job performance. The primary purpose of research, theory development, inquiry, and argument is to improve the practice of school leadership in all of its domains.

• *The purpose of synopsis in the effort is economy.* One can't train forever because life is short, and what one could learn exceeds the time available. Also, everything that could be learned is not of equal value. Our purpose is to provide a new focus for the field of administration and identify what it is that a successful school leader must know and be able to do. This defines the parameters for an economical training program.

• *School administration continues to be an eclectic affair.* The sources of school administration find roots in many different fields, and continue to be highly influenced by ideas from business, economics, and military training. While these ideas appear to be useful, they should be examined carefully. Many business concepts can be applied to schools to result in improved performance.

• *School administration is changing, but there is a core of permanent skills necessary to be successful.* Any reasonable review of the challenges of our times makes this generalization abundantly clear. Yet, it also is true "that the more things change, the more they remain the same." We found in our reviews of literature some skills that were established in the writings of Cubberley, Bobbitt, Mort, and others. Their ideas profoundly impacted the field and continue to do so. We view this work as part of an evolution rather than some arbitrary and finite "ending" to the field of educational administration.

• *Boundaries were made to be changed.* While this book represents the views of both professors and practitioners, there is a chance we could all be wrong on one

267

point or another. For that reason, we invite a reasoned and critical look at the topics and content of what lies within and consideration of what was not included in our treatment of the field. The boundaries of this book are loosely connected and can be expanded or contracted as needed. The authors and AASA hope that this second edition represents the latest concepts to help stimulate the best thinking about the preparation of school leaders for the 21st century.

Resources

1. For information on an alternative to the NASSP Assessment Center see, D. Erlandson, The Management Profile (Principals' Center Press, Texas A&M University, 1988); also see D. Erlandson and J. Hoyle, Administrator Performance Evaluation: A Comparison of Two Measures in the Management Profile, Paper Presented at the Annual Meeting of the American Education Research Association, San Francisco, March, 1989.

2. M.J. McClellan, "A National Study of Public School Superintendents' Perceptions of the Relevance of the Competencies and Related Skills in the Guidelines for the Preparation of School Administrators," (doctoral dissertation, Texas A&M University, 1983).

3. D.L. Piper, "Programs in Educational Administration: State-of-the-Art Perspective, paper presented at the annual meeting of the National Council of Professors of Educational Administration, Missoula, Montana, August 1983, W. Egell, "Educational Administration Professors' Perceptions of the Importance of the Competencies and Skills in the Guidelines for the Preparation of School Administrators," (doctoral dissertation, Texas A&M University, 1983).

4. S. Scalafani, "AASA Guidelines for the Preparation of School Administrators: Do they Represent the Important Job Behaviors of Superintendent?" (doctoral dissertation, the University of Texas, 1987); V. Collier, "Identification of Skills Perceived by Texas School Superintendents as Necessary for Successful Job Performance," (doctoral dissertation, The University of Texas, 1987).

5. M. Hall, "Effective High School Principals' Perceptions of the Importance of the Competencies and Related Skills in the Guidelines for the Preparation of School Administrators," (doctoral dissertation, Texas A&M University, 1988).

6. J.G. Burnham, "Director's Message, *Focus,* Newsletter published by the Texas LEAD Center, Austin, Texas, 1988.

7. The University Council for Educational Administration
Review, 24, 3, (Fall 1988) p. 1.

8. National Commission on Excellence in Educational Administration, *Leaders for America's Schools: The Report of the National Commission on Excellence in Educational Administration*, Tempe, Arizona, Arizona State University, 1987.

9. J. Hoyle, "Uniting University and Public School Systems," *The School Administrator*, April 1989.

Appendix A.

Future Trends and the School Leader

Harold Hodgkinson, Marvin Cetron, and other demographers and futurists have presented detailed lists of social and economic, technological and educational changes that school leaders face. Leaders must understand and assimilate these trends and react to them. By doing so, knowledgeable school leaders can stay on top and develop long-term thinking and strategic planning.

What the Experts Say

Just what do the experts say about the trends education leaders are facing? Here are facts and projections selected from the works of Harold Hodgkinson,[1] Marvin Cetron[2] and John Hoyle.[3] They have been grouped into demographic, social and economic, technological, and educational categories.

Demographic Trends

- Forty percent of the poor in America are *children*.
- Twenty four percent of all children live *below* the poverty level.
- Nearly 60 percent of all children born today will live with only one parent before the age of 18; 90 percent of these children will live in female-headed families; and a majority will be families with incomes under $10,000.
- The teen birth rate in the United States is *twice* that of any other Western nation; most of the babies are born into poverty and will have health and learning difficulties.
- The children come to school speaking over 200 different languages and dialects.
- Nearly 40 percent of all public school students are minorities; one in three of the total population will be a minority by 2005.
- Since 1960, delinquency rates of young people ages 13 to 17 have increased by 130 percent.
- This nation has the highest rate of teen drug use of any industrialized nation,

269

• 15 percent of all children entering school in 1986 were either physically or mentally handicapped, and 10 percent were living with emotional handicaps.

• The birth rate per 1,000 population is declining. In 1950, it was 24.1; that number shrank to 15.7 in 1986, and will shrink to 12 by the year 2006.

• Since 1900, every generation lives three years longer than the last.

• Overall, 34 percent of 18- to 24-year-old high school graduates were enrolled in higher education in 1988 — up two percent since 1983.

• The college-going rate for black high school graduates between the ages of 18 and 24 rose from 26 percent in 1985 to 28.6 percent in 1986 - the first increase since 1981.

• By 1992, there will be as many college students 25 years and older as there will be 24 years and younger.

• In Connecticut, 40 percent of the high school graduates leave the state to go to college. In Texas, only six percent leave the state.

• The number of Americans aged 13 to 19 peaked in the mid-seventies, will decline through early 1990, and will be on the rise by 2006. Most of the increases will be among minority groups.

Some 80 percent of prison inmates in one state are high school dropouts. Each inmate costs approximately $24,000 a year.

Social and Economic Trends

• There will be a recession in 1990, but our long-range forecast for the U.S. economy is good.

• Computers will provide access to all the card catalogs of the world's libraries by the late 1990's.

• The median income of all U.S. families was $29,460 in 1987, well within the accepted bounds of the middle class ($25,000 $50,000). This is a 50 percent increase (after inflation) over 1960.

• A U.S. citizen has twice the buying power today as in 1952.

• Compulsory national service (two years for both males and females) is likely by the year 2006, with three options: military service, VISTA-type (working with the disadvantaged), or Peace Corps.

• More foreign student exchange programs and participation will be available.

• There will be more East-West cultural exchanges, T.V., and radio satellite hookups.

• Diversity will be a growing value. The old idea was to conform, to blend into the group. This is giving way, especially among minorities, to pride in cultural heritage and general acceptance of differences in all aspects of society.

• Only 25 percent of those who graduate from high school go on to graduate from college. In 1986, male high school graduates not enrolling in college were earning an average of 28 percent less in constant dollars than a comparable group in 1973.

• By 2006, 83 percent of doctors will be salaried. This will make medical care less costly to the average person.

- More, smaller medical outlets (surgery centers, Doc-in-theBoxes, etc.) will make high quality medical services available at less cost.
- By 2006, 90 percent of insurance carriers will expand coverage or reduce premiums for policy holders with healthy life-styles.
- By the year 2000, $50 billion will be spent in the U.S. for AIDS research and treatment. Every taxpayer will be paying $500 a year to care for AIDS patients in the year 2006.
- Women will have greater employment opportunities. "Old Girl" networks will become increasingly effective as women fill more positions in middle and upper management.
- By 2006, there will be only three major corporations making up the computer hardware industry: Apple, Digital, and IBM.
- In all organizations, higher education included, as the traditional pyramid is flattened, middle management will be squeezed out.

Technological Trends.

- Superconductors operating at room temperature will be in commercial use by 2001, as will superconductors the size of a three-pound coffee can.
- By 2006, artificial intelligence will be universally used by companies, universities, and government agencies to help assimilate data and solve problems.
- There will be much growth in the engineering, technology, and health industries; and in public school teaching; also, many new biotechnology jobs will open up.
- Thirty-nine percent of the parts used in U.S. manufacturing will be from other countries; 37 percent of parts used in IBM will be imported.
- Naturalistic self-interest will continue to yield to international trade cooperation.
- Telecommunication removes geographic barriers; satellite transmitted data can be set into a computer and transmitted back from anywhere on earth—often at a far lower cost than if the work was done in the U.S.
- "Bloodless surgery" by laser will decrease hospital stays by 90 percent.
- Brain cell and tissue transplants to aid victims of retardation and head traumas will be in the experimental phase by 2006.

Educational Trends.

- Schools at all levels will be used to educate both children and adults. The academic day will be lengthened to seven hours for children; adults will work a 32-hour workweek and prepare for their next job in the remaining hours.
- Professional alliances between public schools and college faculties will continue to grow.
- Telecommunications will allow almost all course work to be shared with other school districts, or colleges in another state or country.
- Personal computers with ultra high resolution screens, 3-D graphics, high level interractivity, and artificial intelligence will enhance the gaming and simulations used in education.
- More businesses will be involved in schools and job training programs. The

investment of corporations in employee education and retraining — now some $80 billion a year - will double by 2006. The Job Training Partnership Act will help workers find jobs or be trained for new ones.

• Institutions increasingly will apply the growing knowledge about individual cognitive (dual brain) and higher order learning to educational institutions.

• The learning environment (place) will not be as important in 2006; students will learn more on their own, in their "place" at all ages.

• Computer-supported approaches to learning will improve learning techniques and allow more material to be learned. Learning time will be reduced by one-sixth.

• Individual students will receive more support from faculty and advisors on decisions about academic programs and career paths.

• The size of higher educational institutions will be reduced-private venture and self-learning and more research will be done elsewhere.

• Seventy percent of U.S. homes will have computers by 2006, compared with 18 percent today.

What School Leaders Can Do

Attempting to peer into the next century is, at best, impossible. School leaders, however, cannot ignore the dynamic trends that unfold before their eyes. They can be ready for the future if they perceive the numerous interacting trends and act to shape our institutions to adjust to them, or to head them off.

How do school leaders alter the societal trends of soaring crime rates, drug abuse, teenage pregnancies, school dropouts, etc.? Through reform yes, but what kind? Are there workable solutions to these complex trends and issues that threaten us all? School leaders must choose to create school systems that are the envy of the world and make a commitment to quality.

Faced with gloomy forecasts in 1989 and beyond for schools, educational leaders at all levels can take the initiative and fight. School leaders can strive to accomplish the following four essential conditions for the successful revitalization and reform of schools[4]:

1. *Create an equitable allocation of resources.* A coalition of leaders must work through national and state professional organizations to propose federal and state legislation similar to the Education of All Handicapped Children Act.

Legislation should require each state to appropriate five percent of new federal dollars for every "at-risk" student beginning at age three. These additional funds, plus a greater percentage of state sales taxes based on the percentage of at-risk students, should provide a major step toward educational equity. These two changes could maintain local control and enable educators to identify and treat students with the greatest need.

Another plan could be a national network called "Support America's Future — its Schools." Underwritten by major corporations, its primary purpose would be to pay for time on network television to tell the education story to all Americans.

2. *Embrace a future-focused school system.* Schools must strive to base learning on the questions of what knowledge and skills will be of most use to students now and in the future. To do this, a "future" learning environment must be estab-

lished that consists of three major components: an operation center, consisting of an elected board that makes policy decisions; an inner learning environment, consisting of teaching and learning activities; and an outer learning environment, which provides a knowledge base from libraries, universities, and other data sources. The plan consists of heavy reliance on participatory democracy among teachers, parents, administrators, board members, business and community leaders, retired persons, social agencies, etc. The future school also would consist of computers, video, and other technology. Each student would learn on word processors. The system would have small and large group computer-aided mastery learning sessions, as well as one-on-one tutoring and counseling.

The keys to success would be: (1) instruction based on how kids actually learn; (2) parents, guardians, and volunteers involved in what the child learns; (3) heavy reliance on technology; and (4) a pervasive, caring, school culture that expects only success and helps each child focus on a successful future.

3. *Utilize the total community.* It is time to take advantage of these rich educational offerings. The above opportunities would include asking parents, retirees, university faculties, and students, business people, and other citizens to assist in teaching, tutoring, and developing and carrying out instruction. Because only 21 percent of school patrons have children in school, the community education concept must become a reality if patrons are to support the schools. In addition, schools would be open from 6:30 a.m. to 6:30 p.m. at least five days a week so early child care and preschool programs can work.

4. *Share a common vision.* Finally, school leaders need to share a common vision of how high school graduates should look, act, and learn. They must establish a shared vision about 21st century schools — what should they be; what kinds of people will be needed; what skills and knowledge must teachers and administrators possess; and what kinds of university, agency, corporation, and professional association collaboration will produce these schools? Then school leaders must identify and select the best and most intellectually demanding, relevant, and humane educational programs.

If school leaders do these things, they can shape the future. Then, 21st century students will think holistically and be aware that all social institutions, countries, and corporations are interconnected. They will become the next futurists and will model intuitive and creative thinking, doing, and being. So armed, they surely will some day lead their states and the nation to greater productivity and world peace.

There is much intellectual excitement in designing the future based on imagery, but it takes clear priorities, hard careful labor, and driving commitment to make the vision a reality.

Resources

1. H. Hodgkinson, "All One System: Demographics of Education, Kindergarten through Graduate School" (Washington, D.C., The Institute for Educational Leadership, 1988).

2. M. Cetron, W. Rocha, and R. Luckins, "Into the 21st Century: Long Term Trends Affecting the United States, "*Futurist,* XXII, no. 4 (1988) 29-40.

3. J. Hoyle and L. McMurrin, *Critical Challenges for Leaders who Anticipate and Mange the Future,* (Tempe, Ariz.: The University Council for Educational Administration, 1982).

4. J. Hoyle, "Urban Education 1999: Alternative· Futures," *Education and Urban Society,* XIII, 3:357-380.

Appendix B.

AASA Professional Standards for the Superintendency

AASA's *Professional Standards for the Superintendency,* sent to every member in early 1994, specifies the benchmarks for improving the selection, preparation, and development of America's school superintendents.

The eight standards were developed during 1993-94 by an AASA blue ribbon national commission composed of six prominent superintendents from school districts of various sizes, three leading university professors, and two executives of national education associations. John R. Hoyle, professor of educational administration at Texas A & M University, chaired the commission. The commission's charge was to commit to paper the knowledge and skills school leaders need on the eve of the 21st century.

Drafts of the commission report were critiqued by a national jury of 100 superintendents, principals, school board representatives, national and state agency officials, selected state governors, business executives, and training officers from corporations. The standards are based on reviews of significant literature and on dialogue among those serving as superintendents, those working for them, and others who prepare, license, and hire them.

Effective superintendents should meet and be able to demonstrate identified competencies and skills related to each of the standards. The knowledge and skill areas of each standard lend themselves to learning that can be gathered from seminars, simulations, case studies, and other classroom or field-based learning methods.

Standard 1: Leadership and District Culture.
Demonstrate executive leadership by developing a collective district vision; shape school culture and climate; provide purpose and direction for individuals and groups; demonstrate an understanding of international issues affecting education; formulate strategic plans, goals, and change efforts with staff and community; set priorities in the context of community, student, and staff needs; serve as an articulate spokesperson for the welfare of all students in a multicultural context.

Indicators. A superintendent should know and be able to:
- Formulate a written vision statement of future direction for the district.
- Demonstrate an awareness of international issues affecting schools and students.
- Promote academic rigor and excellence for staff and students.
- Maintain personal, physical, and emotional wellness.
- Empower others to reach high levels of performance.
- Build self-esteem in staff and students.
- Exhibit creative problem solving.
- Promote and model risk taking.
- Respect and encourage diversity among people and programs.
- Manage time effectively.
- Facilitate comparative planning between constituencies.
- Conduct district school climate assessments.
- Exhibit multicultural and ethnic understanding.
- Promote the value of understanding and celebrating school/community cultures.

Standard 2: Policy and Governance.

Develop procedures for working with the board of education that define mutual expectations, working relationships and strategies for formulating district policy for external and internal programs; adjust local policy to state and federal requirements and constitutional provisions, standards, and regulatory applications; recognize and apply standards involving civil and criminal liabilities.

Indicators. A superintendent should know and be able to:
- Describe the system of public school governance in our democracy.
- Describe procedures for superintendent-board of education interpersonal and working relationships.
- Formulate a district policy for external and internal programs.
- Relate local policy to state and federal regulations and requirements.
- Describe procedures to avoid civil and criminal liabilities.

Standard 3: Communications and Community Relations.

Articulate district purpose and priorities to the community and mass media; request and respond to community feedback; and demonstrate consensus building and conflict mediation. Identify, track, and deal with issues. Formulate and carry out plans for internal and external communications. Exhibit an understanding of school districts as political systems by applying communication skills to strengthen community support of district priorities; build coalitions to gain financial and programmatic support; formulate democratic strategies for referenda; relate political initiatives to the welfare of children.

Indicators. A superintedent should know and be able to:
- Articulate district vision, mission, and priorities to the community and mass media.
- Demonstrate an understanding of political theory and skills needed to build community support for district priorities to the community and mass media.
- Understand and be able to communicate with all cultural groups in the community.
- Demonstrate that good judgment and actions communicate as well as words.

- Develop formal and informal techniques to gain external perception of a district by means of surveys, advisory groups, and personal contact.
- Communicate and project an articulate position for education.
- Write and speak clearly and forcefully.
- Demonstrate formal and informal listening skills.
- Demonstrate group membership and leadership skills.
- Identify the political forces in a community.
- Identify the political context of the community environment.
- Formulate strategies for passing referenda.
- Persuade the community to adopt an initiative for the welfare of students.
- Demonstrate conflict mediation.
- Demonstrate consensus building.
- Demonstrate school/community relations, school business partnerships, and related public service activities.
- Identify, track, and deal with issues.
- Develop and carry out internal and external communication plans.

Standard 4: Organizational Management.
Exhibit an understanding of the school district as a system by defining processes for gathering, analyzing, and using data for decision making; manage the data flow; frame and solve problems; frame and develop priorities and formulate solutions; assist others to form reasoned opinions; reach logical conclusions and make quality decisions to meet internal and external customer expectations; plan and schedule personal and organization work; establish procedures to regulate activities and projects; delegate and empower at appropriate organizational levels; secure and allocate human and material resources; develop and manage the district budget, maintain accurate fiscal records.

Indicators. A superintendent should know and be able to:
- Define processes for gathering, analyzing, and using data for informed decision making.
- Demonstrate a problem-framing process.
- Define the major components of quality management.
- Develop, implement, and monitor change processes to build capacities to serve clients.
- Discuss legal concepts, regulations, and codes for school operations.
- Describe the process of delegating responsibility for decision making.
- Develop a process for maintaining accurate fiscal reporting.
- Acquire, allocate, and manage human, material, and financial resources to effectively and accountably ensure successful student learning.
- Use technological applications to enhance administration of business and support systems.
- Demonstrate financial forecasting, planning, and cash flow management.
- Perform budget planning, management, account auditing, and monitoring.
- Demonstrate a grasp of practices in administering auxiliary programs, such as maintenance, facilities, food services, etc.
- Demonstrate planning and scheduling of personal time and organization work.

Standard 5: Curriculum Planning and Development.

Design curriculum and a strategic plan that enhance teaching and learning in multiple contexts; provide planning and future methods to anticipate occupational trends and their educational implications; identify taxonomies of instructional objectives and validation procedures for curricular units, using theories of cognitive development; align and sequence curriculum; use valid and reliable performance indicators and testing procedures to measure performance outcomes; and describe the proper use of computers and other learning and information technologies.

Indicators. A superintendent should know and be able to:

- Develop core curriculum design and delivery systems for diverse school communities.
- Describe curriculum planning/futures methods to anticipate occupational trends and their educational implications for lifelong learners.
- Demonstrate an understanding of instructional taxonomies, goals, objectives, and processes.
- Describe cognitive development and learning theories and their importance to the sequencing of instruction.
- Demonstrate an understanding of child and adolescent growth and development.
- Describe a process to create developmentally appropriate curriculum and instructional practices for all children and adolescents.
- Demonstrate the use of computers and other technologies in educational programming.
- Conduct assessments of present and future student learning needs.
- Develop a process for faculty input in continued and systematic renewal of the curriculum to ensure appropriate scope, sequence, and content.
- Demonstrate an understanding of curricular alignment to ensure improved student performance and higher order thinking.

Standard 6: Instructional Management.

Exhibit knowledge of instructional management by implementing a system that includes research findings on learning and instructional strategies, instructional time, advanced electronic technologies, and resources to maximize student outcomes; describe and apply research and best practice on integrating curriculum and resources for multicultural sensitivity and assessment strategies to help all students achieve at high levels.

Indicators. A superintendent should know and be able to:

- Develop, implement, and monitor change processes to improve student learning, adult development, and climates for learning.
- Demonstrate an understanding of motivation in the instructional process.
- Describe classroom management theories and techniques.
- Demonstrate an understanding of the development of the total student, including the physical, social, emotional, cognitive, and linguistic needs.
- Formulate a plan to assess appropriate teaching methods and strategies for all learners.
- Analyze available instructional resources and assign them in the most cost-effective and equitable manner to enhance student outcomes.
- Describe instructional strategies that include the role of multicultural sensitivity and learning styles.

- Exhibit applications of computer technology connected to instructional programs.
- Describe alternative methods of monitoring and evaluating student achievement based on objectives and learning outcomes.
- Describe how to interpret and use testing/assessment results to improve education.
- Demonstrate knowledge of research findings on the use of a variety of instructional strategies.
- Describe a student achievement monitoring and reporting sytem.

Standard 7: Human Resources Management.

Develop a staff evaluation and development system to improve the performance of all staff members; select appropriate models for supervision based on adult motivation research; identify alternative employee benefits packages; and describe and apply the legal requirement for personnel selection, development, retention, and dismissal.

Indicators. A superintendent should know and be able to:

- Develop a plan to assess system and staff needs to identify areas for concentrated staff development.
- Demonstrate knowledge of adult learning theory and motivation.
- Evaluate the effectiveness of comprehensive staff development programming to determine its effect on professional performance.
- Demonstrate use of sytem and staff evaluation data for personnel policy and decision making.
- Diagnose and improve organizational health/morale.
- Demonstrate personnel management strategies.
- Understand alternative benefit packages.
- Assess individual and institutional sources of stress and develop methods for reducing stress (e.g., counseling, exercise programs, and diet).
- Demonstrate knowledge of pupil personnel services and categorical programs.

Standard 8: Values and Ethics of Leadership.

Understand and model appropriate values systems, ethics, and moral leadership; know the role of education in a democratic society; exhibit multicultural and ethnic understanding and related behavior; adapt educational programming to the needs of diverse constituencies; balance complex community demands in the best interest of the student; scan and monitor the environment for opportunities for staff and students; respond in an ethical and skillful way to the electronic and printed news media; and coordinate social agencies and human services to help each student grow and develop as a caring, informed citizen.

Indicators. A superintendent should know and be able to:

- Exhibit multicultural and ethnic understanding and sensitivity.
- Describe the role of schooling in a democratic society.
- Demonstrate ethical and personal integrity.
- Model accepted moral and ethical standards in all interactions.
- Describe a strategy to promote the value that moral and ethical practices are established and practiced in each classroom and school.
- Describe how education undergirds a free and democratic society.

- Describe a strategy to ensure that diversity of religion, ethnicity, and way of life in the district are not violated.
- Formulate a plan to coordinate social, health, and other community agencies to support each child in the district.

ACKOWLEDGMENTS

The American Association of School Administrators (AASA) extends its deepest gratitude to those experts in the field of school administration whose vast personal and professional knowledge and experiences made this textbook a reality.

The first edition of *Skills for Successful School Leaders,* published in 1985, was prepared by John R. Hoyle, professor of educational administration at Texas A & M University; Fenwick W. English, professor of educational administration at the University of Kentucky; and Betty E. Steffy, associate professor of educational administration, University of Kentucky. Former AASA Executive Director Paul B. Salmon, and former Senior Executive for Federal Administrator Initiatives Herman R. Goldberg reviewed the initial manuscript and made suggestions that were included in the first edition. Thanks also go to the members of the former National Center for the Improvement of Learning (NCIL), the AASA Committee for the Advancement of School Administration (CASA), and the AASA Advisory Committee on Higher Educational Relationships for their input.

Former AASA Publications Manager Anne Dees served as primary editor for the first edition of *Skills for Successful School Leaders.* She was assisted by Cindy Tursman, then editor of *The School Administrator.* AASA Associate Executive Director Gary Marx served as project director for both the first and second editions of the book.

For the second edition of this book, John Hoyle researched and provided the updated text. AASA Director of Communications Luann Fulbright, and William Henry, executive editor for the Montgomery County Public Schools, provided editorial assistance for the second edition; and AASA Associate Editor Leslie Eckard served as production coordinator. Former AASA Executive Director Richard Miller encouraged and gave full support to updating this valuable work.

This revised version of *Skills for Successful School Leaders* is symbolic of AASA's deep and continuing determination to stay on the forefront in the preparation of school leaders of excellence.

NAME AND TOPIC INDEX

ABOUT THE AUTHORS

John R. Hoyle—Distinguished teacher, consultant, writer, and currently professor of educational administration at Texas A & M University, College Station, Texas. Hoyle is past-president of the National Council of Educational Administration and was AASA's 1982 Cooperative Professor of the Year. He is called a leading reformer in administrator preparation, and is a noted futurist and speaker. Dr. Hoyle was asked by AASA to deliver the 1988 Paul B. Salmon memorial lecture during the association's annual convention.

Fenwick W. English—Professor, educational administration, University of Kentucky, Lexington, Ky. English's many roles have included consultant, author, and experienced school superintendent. Honored as a Distinguished Professor by AASA's National Academy for School Executives (NASE), English has also been recognized by the Association for Supervision and Curriculum Development (ASCD).

Betty E. Steffy—Associate professor, educational administration, University of Kentucky, Lexington, Ky. Steffy is a leading authority on instructional management and school improvement. She is an author and a popular consultant and speaker. She has served as a principal and school superintendent.